2002
A BRAND-NEW YEAR—
A PROMISING NEW START

Enter Sydney Omarr's star-studded world of accurate day-by-day predictions for every aspect of your life. With expert readings and forecasts, you can chart a course to romance, adventure, good health, or career opportunities while gaining valuable insight into yourself and others. Offering a daily outlook for 18 full months, this fascinating guide shows you:

- The important dates in your life
- What to expect from an astrological reading
- How the stars can help you stay healthy and fit
- Your lucky lottery numbers
  And more!

Let this expert's sound advice guide you through a year of heavenly possibilities—for today and for every day of 2002!

SYDNEY OMARR'S DAY-BY-DAY ASTROLOGICAL GUIDE FOR

ARIES—March 21–April 19
TAURUS—April 20–May 20
GEMINI—May 21–June 20
CANCER—June 21–July 22
LEO—July 23–August 22
VIRGO—August 23–September 22
LIBRA—September 23–October 22
SCORPIO—October 23–November 21
SAGITTARIUS—November 22–December 21
CAPRICORN—December 22–January 19
AQUARIUS—January 20–February 18
PISCES—February 19–March 20

IN 2002

SYDNEY OMARR'S

DAY-BY-DAY ASTROLOGICAL GUIDE FOR

TAURUS

April 20–May 20

2002

A SIGNET BOOK

SIGNET
Published by New American Library, a division of
Penguin Putnam Inc., 375 Hudson Street,
New York, New York 10014, U.S.A.
Penguin Books Ltd, 27 Wrights Lane,
London W8 5TZ, England
Penguin Books Australia Ltd, Ringwood,
Victoria, Australia
Penguin Books Canada Ltd, 10 Alcorn Avenue,
Toronto, Ontario, Canada M4V 3B2
Penguin Books (N.Z.) Ltd, 182–190 Wairau Road,
Auckland 10, New Zealand

Penguin Books Ltd, Registered Offices:
Harmondsworth, Middlesex, England

First published by Signet, an imprint of New American Library,
a division of Penguin Putnam Inc.

First Printing, June 2001
10 9 8 7 6 5 4 3 2 1

Copyright © Sydney Omarr, 2001
All rights reserved

Sydney Omarr is syndicated worldwide by
Los Angeles Times Syndicate.

 REGISTERED TRADEMARK—MARCA REGISTRADA

Printed in the United States of America

CONTENTS

INTRODUCTION

Your Cosmic Code

Are you ready for the excitement and challenges of the year 2002? We've cracked the mystery of the human genome, but there's another code that's been used to map the human personality since ancient times. Like your genetic imprint, your astrology chart is uniquely "you." It is a map of your moment in time, which has its own code, based on the position of the sun, moon, and planets at the time and place you were born. What is especially intriguing is that this system can offer specific, practical guidance, even when using only *one* of the elements of the code, your *sun sign*. Though you share that sun sign with others, there are many ways to use it every day to find a more fulfilling lifestyle. Your sun sign "map" can help you find success, attract love, look for a better job, have a healthier body, and even take the vacation of your dreams or decorate your home.

Just knowing the other person's sun sign can give you many clues to how to make your relationship a happy one. You can troubleshoot problems in advance and, if they crop up, find a way to make them work for you. In this year's edition of *Sydney Omarr's Guides,* you'll learn what's best for you and how your sign relates, positively and negatively, with every other sign under the sun.

"For every thing there is a season" could be the theme song of astrology. Will 2002 be the time to charge forward or proceed with caution, to change

1

careers or stick with the job at hand, to fall in love? We'll deal in many ways with the question of timing—when are the potentially difficult times (which also present positive challenges), when can you expect delays and potential misunderstandings, when are the best times to take risks? You'll be able to get your life "on track" and chart your course with full knowledge of the shoals ahead.

For those who are new to astrology or would like to know more about it, there is basic information to give you an inside look at how astrology works. Then you can look up the other planets in your horoscope to find out how each contributes to your unique personality.

Astrologers have been quick to embrace the new technology of the twenty-first century, especially since sophisticated astrological computer programs have eliminated the tedious work of casting a chart and deliver beautiful chart printouts. Now anyone with access to the Internet can view their astrology chart at a free Internet site or buy the same programs professional astrologers use. We'll show you where to do this in chapters devoted especially to Internet resources. We'll also give you Sydney Omarr's updated "Yellow Pages" of the best places for books, tapes, and further astrological studies.

As we explore our inner cosmos via astrology, we are still searching for the same things that always have made life worth living: love, meaningful work, and fulfilling relationships. With Sydney Omarr's astonishingly accurate day-by-day forecasts, you can use your cosmic link to the universe to enhance every aspect of your life. So here's hoping you use your star power wisely and well for a productive and happy 2002!

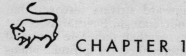

CHAPTER 1

The Coming Trends of 2002!

We're at the beginning of a decisive decade, when many issues are coming to the forefront simultaneously: global expansion, territorial disputes, space travel, biotechnology breakthroughs, overpopulation, dangers of nuclear warfare, and environmental crises. Here are the key planets calling the shots and the trends to watch in 2002.

This year is a "bridge" year, when there are no dramatic shifts in the atmosphere (that comes next year). So it is more a time of consolidation, of taking stock and making plans for the future. The slow-moving planet Pluto is our guide to the hottest trends. Pluto brings about a heightened consciousness and transformation of matters related to the sign it is passing through. Now in Sagittarius, Pluto is emphasizing everything associated with this sign to prepare us philosophically and spiritually for things to come.

Perhaps the most pervasive sign of Pluto in Sagittarius is globalization in all its forms, which has become a main theme of the past few years. We are re-forming boundaries, creating new forms of travel that will definitely include space travel. At this writing, the $60 billion space station is under way, a joint venture between the United States, Russia, Japan, Europe, and Canada. It is scheduled for completion in 2006 and will be one of the brightest objects in the sky.

In true Sagittarius fashion, Pluto will shift our emphasis away from acquiring wealth to a quest for the meaning of it all, as upward strivers discover that money and power are not enough. Sagittarius is the sign of linking everything together; therefore the trend will be to find ways to interconnect on spiritual, philosophical, and intellectual levels.

Pluto in Sagittarius's spiritual emphasis has already filtered down to our home lives. Home altars and private sanctuaries are becoming a part of our personal environment. The oriental art of feng shui has moved westward, giving rise to a more harmonious, spiritual atmosphere in offices and homes, which also promotes luck and prosperity.

Sagittarians are known for their love of animals, and we have never been more pet-happy. Look for extremes related to animal welfare, such as vegetarianism, which will become even more popular and widespread as a lifestyle. As habitats are destroyed, the care, feeding, and control of wild animals will become a larger issue, especially where there are deer, bears, and coyotes in the back yard.

The Sagittarian love of the outdoors combined with Pluto's power has already promoted extreme sports, especially those that require strong legs, like rock climbing, trekking, or snowboarding. Rugged, sporty all-terrain vehicles continue to be popular, as are zippy little scooters which help us get around in a fun way. Expect the trend toward more adventurous travel and fitness or sports-oriented vacations to accelerate: exotic hiking trips to unexplored territories, mountain-climbing expeditions, spa vacations, and sports-associated resorts are part of this trend.

Publishing, which is associated with Sagittarius, has been transformed by the new electronic media, with an enormous variety of books available in print. The Internet bookstore will continue to prosper under Pluto in Sagittarius. It is fascinating that the online bookstore Amazon.com took the Sagittarius-influenced name of the fierce female tribe of archer-warriors who went to the extreme of removing their right breasts to better shoot their arrows.

Who's Lucky? Make Hay, Cancer and Leo!

Good fortune, expansion, and big money opportunities are associated with the movement of Jupiter, the planet that embodies the principle of expansion. Jupiter has a twelve-year cycle, staying in each sign for approximately one year.

When Jupiter enters a sign, the fields associated with that sign usually provide excellent opportunities. Areas of speculation associated with the sign Jupiter is passing through will have the hottest market potential—the ones that currently arouse excitement and enthusiasm.

The flip side of Jupiter is that there are no limits . . . you can expand off the planet under a Jupiter transit, which is why the planet is often called the "Gateway to Heaven." If something is going to burst—such as an artery—or overextend or go over the top in some way, it could happen under a supposedly "lucky" Jupiter transit . . . so be aware.

This year, Jupiter will finish its journey through Cancer in August, when it moves into Leo. So sun sign Cancers and Leos and those with strong Cancer or Leo influence in their horoscopes should have abundant growth opportunities during the year. On the other hand, those born under Capricorn and Aquarius, the signs which occur at the opposite time of year, may have to work harder for success.

Jupiter in Cancer should bring opportunities in home-related industries, child care, the food and shelter industries, cruises, maternal issues, shipping and boating, and water sports. Look for further expansion in home-based business and telecommuting. Combining mothering with an active career will be a key issue for Gen-X women, who'll have a tug of war between family and career.

After Jupiter moves into Leo in August, people will

be looking for more fun in life, more joy, and more opportunities to play. We'll all want to be young again, and chances are that plastic surgery will enjoy a big boom time. Bring on the divas, as larger-than-life personalities take center stage. Look for more self-aggrandizement and self-adornment in flamboyant fashions with plenty of color, style, and piles of gold jewelry. This is an influence which encourages extravagance, showing off, and enjoying the best things in life. On a more serious note, child-raising will very much be on our minds, since the sign of Leo rules children. How will we raise children in a workaholic era? Since this Jupiter encourages love affairs and casual sex, the pull of family ties and responsibilities could be one of the biggest challenges this year.

Saturn Puts on the Brakes in Gemini

Saturn keywords are focus, time, commitment, accomplishment, discipline, and restriction. If Jupiter gives you a handout, then Saturn hands you the bill. With Saturn, nothing's free; you work for what you get, so it's always a good idea to find the areas (or houses) of your horoscope where Saturn is passing through, to learn where to focus your energy on lasting value. With Saturn, you must be sure to finish what you start, be responsible, put in the hard work, and stick with it.

This year, Saturn finishes up its two-year transit of Gemini. The normally light-spirited Geminis have had to deal with the serious, sobering influence of Saturn, just after they enjoyed the expansive period of Jupiter in Gemini in 2000 and 2001. Geminis have to back up the risks they took then and will be required to deliver on promises made. It'll be a powerful challenge for changeable Geminis, who must now pay the piper.

In the world at large, Saturn in Gemini is sure to affect communications. Talk must be followed up by action now. We'll be concerned with Gemini issues of lower education and literacy, reforming the lower educational system. Since Gemini is an air sign, which rules the lungs, there will be further controversy and restriction surrounding smoking and the tobacco industry.

Uranus and Neptune in Aquarius— The High-Tech Signs

Uranus and Neptune are pushing us into the future as they continue their long stays in Aquarius. Uranus overthrows the worn-out status quo and points us toward the future. It rules the sign of Aquarius, so it has been in its most powerful position since 1995, and has created radical breakthroughs in technology, as well as a concern with issues that involve all humanity. It is now preparing to move into Pisces, a sign associated with spirituality, imagination, and creativity. Its coming influence should begin to show up this year, with some dramatic changes in the arts beginning this summer.

Our lust for techno-toys should make this a gadget-crazed time, especially as Jupiter enters playful Leo, reinforcing this trend. Interactive forms of amusement and communication will rival television for our leisure. In fact, television may be on its way out as we opt for more exciting forms of entertainment.

While Jupiter remains in Cancer, the first half of the year, look for more Cancer-related products and events in the news: home furnishings, housing, child care, food products and merchandising, and a surge in restaurants, futuristic cruise ships, and new concepts in living quarters. After Jupiter moves into Leo, it forms an uneasy relationship with Neptune and Uranus on the opposite side of the zodiac, which could engender conflicts between individuals and society at large, between what "I" want and what "they" want.

There will be concern about how technology is negatively affecting personal lives and creativity.

Where there is Neptune, look for imagination and creativity, and since this is the planet of deception and illusion, scams and scandals continue, especially in the high-tech area associated with Aquarius. Neptune is also associated with hospitals, which are acquiring a Neptunian glamour, as well as cutting-edge technology. The atmosphere of many hospitals is already changing from the intimidating sterile surgical environment of the past to that of a health-promoting spa, with alternative therapies such as massage, diet counseling, and aromatherapy available. New procedures in plastic surgery, also a Neptunian glamour field, and antiaging therapies should restore the bloom and the body of youth, as Jupiter in Leo glorifies the everyoung.

CHAPTER 2

Planning Ahead in 2002—
Timing Your Life for Luck,
Prosperity, and Love!

It's no secret that some of the most powerful and famous people, from Julius Caesar to financier J. P.
Morgan, from Ronald Reagan to Cher, have consulted
astrologers before they made their moves. If astrology
helps the rich and famous stay on course through life's
ups and downs, why not put it to work for you?

Take control of your life by coordinating your
schedule with the cosmos. For instance, if you know
the dates that the mischievous planet Mercury will be
creating havoc with communications, you'll back up
that vital fax with a duplicate by Express Mail; you'll
read between the lines of contracts and put off closing
that deal until you have double-checked all the information. When Venus is in your sign, making you the
romantic flavor of the month, you'll be at your most
attractive. That would be a great time to update your
wardrobe, revamp your image, or ask someone you'd
like to know better to dinner. Venus helps you make
that sales pitch and win over the competition.

To find out for yourself if there's truth to the saying
"Timing is everything," mark your own calendar for
love, career moves, vacations, and important events,
using the following information and the tables in this
chapter and the one titled "Look Up Your Planets,"

as well as the moon sign listings under your daily forecast. Here are the happenings to note on your agenda:

- Dates of your sun sign (high-energy period)
- The month previous to your sun sign (low-energy period)
- Dates of planets in your sign this year
- Full and new moons
  (Pay special attention when these fall in your sun sign.)
- Eclipses
- Moon in your sun sign every month, as well as moon in the opposite sign (listed in daily forecast)
- Mercury retrogrades
- Other retrograde periods

Your Personal Power Time

Every birthday starts a cycle of solar energy for you. You should feel a new surge of vitality as the powerful sun enters your sign. This is the time when predominant energies are most favorable to you. So go for it! Start new projects; make your big moves. You'll get the recognition you deserve now, when everyone is attuned to your sun sign. Look in the tables in this book to see if other planets will also be passing through your sun sign at this time. Venus (love, beauty), Mars (energy, drive), or Mercury (communication, mental sharpness) reinforce the sun and give an extra boost to your life in the areas they affect. Venus will rev up your social and love life, making you seem especially attractive. Mars gives you extra energy and drive. Mercury fuels your brain power and helps you communicate. Jupiter signals an especially lucky period of expansion.

There are two "down" times related to the sun. During the month before your birthday period, when you are winding up your annual cycle, you could be feeling especially vulnerable and depleted, so get extra rest, watch your diet, and don't overstress yourself. Use this time to gear up for a big "push" when the sun enters your sign.

Another "down" time is when the sun is in the opposite sign from your sun sign (six months from your birthday) and the prevailing energies are very different from yours. You may feel at odds with the world, and things might not come easily. You'll have to work harder for recognition, because people are not on your wavelength. However, this could be a good time to work on a team, in cooperation with others or behind the scenes.

How to Use the Moon's Phase and Sign

Working with the phases of the moon is as easy as looking up at the night sky. During the new moon, when both the sun and the moon are in the same sign, it's the best time to begin new ventures, especially the activities that are favored by that sign. You'll have powerful energies pulling you in the same direction. You'll be focused outward, toward action and doing. Postpone breaking off, terminating, deliberating, or reflecting, activities that require introspection and passive work.

Get your project under way during the first quarter, then go public at the full moon, a time of high intensity, when feelings come out into the open. This is your time to shine—to express yourself. Be aware, however, that because pressures are being released, other people are also letting off steam and confrontations are possible. So try to avoid arguments. Traditionally, astrologers often advise against surgery at this time, which could produce heavier bleeding.

During the last quarter of the new moon, you'll be most controlled. This is a winding-down phase, a time to cut off unproductive relationships and do serious thinking and inward-directed activities.

You'll feel some new and full moons more strongly than others, especially those new moons that fall in your sun sign and full moons in your opposite sign. Because that full moon happens at your low-energy time of year, it is likely to be an especially stressful time in a relationship, when any hidden problems or unexpressed emotions could surface.

Full and New Moons in 2002

New Moon in Capricorn—January 13
Full Moon in Leo—January 28
New Moon in Aquarius—February 12
Full Moon in Virgo—February 27
New Moon in Pisces—March 13
Full Moon in Libra—March 28
New Moon in Aries—April 12
Full Moon in Scorpio—April 27
New Moon in Taurus—May 12
Full Moon in Sagittarius (lunar eclipse)—May 26
New Moon in Gemini (solar eclipse)—June 10
Full Moon in Capricorn (lunar eclipse)—June 24
New Moon in Cancer—July 10
Full Moon in Aquarius—July 24
New Moon in Leo—August 8
Full Moon in Aquarius (second time)—August 22
New Moon in Virgo—September 6
Full Moon in Pisces—September 21
New Moon in Libra—October 6
Full Moon in Aries—October 21
New Moon in Scorpio—November 4
Full Moon in Taurus (lunar eclipse)—November 19
New Moon in Sagittarius (solar eclipse)—December 4
Full Moon in Gemini—December 19

Moon Sign Timing

To forecast the daily emotional "weather," to determine your monthly high and low days, or to synchronize your activities with the cycles and the sign of the moon, take note of the moon's daily sign under your daily forecast at the end of the book. Here are some of the activities favored and moods you are likely to encounter under each sign.

Moon in Aries

Get moving! The new moon in Aries is an ideal time to start new projects. Everyone is pushy, raring to go, and rather impatient and short-tempered. Leave details and follow-up for later. Competitive sports or martial arts are great ways to let off steam. Quiet types could use some assertiveness, but it's a great day for dynamos. Be careful not to step on too many toes.

Moon in Taurus

It's time to do solid, methodical tasks. This is the time to tackle follow-through or backup work. Lay the foundations for success. Make investments, buy real estate, do appraisals, and do some hard bargaining. Attend to your property—get out in the country. Spend some time in your garden. Enjoy creature comforts, music, a good dinner, and sensual lovemaking. Forget starting a diet.

Moon in Gemini

Talk means action today. Telephone, write a letter, fax! Make new contacts; stay in touch with steady customers. You can handle lots of tasks at once. A great day for mental activity of any kind. Don't try to pin people down—they, too, are feeling restless. Keep it light. Flirtations and socializing are good. Watch gossip—and don't give away secrets.

Moon in Cancer

This is a moody, sensitive, emotional time. People respond to personal attention and mothering. Stay at home; have a family dinner; call your mother. Nostalgia, memories, and psychic powers are heightened. You'll want to hang on to people and things (don't clean out your closets now). You could have some shrewd insights into what others really need and want now. Pay attention to dreams, intuition, and gut reactions.

Moon in Leo

Everybody is in a much more confident, warm, generous mood. It's a good day to ask for a raise, show what you can do, or dress like a star. People will respond to flattery; enjoy a bit of drama and theater. You may be extravagant—treat yourself royally, and show off a bit (but don't break the bank!). Be careful that you don't promise more than you can deliver!

Moon in Virgo

Do practical, down-to-earth chores. Review your budget. Make repairs. Be an efficiency expert. Not a day to ask for a raise. Have a health checkup. Revamp your diet. Buy vitamins or health food. Make your home spotless. Take care of details and piled-up chores. Reorganize your work and life so they run more smoothly and efficiently. Save money. Be prepared for others to be in a critical, faultfinding mood.

Moon in Libra

Attend to legal matters. Negotiate contracts. Arbitrate. Do things with your favorite partner. Socialize.

Be romantic. Buy a special gift, a beautiful object. Decorate yourself or your surroundings. Buy new clothes. Throw a party. Have an elegant, romantic evening. Smooth over any ruffled feathers. Avoid confrontations. Stick to civilized discussions.

Moon in Scorpio

This is a day to do things with passion. You'll have excellent concentration and focus. Try not to get too intense emotionally, however, and avoid sharp exchanges with loved ones. Others may tend to go to extremes, get jealous, and overreact. Great for troubleshooting, problem-solving, research, scientific work—and making love. Pay attention to psychic vibes.

Moon in Sagittarius

A great time for travel. Have philosophical discussions. Set long-range career goals. Work out, do sports, or buy athletic equipment. Others will be feeling upbeat, exuberant, and adventurous. Risk taking is favored—you may feel like taking a gamble, betting on the horses, visiting a local casino, or buying a lottery ticket. Teaching, writing, and spiritual activities also get the green light. Relax outdoors. Take care of animals.

Moon in Capricorn

You can accomplish a lot today, so get on the ball! Issues concerning your basic responsibilities, duties, family and parents could crop up. You'll be expected to deliver on promises now. Weed out the dead wood from your life. Get a dental checkup.

Moon in Aquarius

A great day for doing things with groups—clubs, meetings, outings, politics, and parties. Campaign for your candidate. Work for a worthy cause. Deal with larger issues that affect humanity: the environment and metaphysical questions. Buy a computer or an electronic gadget. Watch TV. Wear something outrageous. Try something you've never done before. Present an original idea. Don't stick to a rigid schedule—go with the flow. Take a class in meditation, mind control, or yoga.

Moon in Pisces

This can be a very creative day, so let your imagination work overtime. Film, theater, music, or ballet could inspire you. Spend some time alone, resting and reflecting, reading or writing poetry. Daydreams can also be profitable. Help those less fortunate or lend a listening ear to someone who may be feeling blue. Don't overindulge in self-pity or escapism, however. People are especially vulnerable to substance abuse now. Turn your thoughts to romance and someone special.

When the Planets Go Backward

All the planets, except for the sun and moon, have times when they appear to move backward—or retrograde—in the sky, or so it seems from our point of view on earth. At these times, planets do not work as they normally do, so it's best to "take a break" from that planet's energies in our life and do some work on an inner level.

Mercury Retrograde

Mercury goes retrograde most often, and its effects can be especially irritating. When it reaches a short distance ahead of the sun three times a year, it seems to move backward from our point of view. Astrologers often compare retrograde motion to the optical illusion that occurs when we ride on a train that passes another train traveling at a different speed—the second train appears to be moving in reverse.

What this means to you is that the Mercury-ruled areas of your life—analytical thought processes, communications, and scheduling—are subject to all kinds of confusion. Be prepared. People will change their minds, or renege on commitments. Communications equipment can break down. Schedules must be changed on short notice. People are late for appointments or don't show up at all. Traffic is terrible. Major purchases malfunction, don't work out, or get delivered in the wrong color. Letters don't arrive or are delivered to the wrong address. Employees will make errors that have to be corrected later. Contracts don't work out or must be renegotiated.

Since most of us can't put our lives on "hold" for nine weeks every year (three Mercury retrograde periods), we should learn to tame the trickster and make it work for us. The key is in the prefix "re-." This is the time to go back over things in your life. Reflect on what you've done during the previous months. Look for deeper insights, spot errors you've missed, and take time to review and reevaluate what has happened. This time is very good for inner spiritual work and meditations. Rest and reward yourself—it's a good time to take a vacation, especially if you revisit a favorite place. Reorganize your work and finish up projects that are backed up. Clean out your desk and closets. Throw away what you can't recycle. If you must sign contracts or agreements, do so with a contingency clause that lets you reevaluate the terms later.

Postpone major purchases or commitments. Don't get married (unless you're remarrying the same person). Try not to rely on other people keeping appointments, contracts, or agreements to the letter—have several alternatives. Double-check and read between the lines. Don't buy anything connected with communications or transportation (if you must, be sure to cover yourself). Mercury retrograding through your sun sign will intensify its effect on your life.

If Mercury was retrograde when you were born, you may be one of the lucky people who don't suffer the frustrations of this period. If so, your mind probably works in a very intuitive, insightful way.

The sign Mercury is retrograding through can give you an idea of what's in store—as well as the sun signs that will be especially challenged.

MERCURY RETROGRADE PERIODS IN 2002
Mercury has three retrograde periods this year: from January 18 to February 8, from May 15 to June 8, and from September 14 to October 6.

Venus Retrograde

Retrograding Venus can cause your relationships to take a backward step, or it can make you extravagant and impractical. Shopping till you drop and buying what you cannot afford are trip-ups at this time. It's *not* a good time to redecorate—you'll hate the color of the walls later. Postpone getting a new hairstyle and try not to fall in love either. But if you wish to make amends in an already troubled relationship, make peaceful overtures at this time. (Note: there is no Mars retrograde period this year.)

VENUS RETROGRADE PERIOD IN 2002
Venus retrogrades from October 10 to November 21.

When Other Planets Retrograde

The slower-moving planets stay retrograde for months at a time (Saturn, Jupiter, Neptune, Uranus, and Pluto). When Saturn is retrograde, it's an uphill battle with self-discipline. You may feel more like hanging out at the beach than getting things done. Neptune retrograde promotes a dreamy escapism from reality, whereas Uranus retrograde may mean setbacks in areas where there have been sudden changes. Think of this as an adjustment period, a time to think things over and allow new ideas to develop. Pluto retrograde is a time to work on establishing proportion and balance in areas where there have been recent dramatic transformations.

When the planets start moving forward again, there's a shift in the atmosphere. Activities connected with each planet start moving ahead, and plans that were stalled get rolling. Make a special note of those days on your calendar and proceed accordingly.

Other Retrogrades in 2002

Jupiter is retrograde from November 2, 2001, until March 1, 2002. It turns retrograde again on December 4, 2002.

Saturn retrogrades from February 7 to October 11.
Uranus retrogrades from June 6 to November 3.
Neptune retrogrades from May 13 to October 20.
Pluto retrogrades from March 20 to August 16.

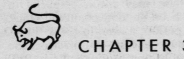

CHAPTER 3

Teach Yourself Astrology

Astrology is a powerful tool of inner transformation that can help you access your personal potential, to understand others, and to interpret events in your life and in the world at large. You don't have to be an expert in astrology to put it to work for you. In this chapter, we'll demystify the horoscope chart and walk you through the basic concepts, so you'll know a sign from a house and what the planets mean. Perhaps from here, you'll upgrade your knowledge with a computer program that calculates charts for everyone you know in a nanosecond, or you'll join an astrology class in your city, or you'll want to explore different techniques of astrology and go on to the asteroids and the fixed stars. The sky's the limit, literally. So let's take off!

The Basics: Signs, Houses, Constellations, and the Zodiac

Everyone knows what a sign is . . . or do they? A *sign* is literally a 30-degree portion of the zodiac, a circular belt of the sky. That is what is meant by a "sign of the zodiac." Things happen within a sign, but a sign does not *do* anything itself—that's the job of the planets. Each sign is simply a portion of celestial real estate and has certain unique characteristics described by four things: an *element* (earth, air, fire, water), a *quality* or mode (cardinal (active), fixed, mutable), by a *polarity* (masculine/feminine, yin/yang) and finally by a *position* in the sequence of zodiac signs.

The *signs* are named after *constellations,* patterns of stars on the zodiac which originally lit up the twelve divisions, like billboards. However, over the centuries, the constellations have shifted from our point of view here on earth. So the constellation which once marked a particular sign may now be in the territory of another sign. (Most Western astrologers use the twelve-equal-part division of the zodiac; however, there are some methods of astrology that still do use the constellations instead of the signs.) However, the *names* of the signs remain the same as their original place-markers.

Most people think of themselves in terms of their *sun sign,* which refers to the sign the sun seems to be passing through at a given moment, from our point of view here on earth. (Of course, we are the ones that are traveling around the sun.) For instance, "I'm an Aries" means that the sun was passing through Aries territory at your birth. However, there are nine other planets (plus asteroids, fixed stars, and sensitive points) which also form our total astrological personality, and some or many of these will be located in other signs. No one is completely "Aries," with all their astrological components in one sign! (Please note that, in astrology, the sun and moon are usually referred to as "planets," though of course they're not.)

Defining the Signs

What makes Aries the sign of go-getters and Taureans savvy with money? And Geminis talk a blue streak and Sagittarians footloose? Descriptions of the signs are not accidental; they are characterized by different combinations of four concepts we have already mentioned: the sign's element, quality, polarity, and position in the sequence of the zodiac.

Take the element of fire: it's associated with passion, heat. Then have it work in an active, energetic way. Give it a jolt of positive energy and place it first in line. And doesn't that sound like the active, me-first, driving, hotheaded, energetic Aries?

Then take the element of earth: it's practical, sensual, where things grow. Make it work in a fixed, stable way or mode. Give it the kind of energy that reacts to its surroundings, that settles in. Make it the consolidating force, coming right after the passionate beginning of Aries. Now you've got a good idea of how sensual, earthy Taurus operates.

Another way to grasp the idea is to pretend you're doing a magical puzzle based on the numbers that can divide into 12 (the total number of signs): 4, 3, and 2. There are 4 "building blocks" or elements, 3 ways a sign operates (qualities or modes), and 2 polarities. These alternate, in turn, around the zodiac, with a different combination coming up for each sign.

THE FOUR ELEMENTS

Here's how they add up. The *four elements* describe the physical concept of the sign. Is it fiery (dynamic), earthy (practical), airy (mental), or watery (emotional)? Divide the 12 signs by the 4 elements and you get 3 zodiac signs of each element: fire (Aries, Leo, Sagittarius); earth (Taurus, Virgo, Capricorn); air (Gemini, Libra, Aquarius); and water (Cancer, Scorpio, Pisces). These are the same elements that make up our planet: earth, air, fire, and water. But astrology uses the elements as *symbols* which link your body and psyche to the rhythms of the cosmos. If major planets in a horoscope are passing through fire signs, the person will be likely to have a warm, enthusiastic personality, able to fire up or motivate others. These are people who make ideas catch fire and spring into existence, but they also have hot tempers. Those with major planets in earth signs are the builders of the zodiac who follow through after the initiative of fire signs to make things happen. These people are solid, practical realists who enjoy material things and sensual pleasures. They are interested in ideas that can be used to achieve concrete results. With major planets in air signs, a person will be more mental, a good communicator. Following the consolidating earth signs, air people reach out to inspire others through the use of words, social contacts, discussion, and debate. Water sign people complete each four-element series, adding the ingredients of emotion, compassion, and imagination. These people are nonverbal communicators who attune themselves to their surroundings and react through the medium of feelings.

THE THREE QUALITIES

The second consideration when defining a sign is how it will operate. Will it take the initiative, or move slowly and deliberately, or adapt easily? Its *quality* (or modality) will tell. There are 3 qualities; therefore, after dividing 3 into 12 signs, it follows that there will be 4 signs of each quality: cardinal, fixed, and mutable.

Cardinal signs begin each season (Aries, Cancer, Libra, Capricorn). People with major planets in cardinal signs tend to be doers. They're active, always involved in projects. They are usually on the fast track to success, impatient to get things under way. Those with major planets in *fixed signs* (Taurus, Leo, Scorpio, Aquarius) move steadily and are always in control. Since these signs happen in the middle of a season, after the initial character of the season is established, it follows that people with major planets in fixed signs would tend to be more centered; they move more deliberately and do things more slowly but thoroughly. The fixed signs fall in parts of your horoscope where you take root and integrate your experiences. *Mutable signs* (Gemini, Virgo, Sagittarius, Pisces) embody the principle of distribution. Planets in these signs will break up the cycle, preparing the way for a change by distributing the energy to the next group. People with predominantly mutable planets are likely to be flexible, adaptable, and communicative. They can move in many directions easily, darting around obstacles.

THE TWO POLARITIES
In addition to an element and a quality, each sign has a *polarity,* either a positive or negative electrical charge that generates energy around the zodiac, like a giant battery. Polarity refers to opposites, which you could also define as masculine/feminine, yin/yang, active/reactive. In their zodiac positions, the six fire and air signs are positive, active, masculine, and yang in polarity. Therefore, planets in these signs will express their energy openly, expanding outward. The six earth and water signs are reactive, negative, and yin—in other words, nurturing and receptive in polarity, which allows the energy to develop and take shape.

All positive energy would be like a car without brakes. All negative energy would be like a stalled vehicle, going nowhere. So both polarities are needed in balanced proportion, to keep the zodiac in a state of equilibrium.

THE ORDER OF THE SIGNS
The specific order of the signs is vital to the balance of the zodiac and the transmission of energy around the cycle. Though each sign is quite different from its neighbors on either side, each seems to grow out of its predecessor like links in a chain, transmitting a synthesis of energy accumulated along the chain to the following sign, beginning with the fire-powered, active, positive, cardinal sign of Aries and ending with watery, mutable, reactive Pisces.

Houses of the Horoscope—
Where the Action Is

We come to the concept of *houses* as we set up a specific horoscope, which is a map of the heavens at a given moment in time. Picture the horoscope chart as a wheel with twelve spokes. In between each of the "spokes" is a section called a *house*. The wheel is stationary, however . . . the houses are always in the same place. Each house represents a different area of life and is influenced or "ruled" by a sign and a planet that are associated with that house. But besides the house's given "rulers," it is colored by the sign which is passing over the spoke (or cusp) at the moment when the horoscope chart is cast. In other words, the first house is naturally ruled by Aries and Mars; however, if Capricorn was the sign passing over the house at the time the chart was cast, it would have a Capricorn influence.

Numerically, the house order begins at the left center spoke (or the 9 position if you were reading a clock) and is read counterclockwise around the chart.

The First House—Home of Aries
and the Planet Mars

This is the house of "firsts"—the first impression you make, how you initiate matters, the image you choose to project. This is where you advertise yourself, where you project your personality. Planets that fall here will intensify the way you come across to others. Often the first house will project an entirely different type of energy from the sun sign. For instance, a Capricorn with Leo in the first house will come across as much more flamboyant than the average Capricorn. The sign on the cusp of this house is known as your *ascendant,* or *rising sign.*

The Second House—Home of Taurus and Venus

Here is your contact with the material world. In this house are your attitudes about money, possessions, finances, whatever belongs to you, and what you own, as well as your earning and spending capacity. On a deeper level, this house reveals your sense of self-worth, the inner values that draw wealth in various forms.

The Third House—Home of Gemini and Mercury

This house describes how you communicate with others—are you understood? Here you reach out to others nearby and interact with the immediate environment. This is how your thinking process works, the way you express your thoughts. In relationships, here are your first experiences with brothers and sisters, and how you handle people close to you, such as your neighbors or pals. It's also where you take short trips, write letters, or use the telephone. It shows how your mind works in terms of left-brain logical and analytical functions.

The Fourth House—Home of Cancer and the Moon

This house shows how you are nurtured and made to feel secure—your roots! Located at the bottom of the chart, the fourth house, like the home, shows the foundation of life, your deepest psychological underpinnings. Here is where you have the deepest confrontation with who you are, and how you make yourself feel secure. It shows your early home environment and the circumstances at the end of your life—your final "home"—as well as the place you call home now. Astrologers look here for information about the primary nurturers in your life.

26

The Fifth House—Home of Leo and the Sun

This is how you express yourself creatively—your idea of play. The Leo house is where the creative potential develops, where you show off your talents. It is also where you procreate, in the sense that your children are outgrowths of your creative ability. It most represents your inner childlike self, the part of you which finds joy in play. If inner security has been established by the time you reach this house, you are now free to have fun, romance, and love affairs—to give of yourself. This is also the place astrologers look for the playful kind of love affairs, flirtations, and brief romantic encounters (rather than long-term commitments).

The Sixth House—Home of Virgo and Mercury

Here is your "care and maintenance" department. It shows how you function in daily life, where you get things done, and where you determine how you look after others and fulfill service duties, such as taking care of pets. Here are your daily survival, your "job" (as opposed to your career, which is the domain of the tenth house), your diet, and your health and fitness regimens. Here is where you take care of your body and organize yourself to perform efficiently.

The Seventh House—Home of Libra and Venus

This house shows your attitude toward partners and those with whom you enter commitments, contracts, or agreements. This house has to do with your relationships—your close, intimate, one-on-one relationships (even your open enemies—those you "face off" with). Open hostilities, lawsuits, divorces, and marriages happen here. If the first house represents the "I," the seventh or opposite house represents the "not-I"—the complementary partner you attract by the way you come across. If you are having trouble with partnerships, consider what you are attracting by the interaction of your first and seventh house.

The Eighth House—Home of Scorpio and Pluto (also Mars)

This refers to how you merge with something or someone, and how you handle power and control. This is one of the most mysterious and powerful houses, where your energy transforms itself from "I" to "we." As you give up your personal power and control by uniting with something or someone, two kinds of energies merge and become something greater, leading to a regeneration of the self on a higher level. Here are your attitudes toward sex, shared resources, and taxes (what you share with the government). Because this house involves what belongs to others, you face issues of control and power struggles, or undergo a deep psychological transformation as you bond with another. Here you transcend yourself with dreams, drugs, and occult or psychic experiences that reflect the collective unconscious.

The Ninth House—Home of Sagittarius and Jupiter

Here is where you search for wisdom and higher knowledge—your belief system. While the third house represents the "lower mind," its opposite on the wheel, the ninth house, is the "higher mind." This is where you ask the "big" questions like "Why are we here?" The ninth house shows what you believe in. After the third house has explored what was close at hand, the ninth stretches out to broaden you with higher education and travel. Here you stretch spiritually with religious activity. Since you are concerned with how everything is related, you tend to take risks, break rules, and push boundaries. Here is where you express your ideas in a book or extensive thesis, where you pontificate, philosophize, or preach.

The Tenth House—Home of Capricorn and Saturn

Here is your public image and how you handle authority. Located directly overhead at the "high noon" position on the horoscope wheel, this house is associated with high-profile activities, where the world sees you. It deals with your career (but not your routine "job"), and your reputation. Here is where you go public and take on responsibilities (as opposed to the fourth house, where you stay home). This will affect the career you choose and your "public relations." This house is also associated with your father or the main authority figure in your life.

The Eleventh House—Home of Aquarius and Uranus

Here is your support system, how you relate to society and your goals. In this house, you extend your identity to belong to a group, a team, a club, a goal, or a belief system. You worry about being popular, winning the election, or making the team; you define what you really want, the kinds of friends you have, your political affiliations, and the kinds of groups you'll belong to. Here is where you become concerned with "what other people think," or you rebel against society. Here is where you could become a socially conscious humanitarian—or a party-going social butterfly. It's where you look to others to stimulate you and discover your kinship to the rest of humanity. The sign on the cusp of this house can help you understand what you gain and lose from friendships.

The Twelfth House—Home of Pisces and Neptune

Here is where the boundaries between yourself and others become blurred, where you become self-less. In your trip around the zodiac, you've gone from the "I" of self-assertion in the first house to the final house, symbolizing the dissolution that happens before rebirth. It's where accumulated experiences are processed in the unconscious. Spiritually oriented astrologers look to this house for evidence of past lives and karma. Places where we go for solitude or to do spiritual or reparatory work belong here, such as retreats, religious institutions, or hospitals. Here are also institutions such as prisons where we withdraw from society or are forced to withdraw because of antisocial behavior. Selfless giving through charitable acts is part of this house, as is helpless receiving or dependence on charity.

In your daily life, the twelfth house reveals your deepest intimacies, your best-kept secrets, especially those you hide from yourself, repressed deep in the unconscious. It is where we surrender a sense of a separate self to a deep feeling of wholeness, such as selfless service in religion or any activity that involves merging with the greater whole. Many sports stars have important planets in the twelfth house that enable them to play in the "zone," finding an inner, almost mystical, strength that transcends their limits.

The Planets Power Up Your Houses

Houses are stronger or weaker depending on how many planets are inhabiting them. If there are many planets occupying a given house, it follows that the activities of that house will be emphasized in your life. If the planet that rules the house naturally is also located there, this too adds power to the house.

Mapping Your Planets

The ten major planets (including the sun and moon) are the doers in your chart. The planets cause things to happen. They will play starring or supporting roles, depending on their positions in your horoscope. A planet in the first house, particularly one that's close to your rising sign, is sure to be a featured player. Planets that are grouped together usually operate together like a team, playing off each other, rather than expressing their energy singularly. A planet that stands alone, away from the others, is usually outstanding and sometimes calls the shots.

The best place for a planet is in the sign or signs it rules; the next best is in a sign where it is *exalted,* or especially harmonious. On the other hand, there are signs where a planet has to work harder to play its role. These are called the planet's *detriment* and *fall.* The sign opposite a planet's rulership, which embodies the opposite area of life, is its *detriment.* The sign opposite its exaltation is its *fall.* Though these terms may suggest unfortunate circumstances for the planet, that is not always true. In fact, a planet that is debilitated can actually be more complete, because it must stretch itself to meet the challenges of living in a more difficult sign. Like world leaders who've had to struggle for greatness, this planet may actually develop more strength and character.

Here's a list of the best places for each planet to be. Note that, as Uranus, Neptune, and Pluto were discovered, they replaced the traditional rulers of signs which best complemented their energies.

ARIES—Mars.
TAURUS—Venus, in its most sensual form.
GEMINI—Mercury in its communicative role.
CANCER—the moon.
LEO—the sun.

VIRGO—Also Mercury, this time in its more critical capacity.

LIBRA—Also Venus, in its more aesthetic, judgmental form.

SCORPIO—Pluto, replacing the sign's original ruler, Mars.

SAGITTARIUS—Jupiter.

CAPRICORN—Saturn.

AQUARIUS—Uranus, replacing Saturn, its original ruler.

PISCES—Neptune, replacing Jupiter, its original ruler.

A person who has many planets in exalted signs is lucky indeed, for here is where the planet can accomplish the most and be its most influential and creative.

SUN—Exalted in Aries, where its energy creates action.

MOON—Exalted in Taurus, where instincts and reactions operate on a highly creative level.

MERCURY—Exalted in Aquarius, where it can reach analytical heights.

VENUS—Exalted in Pisces, a sign whose sensitivity encourages love and creativity.

MARS—Exalted in Capricorn, a sign that puts energy to work productively.

JUPITER—Exalted in Cancer, where it encourages nurturing and growth.

SATURN—At home in Libra, where it steadies the scales of justice and promotes balanced, responsible judgment.

URANUS—Powerful in Scorpio, where it promotes transformation.

NEPTUNE—Especially favored in Cancer, where it gains the security to transcend to a higher state.

PLUTO—Exalted in Pisces, where it dissolves the old cycle, to make way for transition to the new.

The Sun and the Moon

Since the sun is always the first consideration, it is important to treat it as the star of the show. It is your conscious ego and it is always center stage, even when sharing a house or a sign with several other planets. This is why sun sign astrology works for so many people.

The sun rules the sign of Leo, gaining strength through the pride, dignity, and confidence of the fixed-fire personality. It is exalted in "me-first" Aries. In its detriment, Aquarius, the sun-ego is strengthened through group participation and social consciousness, rather than through self-centeredness. (Note how many Aquarius people are involved in politics, social work, and public life. They are following the demands of their sun sign to be spokesperson for a group.) In its fall, Libra, the sun needs the strength of a partner—an "other"—to enhance its own balance and self-expression.

As the sun represents your outer light, the moon represents the inner "you," your deep emotional nature. We go into more detail about the moon and its influence in your life and moods in a separate chapter in this book. Read it for details about this all-important planet.

Each of the other eight planets is colored by the sign it is passing through. For example, Mercury, the planet that rules the way you communicate, will express itself in a dynamic, headstrong way if it was passing through the sign of Aries when you were born. You will speak differently if it was passing through the slower, more patient sign of Taurus. And so on through the list. Here's a rundown of the planets and how they behave in every sign.

The Personal Planets—Mercury, Venus, and Mars

These planets work in your immediate personal life.

Mercury affects how you communicate and how your mental processes work. Are you a quick study who grasps information rapidly, or do you learn more slowly and thoroughly? How is your concentration? Can you express yourself easily? Are you a good writer? All these questions can be answered by your Mercury placement.

Venus shows what you react to. What turns you on? What appeals to you aesthetically? Are you charming to others? Are you attractive to look at? Your taste, your refinement, your sense of balance and proportion are all Venus-ruled.

Mars is your outgoing energy, your drive and ambition. Do you reach out for new adventures? Are you assertive? Are you motivated? Self-confident? Hot-tempered? How you channel your energy and drive is revealed by your Mars placement.

Mercury Communicates

Since Mercury never travels far from the sun, read Mercury in your sun sign, then the signs preceding and following it. Then decide which reflects the way your mind works.

Mercury in Aries

Your mind is very active and assertive. You never hesitate to say what you think or shy away from a battle. In fact, you may relish a verbal confrontation. Tact is not your strong point, so you may have to learn not to trip over your tongue.

Mercury in Taurus

Though you may be a slow learner, you have good concentration and mental stamina. You want to make your ideas really happen. You'll attack a problem methodically and consider every angle thoroughly, never jumping to conclusions. You'll stick with a subject until you master it.

Mercury in Gemini

A wonderful communicator with great facility for expressing yourself both verbally and in writing. You talk and talk, love gathering all kinds of information. You probably finish other people's sentences and talk with hand gestures. You can talk to anybody anytime and probably have phone and e-mail bills to prove it. You read anything from sci-fi to Shakespeare and might need an extra room just for your book collection. Though you learn fast, you may lack focus and discipline. Watch a tendency to jump from subject to subject.

Mercury in Cancer

You rely on intuition more than logic. Your mental processes are usually colored by your emotions, so you may seem shy or hesitant to voice your opinions. However, this placement gives you the advantage of great imagination and empathy in the way you communicate with others.

Mercury in Leo

You are enthusiastic and very dramatic in the way you express yourself. You like to hold the attention of groups and could be a great public speaker. Your mind thinks big, so you'd prefer to deal with the overall picture rather than with the details.

Mercury in Virgo

This is one of the best places for Mercury. It should give you critical ability, attention to details, and thorough analysis. Your mind focuses on the practical side of things. This type of thinking is very well suited to being a teacher or an editor.

Mercury in Libra

You're either a born diplomat who smoothes over ruffled feathers or a talented debater. However, since you're forever weighing the pros and cons of a situation, you may vacillate when making decisions.

Mercury in Scorpio

This is an investigative mind which stops at nothing to get the answers. You may have a sarcastic, stinging wit or a gift for the cutting remark. There's always a grain of truth to your verbal sallies, thanks to your penetrating insight.

Mercury in Sagittarius

You're a super salesman with a tendency to expound. Though you are very broad-minded, you can be dogmatic when it comes to telling others what's good for them. You won't hesitate to tell the truth as you see it, so watch a tendency toward tactlessness. On the plus side, you have a great sense of humor. This position of Mercury is often considered by astrologers to be at a disadvantage because Sagittarius opposes Gemini, the sign Mercury rules, and squares off with Virgo, another Mercury-ruled sign. What often happens is that Mercury in Sagittarius oversteps its bounds and loses sight of the facts in a situation. Do a reality check before making promises that you may not be able to keep.

Mercury in Capricorn

This placement endows good mental discipline. You have a love of learning and a very orderly approach to your subjects. You will patiently plod through the facts and figures until you have mastered the tasks. You grasp structured situations easily, but may be short on creativity.

Mercury in Aquarius

With Uranus and Neptune in Aquarius now energizing your Mercury, you're sure to be on the cutting edge of new ideas. An independent, original thinker, you'll have more far-out ideas than the average person and be quick to check out any unusual opportunities. Your opinions are so well researched and grounded, in fact, that once your mind is made up, it is difficult to change.

Mercury in Pisces

You have the psychic intuitive mind of a natural poet. Learn to make use of your creative imagination. You may think in terms of helping others, but check a tendency to be vague and forgetful of details.

Venus Relates

Venus tells how you relate to others and to your environment. It shows where you receive pleasure, what you love to do. Find your Venus placement on the chart on pages 68–75 by looking for the year of your birth in the left-hand column. Then follow the line of that year across the page until you reach the time period of your birthday. The sign heading that column will be your Venus. If you were born on a day when Venus was changing signs, check the signs preceding or following that day to determine if that feels more like your Venus nature.

Venus in Aries

You can't stand to be bored, confined, or ordered around. But a good challenge, maybe even a rousing row, turns you on. Don't you pick a fight now and then just to get someone stirred up? You're attracted by the chase, not the catch, which could cause some problems in your love life, if the object of your affection becomes too attainable. You love someone who keeps you on your toes. You like to wear red and be first with the latest fashion. You'll spot a trend before anyone else.

Venus in Taurus

All your senses work in high gear. You love to be surrounded by glorious tastes, smells, textures, sounds, and visuals. Austere minimalism is not your style. Neither is being rushed. You like time to enjoy your pleasures. Soothing surroundings with plenty of creature comforts are your cup of tea. You like to feel secure in your nest, with no sudden jolts or surprises. You like familiar objects—in fact, you may hate to let anything or anyone go.

Venus in Gemini

You are a lively, sparkling personality who thrives in a situation that affords a constant variety and a frequent change of scenery. A varied social life is important to you, with plenty of stimulation and a chance to engage in some light flirtation. Commitment may be difficult, because playing the field is so much fun.

Venus in Cancer

An atmosphere where you feel protected, coddled, and mothered is best for you. You love to be surrounded by children in a cozy, homelike situation. You are attracted to those who are tender and nurturing, who make you feel secure and well provided for. You may be quite secretive about your emotional life or attracted to clandestine relationships.

Venus in Leo

First-class attention in large doses turns you on, and so do the glitter of real gold and the flash of mirrors. You like to feel like a star at all times, surrounded by your admiring audience. The side effect is that you may be attracted to flatterers and tinsel, while the real gold requires some digging.

Venus in Virgo

Everything neatly in its place? On the surface, you are attracted to an atmosphere where everything is in perfect order, but underneath are some basic, earthy urges. You are attracted to those who appeal to your need to teach, be of service, or play out a Pygmalion fantasy. You are at your best when you are busy doing something useful, helping someone improve.

Venus in Libra

"Elegance" and "harmony" are your key words. You can't abide an atmosphere of contention. Your taste tends toward the classic, with light harmonies of color— nothing clashing, trendy, or outrageous. You love doing things with a partner and should be careful to pick one who is decisive, but patient enough to let you weigh the pros and cons. And steer clear of argumentative types. It helps a lot if your partner is attractive and stylish, as well as charming, and appreciates the finer things in life.

Venus in Scorpio

Hidden mysteries intrigue you. In fact, anything that is too open and aboveboard is a bit of a bore. You surely have a stack of whodunits by the bed, along with an erotic magazine or two. You like to solve puzzles, and may also be fascinated with the occult, crime, or scientific research. Intense, all-or-nothing situations add spice to your life, and you love to ferret out the secrets of others. But you could get burned by your flair for living dangerously. The color black, spicy food, dark wood furniture, and heady perfume all get you in the right mood.

Venus in Sagittarius

If you are not actually a world traveler, your surroundings are sure to reflect your love of faraway places. You like a casual outdoor atmosphere and a dog or two to pet. There should be plenty of room for athletic equipment and suitcases. You're attracted to kindred souls who love to travel and who share your freedom-loving philosophy of life. Athletics, spiritual, or New Age pursuits could be other interests.

Venus in Capricorn

No fly-by-night relationships for you! You want substance in life and you are attracted to whatever will help you get where you are going. Status objects turn you on. And so do those who have a serious, responsible, businesslike approach, or who remind you of a beloved parent. It is characteristic of this placement to be attracted to someone of a different generation. Antiques, traditional clothing, and dignified behavior favor you.

Venus in Aquarius

This Venus wants to make friends more than to make love. You like to be in a group, particularly one pushing a worthy cause. In fact, fame of one sort or another is fascinating to you. You feel quite at home surrounded by people, but may remain detached from any intense commitment. Original ideas and unpredictable people attract you. You don't like everything to be planned out in advance, preferring spontaneity and delightful surprises.

Venus in Pisces

Venus is exalted in Pisces, which makes this one of the more desirable Venuses to have. This Venus loves to give of the self, and you'll find plenty of takers. Stray animals and people appeal to your heart and your pocketbook, but be careful to look at their motives realistically once in a while. You are extremely vulnerable to sob stories of all kinds. Fantasy, theater, and psychic or spiritual activities also speak to you.

Mars Moves and Shakes

Mars shows how you pursue your goals, whether you have energy to burn or proceed at a slow, steady pace. Or are you nervous, restless, unable to sit still? Mars will also show how you get angry. Will you explode, do a slow burn, or hold everything inside, then get revenge later?

To find your Mars, turn to the chart on pages 76–87. Then find your birth year in the left-hand column and trace the line across horizontally until you come to the column headed by the month of your birth. There you will find an abbreviation of your Mars sign. If the description of your Mars sign doesn't ring true, read the description of the signs preceding and following it. You may have been born on a day when Mars was changing signs, and your Mars would then be in the adjacent sign.

Mars in Aries

In the sign it rules, Mars shows its brilliant fiery nature. You have an explosive temper and can be quite impatient, but on the other hand, you possess tremendous courage, energy, and drive. You'll let nothing stand in your way as you race to be first! Obstacles are met head-on and broken through by force. However, situations that require patience and persistence could make you explode in rage. You're a great starter, but not necessarily there at the finish.

Mars in Taurus

Slow, steady, concentrated energy gives you staying power. You've got great stamina and you never give up. Your tactic is to wear away obstacles with your persistence. Often you come out a winner because you've had the patience to hang in there. When angered, you do a slow burn.

Mars in Gemini

You can't sit still for long. This Mars craves variety. You often have two or more things going on at once. It's all an amusing game to you. Your life can get very complicated, which only adds spice and stimulation. What drives you into a nervous, hyper state? Boredom, sameness, routine, and confinement. You can do wonderful things with your hands, and you have a way with words.

Mars in Cancer

You rarely attack head-on. Instead, you'll keep things to yourself, make plans in secret, and always cover your actions. This might be interpreted by some as manipulative, but it's really your method of self-protection. You get furious when anyone knows too much about you, though you do like to know all about others. Your mothering and feeding instincts can be put to good use, if you work in food, hotel, or child-care-related businesses. You may have to overcome your fragile sense of security, which prompts you not to take risks and to get physically upset when criticized. Don't take things so personally!

Mars in Leo

You have a very dominant personality that takes center stage. Modesty is not one of your stellar traits, nor is taking a back seat, ever. You prefer giving the orders and have been known to make a dramatic scene if they are not obeyed. Properly used, this Mars confers leadership ability, endurance, and courage.

Mars in Virgo

You are the faultfinder of the zodiac, who notices every detail. Mistakes of any kind make you nervous, and you are sure you can do the job better than anyone else. You may worry, even if everything is going smoothly. Though you might not express anger directly, you sure can nag. You have definite likes and dislikes. You are certainly more industrious and detail-oriented than other signs. Your Mars energy is often most positively expressed in some kind of teaching role.

Mars in Libra

This Mars will have a passion for beauty, justice, and art. Generally, you will avoid confrontations at all costs. You prefer to spend your energy finding diplomatic solutions or weighing pros and cons. Your other techniques are passive aggression or exercising your well-known charm to get people to do what you want.

Mars in Scorpio

This is a powerful placement, so intense that it demands careful channeling into worthwhile activities. Otherwise, you could become obsessed with your sexuality or might use your need for power and control to manipulate others. You are strong-willed, shrewd, and very private about your affairs, and you'll usually have a secret agenda behind your actions. Your great stamina, focus, and discipline would be excellent assets for careers in the military or medical fields, especially research or surgery. When angry, you don't get mad—you get even!

Mars in Sagittarius

This expansive Mars often propels people into sales, travel, athletics, or philosophy. Your energies function well when you are on the move. You have a hot temper and are inclined to say what you think before you consider the consequences. You shoot for high goals and talk endlessly about them, but you may be weak on groundwork. This Mars needs a solid foundation. Watch a tendency to take unnecessary risks.

Mars in Capricorn

This is an ambitious Mars with an excellent sense of timing. You have an eye for those who can be useful to you, and you may dismiss people ruthlessly when you're angry. But you drive yourself hard and deliver full value. This is a good placement for an executive. You'll aim for status and a high material position in life, and keep climbing despite the odds. A great Mars to have!

Mars in Aquarius

This is the most rebellious Mars. You seem to have a drive to assert yourself against the status quo. You may enjoy provoking people, shocking them out of traditional views. Or this placement could express itself in an offbeat sex life. Somehow you often find yourself in unconventional situations. You enjoy being a leader of an active avant-garde group, which pursues forward-looking studies, politics, or goals.

Mars in Pisces

This Mars is a good actor who knows just how to appeal to the sympathies of others. You create and project wonderful fantasies or use your sensitive antennae to crusade for those less fortunate. You get what you want through creating a veil of illusion and glamour. This is a good Mars for someone in the creative fields—a dancer, performer, or photographer—or for someone in motion pictures. Many famous film stars have this placement. Watch a tendency to manipulate by making others feel sorry for you.

Jupiter Expands

Jupiter is the planet in your horoscope that makes you want *more*. This big, bright, swirling mass of gases is associated with abundance, prosperity, and the kind of windfall you get without too much hard work. You're optimistic under Jupiter's influence, when anything seems possible. You'll travel, expand your mind with higher education, and publish to share your knowledge widely. But a strong Jupiter has its downside, too, because Jupiter's influence is neither discriminating nor disciplined. It represents the principle of growth without judgment, and could result in extravagance, weight gain, laziness, and carelessness, if not kept in check.

Be sure to look up your Jupiter in the tables in this book. When the current position of Jupiter is favorable, you may get that lucky break. This is a great time to try new things, take risks, travel, or get more education. Opportunities seem to open up easily, so take advantage of them.

Once a year, Jupiter changes signs. That means you are due for an expansive time every twelve years, when Jupiter travels through your sun sign. You'll also have "up" periods every four years, when Jupiter is in the same element as your sun sign.

Jupiter in Aries

You are the soul of enthusiasm and optimism. Your luckiest times are when you are getting started on an exciting project or selling an ideal that you really believe in. You may have to watch a tendency to be arrogant with those who do not share your enthusiasm. You follow your impulses, often ignoring budget or other commonsense limitations. To produce real, solid benefits, you'll need patience and follow-through wherever this Jupiter falls in your horoscope.

Jupiter in Taurus

You'll spend on beautiful material things, especially those that come from nature—items made of rare woods, natural fabrics, or precious gems, for instance. You can't have too much comfort or too many sensual pleasures. Watch a tendency to overindulge in good food, or to overpamper yourself with nothing but the best. Spartan living is not for you! You may be especially lucky in matters of real estate.

Jupiter in Gemini

You are the great talker of the zodiac, and you may be a great writer, too. But restlessness could be your weak point. You jump around, talk too much, and could be a jack-of-all-trades. Keeping a secret is especially difficult, so you'll also have to watch a tendency to spill the beans. Since you love to be at the center of a beehive of activity, you'll have a vibrant social life. Your best opportunities will come through your talent for language—speaking, writing, communicating, and selling.

Jupiter in Cancer

You are luckiest in situations where you can find emotional closeness or deal with basic security needs, such as food, nurturing, or shelter. You may be a great collector and you may simply love to accumulate things—you are the one who stashes things away for a rainy day. You probably have a very good memory and love children—in fact, you may have many children to care for. The food, hotel, child-care, and shipping businesses hold good opportunities for you.

Jupiter in Leo

You are a natural showman who loves to live in a larger-than-life way. Yours is a personality full of color that always finds its way into the limelight. You can't have too much attention or applause. Show biz is a natural place for you, and so is any area where you can play to a crowd. Exercising your flair for drama, your natural playfulness, and your romantic nature brings you good fortune. But watch a tendency to be overly extravagant or to monopolize center stage.

Jupiter in Virgo

You actually love those minute details others find boring. To you, they make all the difference between the perfect and the ordinary. You are the fine craftsman who spots every flaw. You expand your awareness by finding the most efficient methods and by being of service to others. Many will be drawn to medical or teaching fields. You'll also have luck in publishing, crafts, nutrition, and service professions. Watch out for a tendency to overwork.

Jupiter in Libra

This is an other-directed Jupiter that develops best with a partner, for the stimulation of others helps you grow. You are also most comfortable in harmonious, beautiful situations, and you work well with artistic people. You have a great sense of fair play and an ability to evaluate the pros and cons of a situation. You usually prefer to play the role of diplomat rather than adversary.

Jupiter in Scorpio

You love the feeling of power and control, of taking things to their limit. You can't resist a mystery, and your shrewd, penetrating mind sees right through to the heart of most situations and people. You have luck in work that provides for solutions to matters of life and death. You may be drawn to undercover work, behind-the-scenes intrigue, psychotherapy, the occult, and sex-related ventures. Your challenge will be to develop a sense of moderation and tolerance for other beliefs. This Jupiter can be fanatical. You may have luck in handling other people's money—insurance, taxes, and inheritance can bring you a windfall.

Jupiter in Sagittarius

Independent, outgoing, and idealistic, you'll shoot for the stars. This Jupiter compels you to travel far and wide, both physically and mentally, via higher education. You may have luck while traveling in an exotic place. You also have luck with outdoor ventures, exercise, and animals, particularly horses. Since you tend to be very open about your opinions, watch a tendency to be tactless and to exaggerate. Instead, use your wonderful sense of humor to make your point.

Jupiter in Capricorn

Jupiter is much more restrained in Capricorn, the sign of rules and authority. Here, Jupiter can make you overwork and heighten any ambition or sense of duty you may have. You'll expand in areas that advance your position, putting you farther up the social or corporate ladder. You are lucky working within the establishment in a very structured situation, where you can show off your ability to organize and reap rewards for your hard work.

Jupiter in Aquarius

This is another freedom-loving Jupiter, with great tolerance and originality. You are at your best when you are working for a humanitarian cause and in the company of many supporters. This is a good Jupiter for a political career. You'll relate to all kinds of people on all social levels. You have an abundance of original ideas, but you are best off away from routine and any situation that imposes rigid rules. You need mental stimulation!

Jupiter in Pisces

You are a giver whose feelings and pocketbook are easily touched by others, so choose your companions with care. You could be the original sucker for a hard-luck story. Better find a worthy hospital or charity to appreciate your selfless support. You have a great creative imagination and may attract good fortune in fields related to oil, perfume, pharmaceuticals, petroleum, dance, footwear, and alcohol. But beware of overindulgence in alcohol—focus on a creative outlet instead.

Saturn Brakes

Jupiter speeds you up with *lucky breaks,* then along comes Saturn to slow you down with the *disciplinary brakes.* Saturn has unfairly been called a malefic planet, one of the bad guys of the zodiac. On the contrary, Saturn is one of our best friends, the kind who tells you what you need to hear, even if it's not good news. Under a Saturn transit, we grow up, take responsibility for our lives, and emerge from whatever test this planet has in store, far wiser, more capable, and more mature.

When Saturn hits a critical point in your horoscope, you can count on an experience that will make you slow up, pull back, and reexamine your life. It is a call to eliminate what is not working and to shape up. By the end of its twenty-eight-year trip around the zodiac,

Saturn will have tested you in all areas of your life. The major tests happen in seven-year cycles, when Saturn passes over the *angles* of your chart—your rising sign, midheaven, descendant, and nadir. This is when the real life-changing experiences happen. But you are also in for a testing period whenever Saturn passes a *planet* in your chart or stresses that planet from a distance. Therefore, it is useful to check your planetary positions with the timetable of Saturn to prepare in advance, or at least to brace yourself.

When Saturn returns to its location at the time of your birth, at approximately age twenty-eight, you'll have your first Saturn return. At this time, a person usually takes stock or settles down to find his mission in life and assumes full adult duties and responsibilities.

Another way Saturn helps us is to reveal the karmic lessons from previous lives and give us the chance to overcome them. So look at Saturn's challenges as much-needed opportunities for self-improvement. Under a Jupiter influence, you'll have more fun, but Saturn gives you solid, long-lasting results.

Look up your natal Saturn in the tables in this book for clues on where you need work.

Saturn in Aries

Saturn here puts the brakes on Aries's natural drive and enthusiasm. You don't let anyone push you around and you know what's best for yourself. Following orders is not your strong point, and neither is diplomacy. You tend to be quick to go on the offensive in relationships, attacking first, before anyone attacks you. Because no one quite lives up to your standards, you often wind up doing everything yourself. You'll have to learn to cooperate and tone down self-centeredness.

Saturn in Taurus

A big issue is taking control of your cash flow. There will be lean periods that can be frightening, but you have the patience and endurance to stick them out and the methodical drive to prosper in the end. Learn to take a philosophical attitude like Ben Franklin, who had this placement and who said, "A penny saved is a penny earned."

Saturn in Gemini

You are a serious student of life, who may have difficulty communicating or sharing your knowledge. You may be shy, speak slowly, or have fears about communicating, like Eleanor Roosevelt. You dwell in the realms of science, theory, or abstract analysis, even when you are dealing with the emotions, like Sigmund Freud, who also had this placement.

Saturn in Cancer

Your tests come with establishing a secure emotional base. In doing so, you may have to deal with some very basic fears centering on your early home environment. Most of your Saturn tests will have emotional roots in those early childhood experiences. You may have difficulty remaining objective in terms of what you try to achieve, so it will be especially important for you to deal with negative feelings such as guilt, paranoia, jealousy, resentment, and suspicion. Galileo and Michaelangelo also navigated these murky waters.

Saturn in Leo

This is an authoritarian Saturn, a strict, demanding parent who may deny the pleasure principle in your zeal to see that rules are followed. Though you may feel guilty about taking the spotlight, you are very ambitious and loyal. You have to watch a tendency toward rigidity, also toward overwork and holding back affection. Joseph Kennedy and Billy Graham share this placement.

Saturn in Virgo

This is a cautious, exacting Saturn, intensely hard on yourself. Most of all, you give yourself the roughest time with your constant worries about every little detail, often making yourself sick. You may have difficulties setting priorities and getting the job done. Your tests will come in learning tolerance and understanding of others. Charles de Gaulle, Mae West, and Nathaniel Hawthorne had this meticulous Saturn.

Saturn in Libra

Saturn is exalted here, which makes this planet an ally. However, there are very likely to be commitment issues. You must learn to stand solidly on your own before you can have a successful relationship. You may choose very serious, older partners in life. You are extremely cautious as you deliberate every involvement—with good reason. It is best that you find an occupation that makes good use of your sense of duty and honor. Steer clear of fly-by-night situations. Both Khrushchev and Mao Tse-tung had this placement, too.

Saturn in Scorpio

You have great staying power. This Saturn tests you in situations involving control of others. You may feel drawn to some kind of intrigue or undercover work, like J. Edgar Hoover. Or there may be an air of mystery surrounding your life and death, like Marilyn Monroe and Robert Kennedy, who had this placement. There are lessons to be learned from your sexual involvements. Often sex is used for manipulation or is somehow out of the ordinary. The Roman emperor Caligula and the transvestite Christine Jorgensen are extreme cases.

Saturn in Sagittarius

Your challenges and lessons will come from tests of your spiritual and philosophical values, as happened to Martin Luther King and Gandhi. You are high-minded and sincere with this reflective, moral placement. Uncompromising in your ethical standards, you could become a benevolent despot.

Saturn in Capricorn

With the help of Saturn at maximum strength, your judgment will improve with age. And like Spencer Tracy's screen image, you'll be the gray-haired hero with a strong sense of responsibility. You advance in life slowly but steadily, always with a strong hand at the helm and an eye for the advantageous situation. Like Pat Robertson, you're likely to stand for conservative values. Negatively, you may be a loner, prone to periods of melancholy.

Saturn in Aquarius

Your tests come from relationships with groups. Do you care too much about what others think? Do you feel like an outsider, as Greta Garbo did? You may fear being different from others and therefore demean your own unique, forward-looking gifts, or like Lord Byron and Howard Hughes, take the opposite tack and rebel in the extreme. However, others with this placement have been able to apply discipline to accomplish great humanitarian goals, as Albert Schweitzer did.

Saturn in Pisces

Your fear of the unknown and the irrational may lead you to the safety and protection of an institution. You may go on the run like Jesse James, who had this placement, to avoid looking too deeply inside. Or you might go in the opposite, more positive direction and develop a disciplined psychoanalytic approach, which puts you more in control of your feelings. Some of you will take refuge in work with hospitals, charities, or religious institutions. Queen Victoria, who had this placement, symbolized an era when institutions of all kinds were sustained. Discipline applied to artistic work, especially poetry and dance, or spiritual work, such as yoga or meditation, might be helpful.

Uranus, Neptune, and Pluto Affect Your Whole Generation

These three planets remain in signs such a long time that a whole generation bears the imprint of the sign. Mass movements, great sweeping changes, fads that characterize a generation, even the issues of the conflicts and wars of the time are influenced by the "outer three." When one of these distant planets changes signs, there is a definite shift in the atmosphere, the feeling of the end of an era.

Since these planets are so far away from the sun—too distant to be seen by the naked eye—they pick up signals from the universe at large. These planetary receivers literally link the sun with distant energies, and then perform a similar function in your horoscope by linking your central character with intuitive, spiritual, transformative forces from the cosmos. Each planet has a special domain and will reflect this in the area of your chart where it falls.

Uranus Wakes You Up

There is nothing ordinary about this quirky green planet that seems to be traveling on its side, surrounded by a swarm of moons. Is it any wonder that astrologers assigned it to Aquarius, the most eccentric and gregarious sign? Uranus seems to wend its way around the sun, marching to its own tune.

Uranus's energy is electrical, happening in sudden flashes. It is not influenced by karma or past events, nor does it regard tradition, sex, or sentiment. The Uranian key words are "surprise" and "awakening." Uranus wakes you up, jolts you out of your comfortable rut. Suddenly, there's that flash of inspiration, that bright idea, a totally new approach that revolutionizes whatever you're doing. A Uranus event takes you by surprise, happens from out of the blue, for better or for worse. The Uranus place in your life is where you wake up to your own special qualities and become your own person, leaving the structures of Saturn behind.

Look up the sign of Uranus at the time of your birth. Then place it in the appropriate house in your chart and see where you follow your own tune.

Uranus in Aries

BIRTH DATES:
    March 31, 1927–November 4, 1927
    January 13, 1928—June 6, 1934
    October 10, 1934—March 28, 1935

Your generation is original, creative, pioneering. It developed the computer, the airplane, and the cyclotron. You let nothing hold you back from exploring the unknown and have a powerful mixture of fire and electricity behind you. Women of your generation were among the first to be liberated. You were the unforgettable style setters. You have a surprise in store for everyone. Like Yoko Ono, Grace Kelly, and Jacqueline Onassis, your life may be jolted by sudden and violent changes.

Uranus in Taurus

BIRTH DATES:
    June 6, 1934–October 10, 1934
    March 28, 1935–August 7, 1941
    October 5, 1941–May 15, 1942

World War II began during your generation. You are probably self-employed or would like to be. You have original ideas about making money, and you brace yourself for sudden changes of fortune. This Uranus can cause shakeups, particularly in finances, but it can also make you a born entrepreneur.

Uranus in Gemini

BIRTH DATES:
    August 7, 1941–October 5, 1941
    May 15, 1942–August 30, 1948
    November 12, 1948–June 10, 1949

You were the first children to be influenced by television. Now, in your adult years, your generation stocks up on answering machines, cordless phones, car phones, computers, and fax machines—any new way you can communicate. You have an inquiring mind, but your interests may be rather short-lived. This Uranus can be easily fragmented if there is no structure and focus.

Uranus in Cancer

BIRTH DATES:
    August 30, 1948–November 12, 1948
    June 10, 1949–August 24, 1955
    January 28, 1956–June 10, 1956

This generation came at a time when divorce was becoming commonplace, so your home image is unconventional. You may have an unusual relationship with your parents; you may have come from a broken home or an unconventional one. You'll have unorthodox ideas about parenting, intimacy, food, and shelter. You may also be interested in dreams, psychic phenomena, and memory work.

Uranus in Leo

BIRTH DATES:
  August 24, 1955–January 28, 1956
  June 10, 1956–November 1, 1961
  January 10, 1962–August 10, 1962

This generation understands how to use electronic media. Many of your group are now leaders in the high-tech industries, and you also understand how to use the new media to promote yourself. Like Isadora Duncan, you may have a very eccentric kind of charisma and a life that is sparked by unusual love affairs. Your children, too, may have traits that are out of the ordinary. Where this planet falls in your chart, you'll have a love of freedom, be a bit of an egomaniac, and show the full force of your personality in a unique way, like tennis great Martina Navratilova.

Uranus in Virgo

BIRTH DATES:
  November 1, 1961–January 10, 1962
  August 10, 1962–September 28, 1968
  May 20, 1969–June 24, 1969

You'll have highly individual work methods, and many will be finding newer, more practical ways to use computers. Like Einstein, who had this placement, you'll break the rules brilliantly. Your generation came at a time of student rebellions, the civil rights movement, and the general acceptance of health foods. Chances are, you're concerned about pollution and cleaning up the environment. You may also be involved with non-traditional healing methods. Heavyweight champ Mike Tyson has this placement.

Uranus in Libra

BIRTH DATES:
  September 28, 1968–May 20, 1969
  June 24, 1969–November 21, 1974
  May 1, 1975–September 8, 1975

Your generation will be always changing partners.
Born during the era of women's liberation, you may
have come from a broken home and have no clear
image of what a marriage entails. There will be many
sudden splits and experiments before you settle down.
Your generation will be much involved in legal and
political reforms and in changing artistic and fashion
looks.

Uranus in Scorpio

BIRTH DATES:
  November 21, 1974–May 1, 1975
  September 8, 1975–February 17, 1981
  March 20, 1981–November 16, 1981

Interest in transformation, meditation, and life after
death signaled the beginning of New Age consciousness. Your generation recognizes no boundaries, no
limits, and no external controls. You'll have new attitudes toward death and dying, psychic phenomena,
and the occult. Like Mae West and Casanova, you'll
shock 'em sexually, too.

Uranus in Sagittarius

BIRTH DATES:
  February 17, 1981–March 20, 1981
  November 16, 1981–February 15, 1988
  May 27, 1988–December 2, 1988

Could this generation be the first to travel in outer space? An earlier generation with this placement included Charles Lindbergh—at that time, the first Zeppelins and the Wright Brothers were conquering the skies. Uranus here forecasts great discoveries, mind expansion, and long-distance travel. Like Galileo and Martin Luther, this generation will formulate new theories about the cosmos and man's relation to it.

Uranus in Capricorn

BIRTH DATES:
  December 20, 1904–January 30, 1912
  September 4, 1912–November 12, 1912
  February 15, 1988–May 27, 1988
  December 2, 1988–April 1, 1995
  June 9, 1995–January 12, 1996

This generation will challenge traditions with the help of electronic gadgets. During the mid-1990s, we got organized with the help of technology put to practical use. Home computers and handheld devices became widely used. Great leaders, who were movers and shakers of history, like Julius Caesar and Henry VIII, were born under this placement.

Uranus in Aquarius

BIRTH DATES:
  January 30, 1912–September 4, 1912
  November 12, 1912–April 1, 1919
  August 16, 1919–January 22, 1920
  April 1, 1995–June 9, 1995
  January 12, 1996–March 10, 2003

The last generation with this placement produced great innovative minds such as Leonard Bernstein and Orson Welles. Babies who are born now will become another radical breakthrough generation, much concerned with global issues that involve all humanity. Intuition, innovation, and sudden changes will continue to surprise everyone while Uranus is in its home sign.

Uranus in Pisces

BIRTH DATES:
  April 1, 1919–August 16, 1919
  January 22, 1920–March 31, 1927
  November 4, 1927–January 12, 1928
  March 10, 2003–May 28, 2010

Uranus in Pisces previously focused attention on the rise of electronic entertainment—radio and the cinema—and the secretiveness of Prohibition. This produced a generation of idealists exemplified by Judy Garland's theme, "Somewhere Over the Rainbow." Coming up next year will be the dramatic return of Uranus to Pisces, which should spark a wonderful spurt of creativity and innovation in the arts.

Neptune Takes You out of This World

Under Neptune's influence, you see what you want to see. But Neptune also encourages you to create, letting your fantasies and daydreams run free. Neptune is often maligned as the planet of illusions, drugs, and alcohol, where you can't bear to face reality. But it also embodies the energy of glamour, subtlety, mystery, and mysticism, and governs anything that takes you beyond the mundane world, including out-of-body experiences.

Neptune acts to break through your ordinary perceptions and take you to another level of reality, where you experience either confusion or ecstasy. Neptune's force can pull you off-course, the way this planet affects its neighbor, Uranus, but only if you allow this to happen. Those who use Neptune wisely can translate their daydreams into poetry, theater, design, or inspired moves in the business world, avoiding the tricky "con artist" side of this planet.

Find your Neptune listed below:

Neptune in Cancer

BIRTH DATES:
 July 19, 1901–December 25, 1901
 May 21, 1902–September 23, 1914
 December 14, 1914–July 19, 1915
 March 1916–May 2, 1916

Dreams of the homeland, idealistic patriotism, and glamorization of the nurturing assets of women characterized this time. You who were born here have unusual psychic ability and deep insights into the basic needs of others.

Neptune in Leo

BIRTH DATES:
 September 23, 1914–December 14, 1914
 July 19, 1915–March 19, 1916
 May 2, 1916–September 21, 1928
 February 19, 1929–July 24, 1929

Neptune here brought us the glamour and high living of the 1920s and the big spenders of that time. The Neptunian temptations of gambling, seduction, theater, and lavish entertaining distracted us from the realities of the age. Those born in this generation also made great advances in the arts.

Neptune in Virgo

BIRTH DATES:
  September 21, 1928–February 19, 1929
  July 24, 1929–October 3, 1942
  April 17, 1943–August 2, 1943

Neptune in Virgo encompassed the Great Depression and World War II, while those born at this time later spread the gospel of health and fitness. This generation's devotion to spending hours at the office inspired the term "workaholic."

Neptune in Libra

BIRTH DATES:
  October 3, 1942–April 17, 1943
  August 2, 1943–December 24, 1955
  March 12, 1956–October 19, 1956
  June 15, 1957–August 6, 1957

Neptune in Libra produced the romantic generation who would later be extremely concerned with relating. As this generation matured, there was a new trend toward marriage and commitment. Racial and sexual equality become important issues, as they redesigned traditional relationship roles to suit modern times.

Neptune in Scorpio

BIRTH DATES:
  December 24, 1955–March 12, 1956
  October 19, 1956–June 15, 1957
  August 6, 1957–January 4, 1970
  May 3, 1970–November 6, 1970

Neptune in Scorpio ushered in a generation that would become interested in transformative power. Born in an era that glamorized sex, drugs, rock and roll, and Eastern religion, they matured in a more sobering time of AIDS, cocaine abuse, and New Age spirituality. As they evolve, they will become active in healing the planet from the results of the abuse of power.

Neptune in Sagittarius

BIRTH DATES:
  January 4, 1970–May 3, 1970
  November 6, 1970–January 19, 1984
  June 23, 1984–November 21, 1984

Neptune in Sagittarius was the time when space and astronaut travel became a reality. The Neptune influence glamorized new approaches to mysticism, religion, and mind expansion. This generation will take a new approach to spiritual life, with emphasis on visions, mysticism, and clairvoyance.

Neptune in Capricorn

BIRTH DATES:
  January 19, 1984–June 23, 1984
  November 21, 1984–January 29, 1998

Neptune in Capricorn brought a time when delusions about material power were first glamorized, then dashed on the rocks of reality. It was also a time when the psychic and occult worlds spawned a new category of business enterprise, and sold services on television.

Neptune in Aquarius

BIRTH DATES:
  January 29, 1998–April 4, 2111

This should continue to be a time of breakthroughs, when the creative influence of Neptune reaches a universal audience. This is a time of dissolving barriers, of globalization, when we truly become one world. Computer technology used for the creative arts, innovative drug therapies, and high-tech "highs" such as trance music are recent manifestations.

Pluto Transforms You

Pluto is a mysterious little planet with a strange elliptical orbit that occasionally runs inside the orbit of its neighbor Neptune. Because of its eccentric path, the length of time Pluto stays in any given sign can vary from thirteen to thirty-two years. It has covered only seven signs in the past century. Though it is a tiny planet, its influence is great. When Pluto zaps a strategic point in your horoscope, your life changes dramatically.

This little planet is the power behind the scenes; it affects you at deep levels of consciousness, causing events to come to the surface that will transform you and your generation. Nothing escapes, or is sacred, with this probing planet. The Pluto place in your horoscope is where you have invisible power (Mars governs the visible power), where you can transform, heal, and affect the unconscious needs of the masses. Pluto tells how your generation projects power, what makes it seem "cool" to others. And when Pluto changes signs, there's a whole new concept of what's cool.

Pluto in Gemini

BIRTH DATES:
  Late 1800s–May 26, 1914

This was a time of mass suggestion and breakthroughs in communications, when many brilliant writers, such as Ernest Hemingway and F. Scott Fitzgerald, were born. Henry Miller, D. H. Lawrence, and James Joyce scandalized society by using explicit sexual images and language in their literature. "Muckraking" journalists exposed corruption. Pluto-ruled Scorpio President Theodore Roosevelt said, "Speak softly, but carry a big stick." This generation had an intense need to communicate and made major breakthroughs in knowledge. A compulsive restlessness and a thirst for a variety of experiences characterizes many of this generation.

Pluto in Cancer

BIRTH DATES:
May 26, 1914–June 14, 1939

Dictators and mass media rose up to wield emotional power over the masses. Women's rights was a popular issue. Deep sentimental feelings, acquisitiveness, and possessiveness characterized these times and people. The great Hollywood stars who embodied the American image were born during this period: Grace Kelly, Esther Williams, Frank Sinatra, Lana Turner, etc.

Pluto in Leo

BIRTH DATES:
June 14, 1939–August 19, 1957

The performing arts played on the emotions of the masses. Mick Jagger, John Lennon, and rock and roll were born at this time. So were "baby boomers" like Bill and Hillary Clinton. Those born here tend to be self-centered, powerful, and boisterous. This generation does its own thing, for better or for worse.

Pluto in Virgo

BIRTH DATES:
August 19, 1957–October 5, 1971
April 17, 1972–July 30, 1972

This is the "yuppie" generation that sparked a mass movement toward fitness, health, and career. A much more sober, serious, driven generation than the fun-loving Pluto in Leos. During this time, machines were invented to process detail work efficiently. Inventions took a practical turn, as answering machines, fax machines, car phones, and home office equipment contributed to transform the workplace.

Pluto in Libra

BIRTH DATES:
  October 5, 1971–April 17, 1972
  July 30, 1972–August 28, 1984

A mellower generation concerned with partnerships, working together, and finding diplomatic solutions to problems. Marriage is important to this generation, who will redefine it, combining traditional values with equal partnership. This was a time of women's liberation, gay rights, ERA, and legal battles over abortion, all of which transformed our ideas about relationships.

Pluto in Scorpio

BIRTH DATES:
  August 28, 1984–January 17, 1995

Pluto was in its ruling sign for a comparatively short period of time. In 1989, it was at its perihelion, or closest point to the sun and Earth. We have all felt the transforming power somewhere in our lives. This was a time of record achievements, destructive sexually transmitted diseases, nuclear power controversies, and explosive political issues. Pluto destroys in order to create new understanding—the phoenix rising from the ashes, which should be some consolation for those of you who felt Pluto's force before 1995. Sexual shockers were par for the course during these intense years, when black clothing, transvestites, body piercing, tattoos, and sexually explicit advertising pushed the boundaries of good taste.

Pluto in Sagittarius

BIRTH DATES:
 January 17, 1995–January 27, 2008

During our current Pluto transit, we are being pushed to expand our horizons. For many of us, this will mean rolling down the information superhighway into the future. Another trend is to find deeper spiritual meaning in life. This is a time when spiritual emphasis will become pervasive, when religious convictions will exert more power in our political life as well.

Since Sagittarius is the sign that rules travel, there's a good possibility that Pluto, the planet of extremes, will make space travel a reality for some of us. Discovery of life on Mars, which traveled here on meteors, could transform our ideas about where we came from.

New dimensions in electronic publishing, concern with animal rights and the environment, and an increasing emphasis on extreme forms of religion are other signs of these times. Look for charismatic religious leaders to arise now. We'll also be developing far-reaching philosophies designed to elevate our lives with a new sense of purpose.

VENUS SIGNS 1901–2002

	Aries	Taurus	Gemini	Cancer	Leo	Virgo
1901	3/29–4/22	4/22–5/17	5/17–6/10	6/10–7/5	7/5–7/29	7/29–8/23
1902	5/7–6/3	6/3–6/30	6/30–7/25	7/25–8/19	8/19–9/13	9/13–10/7
1903	2/28–3/24	3/24–4/18	4/18–5/13	5/13–6/9	6/9–7/7	7/7–8/17
						9/6–11/8
1904	3/13–5/7	5/7–6/1	6/1–6/25	6/25–7/19	7/19–8/13	8/13–9/6
1905	2/3–3/6	3/6–4/9	7/8–8/6	8/6–9/1	9/1–9/27	9/27–10/21
	4/9–5/28	5/28–7/8				
1906	3/1–4/7	4/7–5/2	5/2–5/26	5/26–6/20	6/20–7/16	7/16–8/11
1907	4/27–5/22	5/22–6/16	6/16–7/11	7/11–8/4	8/4–8/29	8/29–9/22
1908	2/14–3/10	3/10–4/5	4/5–5/5	5/5–9/8	9/8–10/8	10/8–11/3
1909	3/29–4/22	4/22–5/16	5/16–6/10	6/10–7/4	7/4–7/29	7/29–8/23
1910	5/7–6/3	6/4–6/29	6/30–7/24	7/25–8/18	8/19–9/12	9/13–10/6
1911	2/28–3/23	3/24–4/17	4/18–5/12	5/13–6/8	6/9–7/7	7/8–11/8
1912	4/13–5/6	5/7–5/31	6/1–6/24	6/24–7/18	7/19–8/12	8/13–9/5
1913	2/3–3/6	3/7–5/1	7/8–8/5	8/6–8/31	9/1–9/26	9/27–10/20
	5/2–5/30	5/31–7/7				
1914	3/14–4/6	4/7–5/1	5/2–5/25	5/26–6/19	6/20–7/15	7/16–8/10
1915	4/27–5/21	5/22–6/15	6/16–7/10	7/11–8/3	8/4–8/28	8/29–9/21
1916	2/14–3/9	3/10–4/5	4/6–5/5	5/6–9/8	9/9–10/7	10/8–11/2
1917	3/29–4/21	4/22–5/15	5/16–6/9	6/10–7/3	7/4–7/28	7/29–8/21
1918	5/7–6/2	6/3–6/28	6/29–7/24	7/25–8/18	8/19–9/11	9/12–10/5
1919	2/27–3/22	3/23–4/16	4/17–5/12	5/13–6/7	6/8–7/7	7/8–11/8
1920	4/12–5/6	5/7–5/30	5/31–6/23	6/24–7/18	7/19–8/11	8/12–9/4
1921	2/3–3/6	3/7–4/25	7/8–8/5	8/6–8/31	9/1–9/25	9/26–10/20
	4/26–6/1	6/2–7/7				
1922	3/13–4/6	4/7–4/30	5/1–5/25	5/26–6/19	6/20–7/14	7/15–8/9
1923	4/27–5/21	5/22–6/14	6/15–7/9	7/10–8/3	8/4–8/27	8/28–9/20
1924	2/13–3/8	3/9–4/4	4/5–5/5	5/6–9/8	9/9–10/7	10/8–11/12
1925	3/28–4/20	4/21–5/15	5/16–6/8	6/9–7/3	7/4–7/27	7/28–8/21

Libra	Scorpio	Sagittarius	Capricorn	Aquarius	Pisces
8/23–9/17	9/17–10/12	10/12–1/16	1/16–2/9	2/9–3/5	3/5–3/29
			11/7–12/5	12/5–1/11	
10/7–10/31	10/31–11/24	11/24–12/18	12/18–1/11	2/6–4/4	1/11–2/6
					4/4–5/7
8/17–9/6	12/9–1/5			1/11–2/4	2/4–2/28
11/8–12/9					
9/6–9/30	9/30–10/25	1/5–1/30	1/30–2/24	2/24–3/19	3/19–4/13
		10/25–11/18	11/18–12/13	12/13–1/7	
10/21–11/14	11/14–12/8	12/8–1/1/06			1/7–2/3
8/11–9/7	9/7–10/9	10/9–12/15	1/1–1/25	1/25–2/18	2/18–3/14
	12/15–12/25	12/25–2/6			
9/22–10/16	10/16–11/9	11/9–12/3	2/6–3/6	3/6–4/2	4/2–4/27
			12/3–12/27	12/27–1/20	
11/3–11/28	11/28–12/22	12/22–1/15			1/20–2/4
8/23–9/17	9/17–10/12	10/12–11/17	1/15–2/9	2/9–3/5	3/5–3/29
			11/17–12/5	12/5–1/15	
10/7–10/30	10/31–11/23	11/24–12/17	12/18–12/31	1/1–1/15	1/16–1/28
				1/29–4/4	4/5–5/6
11/19–12/8	12/9–12/31		1/1–1/10	1/11–2/2	2/3–2/27
9/6–9/30	1/1–1/4	1/5–1/29	1/30–2/23	2/24–3/18	3/19–4/12
	10/1–10/24	10/25–11/17	11/18–12/12	12/13–12/31	
10/21–11/13	11/14–12/7	12/8–12/31		1/1–1/6	1/7–2/2
8/11–9/6	9/7–10/9	10/10–12/5	1/1–1/24	1/25–2/17	2/18–3/13
	12/6–12/30	12/31			
9/22–10/15	10/16–11/8	1/1–2/6	2/7–3/6	3/7–4/1	4/2–4/26
		11/9–12/2	12/3–12/26	12/27–12/31	
11/3–11/27	11/28–12/21	12/22–12/31		1/1–1/19	1/20–2/13
8/22–9/16	9/17–10/11	1/1–1/14	1/15–2/7	2/8–3/4	3/5–3/28
		10/12–11/6	11/7–12/5	12/6–12/31	
10/6–10/29	10/30–11/22	11/23–12/16	12/17–12/31	1/1–4/5	4/6–5/6
11/9–12/8	12/9–12/31		1/1–1/9	1/10–2/2	2/3–2/26
9/5–9/30	1/1–1/3	1/4–1/28	1/29–2/22	2/23–3/18	3/19–4/11
	9/31–10/23	10/24–11/17	11/18–12/11	12/12–12/31	
10/21–11/13	11/14–12/7	12/8–12/31		1/1–1/6	1/7–2/2
8/10–9/6	9/7–10/10	10/11–11/28	1/1–1/24	1/25–2/16	2/17–3/12
	11/29–12/31				
9/21–10/14	1/1	1/2–2/6	2/7–3/5	3/6–3/31	4/1–4/26
	10/15–11/7	11/8–12/1	12/2–12/25	12/26–12/31	
11/13–11/26	11/27–12/21	12/22–12/31		1/1–1/19	1/20–2/12
8/22–9/15	9/16–10/11	1/1–1/14	1/15–2/7	2/8–3/3	3/4–3/27
		10/12–11/6	11/7–12/5	12/6–12/31	

VENUS SIGNS 1901–2002

	Aries	Taurus	Gemini	Cancer	Leo	Virgo
1926	5/7–6/2	6/3–6/28	6/29–7/23	7/24–8/17	8/18–9/11	9/12–10/5
1927	2/27–3/22	3/23–4/16	4/17–5/11	5/12–6/7	6/8–7/7	7/8–11/9
1928	4/12–5/5	5/6–5/29	5/30–6/23	6/24–7/17	7/18–8/11	8/12–9/4
1929	2/3–3/7	3/8–4/19	7/8–8/4	8/5–8/30	8/31–9/25	9/26–10/19
	4/20–6/2	6/3–7/7				
1930	3/13–4/5	4/6–4/30	5/1–5/24	5/25–6/18	6/19–7/14	7/15–8/9
1931	4/26–5/20	5/21–6/13	6/14–7/8	7/9–8/2	8/3–8/26	8/27–9/19
1932	2/12–3/8	3/9–4/3	4/4–5/5	5/6–7/12	9/9–10/6	10/7–11/1
			7/13–7/27	7/28–9/8		
1933	3/27–4/19	4/20–5/28	5/29–6/8	6/9–7/2	7/3–7/26	7/27–8/20
1934	5/6–6/1	6/2–6/27	6/28–7/22	7/23–8/16	8/17–9/10	9/11–10/4
1935	2/26–3/21	3/22–4/15	4/16–5/10	5/11–6/6	6/7–7/6	7/7–11/8
1936	4/11–5/4	5/5–5/28	5/29–6/22	6/23–7/16	7/17–8/10	8/11–9/4
1937	2/2–3/8	3/9–4/13	7/7–8/3	8/4–8/29	8/30–9/24	9/25–10/18
	4/14–6/3	6/4–7/6				
1938	3/12–4/4	4/5–4/28	4/29–5/23	5/24–6/18	6/19–7/13	7/14–8/8
1939	4/25–5/19	5/20–6/13	6/14–7/8	7/9–8/1	8/2–8/25	8/26–9/19
1940	2/12–3/7	3/8–4/3	4/4–5/5	5/6–7/4	9/9–10/5	10/6–10/31
			7/5–7/31	8/1–9/8		
1941	3/27–4/19	4/20–5/13	5/14–6/6	6/7–7/1	7/2–7/26	7/27–8/20
1942	5/6–6/1	6/2–6/26	6/27–7/22	7/23–8/16	8/17–9/9	9/10–10/3
1943	2/25–3/20	3/21–4/14	4/15–5/10	5/11–6/6	6/7–7/6	7/7–11/8
1944	4/10–5/3	5/4–5/28	5/29–6/21	6/22–7/16	7/17–8/9	8/10–9/2
1945	2/2–3/10	3/11–4/6	7/7–8/3	8/4–8/29	8/30–9/23	9/24–10/18
	4/7–6/3	6/4–7/6				
1946	3/11–4/4	4/5–4/28	4/29–5/23	5/24–6/17	6/18–7/12	7/13–8/8
1947	4/25–5/19	5/20–6/12	6/13–7/7	7/8–8/1	8/2–8/25	8/26–9/18
1948	2/11–3/7	3/8–4/3	4/4–5/6	5/7–6/28	9/8–10/5	10/6–10/31
			6/29–8/2	8/3–9/7		
1949	3/26–4/19	4/20–5/13	5/14–6/6	6/7–6/30	7/1–7/25	7/26–8/19
1950	5/5–5/31	6/1–6/26	6/27–7/21	7/22–8/15	8/16–9/9	9/10–10/3
1951	2/25–3/21	3/22–4/15	4/16–5/10	5/11–6/6	6/7–7/7	7/8–11/9

Libra	Scorpio	Sagittarius	Capricorn	Aquarius	Pisces
10/6–10/29	10/30–11/22	11/23–12/16	12/17–12/31	1/1–4/5	4/6–5/6
11/10–12/8	12/9–12/31	1/1–1/7	1/8	1/9–2/1	2/2–2/26
9/5–9/28	1/1–1/3	1/4–1/28	1/29–2/22	2/23–3/17	3/18–4/11
	9/29–10/23	10/24–11/16	11/17–12/11	12/12–12/31	
10/20–11/12	11/13–12/6	12/7–12/30	12/31	1/1–1/5	1/6–2/2
8/10–9/6	9/7–10/11	10/12–11/21	1/1–1/23	1/24–2/16	2/17–3/12
	11/22–12/31				
9/20–10/13	1/1–1/3	1/4–2/6	2/7–3/4	3/5–3/31	4/1–4/25
	10/14–11/6	11/7–11/30	12/1–12/24	12/25–12/31	
11/2–11/25	11/26–12/20	12/21–12/31		1/1–1/18	1/19–2/11
8/21–9/14	9/15–10/10	1/1–1/13	1/14–2/6	2/7–3/2	3/3–3/26
		10/11–11/5	11/6–12/4	12/5–12/31	
10/5–10/28	10/29–11/21	11/22–12/15	12/16–12/31	1/1–4/5	4/6–5/5
11/9–12/7	12/8–12/31		1/1–1/7	1/8–1/31	2/1–2/25
9/5–9/27	1/1–1/2	1/3–1/27	1/28–2/21	2/22–3/16	3/17–4/10
	9/28–10/22	10/23–11/15	11/16–12/10	12/11–12/31	
10/19–11/11	11/12–12/5	12/6–12/29	12/30–12/31	1/1–1/5	1/6–2/1
8/9–9/6	9/7–10/13	10/14–11/14	1/1–1/22	1/23–2/15	2/16–3/11
	11/15–12/31				
9/20–10/13	1/1–1/3	1/4–2/5	2/6–3/4	3/5–3/30	3/31–4/24
	10/14–11/6	11/7–11/30	12/1–12/24	12/25–12/31	
11/1–11/25	11/26–12/19	12/20–12/31		1/1–1/18	1/19–2/11
8/21–9/14	9/15–10/9	1/1–1/12	1/13–2/5	2/6–3/1	3/2–3/26
		10/10–11/5	11/6–12/4	12/5–12/31	
10/4–10/27	10/28–11/20	11/21–12/14	12/15–12/31	1/1–4/4	4/6–5/5
11/9–12/7	12/8–12/31		1/1–1/7	1/8–1/31	2/1–2/24
9/3–9/27	1/1–1/2	1/3–1/27	1/28–2/20	2/21–3/16	3/17–4/9
	9/28–10/21	10/22–11/15	11/16–12/10	12/11–12/31	
10/19–11/11	11/12–12/5	12/6–12/29	12/30–12/31	1/1–1/4	1/5–2/1
8/9–9/6	9/7–10/15	10/16–11/7	1/1–1/21	1/22–2/14	2/15–3/10
	11/8–12/31				
9/19–10/12	1/1–1/4	1/5–2/5	2/6–3/4	3/5–3/29	3/30–4/24
	10/13–11/5	11/6–11/29	11/30–12/23	12/24–12/31	
11/1–11/25	11/26–12/19	12/20–12/31		1/1–1/17	1/18–2/10
8/20–9/14	9/15–10/9	1/1–1/12	1/13–2/5	2/6–3/1	3/2–3/25
		10/10–11/5	11/6–12/5	12/6–12/31	
10/4–10/27	10/28–11/20	11/21–12/13	12/14–12/31	1/1–4/5	4/6–5/4
11/10–12/7	12/8–12/31		1/1–1/7	1/8–1/31	2/1–2/24

VENUS SIGNS 1901–2002

	Aries	Taurus	Gemini	Cancer	Leo	Virgo
1952	4/10–5/4	5/5–5/28	5/29–6/21	6/22–7/16	7/17–8/9	8/10–9/3
1953	2/2–3/3 4/1–6/5	3/4–3/31 6/6–7/7	7/8–8/3	8/4–8/29	8/30–9/24	9/25–10/18
1954	3/12–4/4	4/5–4/28	4/29–5/23	5/24–6/17	6/18–7/13	7/14–8/8
1955	4/25–5/19	5/20–6/13	6/14–7/7	7/8–8/1	8/2–8/25	8/26–9/18
1956	2/12–3/7	3/8–4/4	4/5–5/7 6/24–8/4	5/8–6/23 8/5–9/8	9/9–10/5	10/6–10/31
1957	3/26–4/19	4/20–5/13	5/14–6/6	6/7–7/1	7/2–7/26	7/27–8/19
1958	5/6–5/31	6/1–6/26	6/27–7/22	7/23–8/15	8/16–9/9	9/10–10/3
1959	2/25–3/20	3/21–4/14	4/15–5/10	5/11–6/6	6/7–7/8 9/21–9/24	7/9–9/20 9/25–11/9
1960	4/10–5/3	5/4–5/28	5/29–6/21	6/22–7/15	7/16–8/9	8/10–9/2
1961	2/3–6/5	6/6–7/7	7/8–8/3	8/4–8/29	8/30–9/23	9/24–10/17
1962	3/11–4/3	4/4–4/28	4/29–5/22	5/23–6/17	6/18–7/12	7/13–8/8
1963	4/24–5/18	5/19–6/12	6/13–7/7	7/8–7/31	8/1–8/25	8/26–9/18
1964	2/11–3/7	3/8–4/4	4/5–5/9 6/18–8/5	5/10–6/17 8/6–9/8	9/9–10/5	10/6–10/31
1965	3/26–4/18	4/19–5/12	5/13–6/6	6/7–6/30	7/1–7/25	7/26–8/19
1966	5/6–6/31	6/1–6/26	6/27–7/21	7/22–8/15	8/16–9/8	9/9–10/2
1967	2/24–3/20	3/21–4/14	4/15–5/10	5/11–6/6	6/7–7/8 9/10–10/1	7/9–9/9 10/2–11/9
1968	4/9–5/3	5/4–5/27	5/28–6/20	6/21–7/15	7/16–8/8	8/9–9/2
1969	2/3–6/6	6/7–7/6	7/7–8/3	8/4–8/28	8/29–9/22	9/23–10/17
1970	3/11–4/3	4/4–4/27	4/28–5/22	5/23–6/16	6/17–7/12	7/13–8/8
1971	4/24–5/18	5/19–6/12	6/13–7/6	7/7–7/31	8/1–8/24	8/25–9/17
1972	2/11–3/7	3/8–4/3	4/4–5/10 6/12–8/6	5/11–6/11 8/7–9/8	9/9–10/5	10/6–10/30
1973	3/25–4/18	4/18–5/12	5/13–6/5	6/6–6/29	7/1–7/25	7/26–8/19
1974	5/5–5/31	6/1–6/25	6/26–7/21	7/22–8/14	8/15–9/8	9/9–10/2
1975	2/24–3/20	3/21–4/13	4/14–5/9	5/10–6/6	6/7–7/9 9/3–10/4	7/10–9/2 10/5–11/9

Libra	Scorpio	Sagittarius	Capricorn	Aquarius	Pisces
9/4–9/27	1/1–1/2	1/3–1/27	1/28–2/20	2/21–3/16	3/17–4/9
	9/28–10/21	10/22–11/15	11/16–12/10	12/11–12/31	
10/19–11/11	11/12–12/5	12/6–12/29	12/30–12/31	1/1–1/5	1/6–2/1
8/9–9/6	9/7–10/22	10/23–10/27	1/1–1/22	1/23–2/15	2/16–3/11
	10/28–12/31				
9/19–10/13	1/1–1/6	1/7–2/5	2/6–3/4	3/5–3/30	3/31–4/24
	10/14–11/5	11/6–11/30	12/1–12/24	12/25–12/31	
11/1–11/25	11/26–12/19	12/20–12/31		1/1–1/17	1/18–2/11
8/20–9/14	9/15–10/9	1/1–1/12	1/13–2/5	2/6–3/1	3/2–3/25
		10/10–11/5	11/6–12/6	12/7–12/31	
10/4–10/27	10/28–11/20	11/21–12/14	12/15–12/31	1/1–4/6	4/7–5/5
11/10–12/7	12/8–12/31		1/1–1/7	1/8–1/31	2/1–2/24
9/3–9/26	1/1–1/2	1/3–1/27	1/28–2/20	2/21–3/15	3/16–4/9
	9/27–10/21	10/22–11/15	11/16–12/10	12/11–12/31	
10/18–11/11	11/12–12/4	12/5–12/28	12/29–12/31	1/1–1/5	1/6–2/2
8/9–9/6	9/7–12/31		1/1–1/21	1/22–2/14	2/15–3/10
9/19–10/12	1/1–1/6	1/7–2/5	2/6–3/4	3/5–3/29	3/30–4/23
	10/13–11/5	11/6–11/29	11/30–12/23	12/24–12/31	
11/1–11/24	11/25–12/19	12/20–12/31		1/1–1/16	1/17–2/10
8/20–9/13	9/14–10/9	1/1–1/12	1/13–2/5	2/6–3/1	3/2–3/25
		10/10–11/5	11/6–12/7	12/8–12/31	
10/3–10/26	10/27–11/19	11/20–12/13	2/7–2/25	1/1–2/6	4/7–5/5
			12/14–12/31	2/26–4/6	
11/10–12/7	12/8–12/31		1/1–1/6	1/7–1/30	1/31–2/23
9/3–9/26	1/1	1/2–1/26	1/27–2/20	2/21–3/15	3/16–4/8
	9/27–10/21	10/22–11/14	11/15–12/9	12/10–12/31	
10/18–11/10	11/11–12/4	12/5–12/28	12/29–12/31	1/1–1/4	1/5–2/2
8/9–9/7	9/8–12/31		1/1–1/21	1/22–2/14	2/15–3/10
9/18–10/11	1/1–1/7	1/8–2/5	2/6–3/4	3/5–3/29	3/30–4/23
	10/12–11/5	11/6–11/29	11/30–12/23	12/24–12/31	
	11/25–12/18	12/19–12/31		1/1–1/16	1/17–2/10
10/31–11/24					
8/20–9/13	9/14–10/8	1/1–1/12	1/13–2/4	2/5–2/28	3/1–3/24
		10/9–11/5	11/6–12/7	12/8–12/31	
			1/30–2/28	1/1–1/29	
10/3–10/26	10/27–11/19	11/20–12/13	12/14–12/31	3/1–4/6	4/7–5/4
			1/1–1/6	1/7–1/30	1/31–2/23
11/10–12/7	12/8–12/31				

VENUS SIGNS 1901–2002

	Aries	Taurus	Gemini	Cancer	Leo	Virgo
1976	4/8–5/2	5/2–5/27	5/27–6/20	6/20–7/14	7/14–8/8	8/8–9/1
1977	2/2–6/6	6/6–7/6	7/6–8/2	8/2–8/28	8/28–9/22	9/22–10/17
1978	3/9–4/2	4/2–4/27	4/27–5/22	5/22–6/16	6/16–7/12	7/12–8/6
1979	4/23–5/18	5/18–6/11	6/11–7/6	7/6–7/30	7/30–8/24	8/24–9/17
1980	2/9–3/6	3/6–4/3	4/3–5/12	5/12–6/5	9/7–10/4	10/4–10/30
			6/5–8/6	8/6–9/7		
1981	3/24–4/17	4/17–5/11	5/11–6/5	6/5–6/29	6/29–7/24	7/24–8/18
1982	5/4–5/30	5/30–6/25	6/25–7/20	7/20–8/14	8/14–9/7	9/7–10/2
1983	2/22–3/19	3/19–4/13	4/13–5/9	5/9–6/6	6/6–7/10	7/10–8/27
					8/27–10/5	10/5–11/9
1984	4/7–5/2	5/2–5/26	5/26–6/20	6/20–7/14	7/14–8/7	8/7–9/1
1985	2/2–6/6	6/7–7/6	7/6–8/2	8/2–8/28	8/28–9/22	9/22–10/16
1986	3/9–4/2	4/2–4/26	4/26–5/21	5/21–6/15	6/15–7/11	7/11–8/7
1987	4/22–5/17	5/17–6/11	6/11–7/5	7/5–7/30	7/30–8/23	8/23–9/16
1988	2/9–3/6	3/6–4/3	4/3–5/17	5/17–5/27	9/7–10/4	10/4–10/29
			5/27–8/6	8/28–9/22	9/22–10/16	
1989	3/23–4/16	4/16–5/11	5/11–6/4	6/4–6/29	6/29–7/24	7/24–8/18
1990	5/4–5/30	5/30–6/25	6/25–7/20	7/20–8/13	8/13–9/7	9/7–10/1
1991	2/22–3/18	3/18–4/13	4/13–5/9	5/9–6/6	6/6–7/11	7/11–8/21
					8/21–10/6	10/6–11/9
1992	4/7–5/1	5/1–5/26	5/26–6/19	6/19–7/13	7/13–8/7	8/7–8/31
1993	2/2–6/6	6/6–7/6	7/6–8/1	8/1–8/27	8/27–9/21	9/21–10/16
1994	3/8–4/1	4/1–4/26	4/26–5/21	5/21–6/15	6/15–7/11	7/11–8/7
1995	4/22–5/17	5/16–6/10	6/10–7/5	7/5–7/29	7/29–8/23	8/23–9/16
1996	2/9–3/6	3/6–4/3	4/3–8/7	8/7–9/7	9/7–10/4	10/4–10/29
1997	3/23–4/16	4/16–5/10	5/10–6/4	6/4–6/28	6/28–7/23	7/23–8/17
1998	5/3–5/29	5/29–6/24	6/24–7/19	7/19–8/13	8/13–9/6	9/6–9/30
1999	2/21–3/18	3/18–4/12	4/12–5/8	5/8–6/5	6/5–7/12	7/12–8/15
					8/15–10/7	10/7–11/9
2000	4/6–5/1	5/1–5/25	5/25–6/13	6/13–7/13	7/13–8/6	8/6–8/31
2001	2/2–6/6	6/6–7/5	7/5–8/1	8/1–8/26	8/26–9/20	9/20–10/15
2002	3/7–4/1	4/1–4/25	4/25–5/20	5/20–6/14	6/14–7/10	7/10–8/7

Libra	Scorpio	Sagittarius	Capricorn	Aquarius	Pisces
9/1–9/26	9/26–10/20	1/1–1/26	1/26–2/19	2/19–3/15	3/15–4/8
		10/20–11/14	11/14–12/8	12/9–1/4	
10/17–11/10	11/10–12/4	12/4–12/27	12/27–1/20/78		1/4–2/2
8/6–9/7	9/7–1/7			1/20–2/13	2/13–3/9
9/17–10/11	10/11–11/4		2/5–3/3	3/3–3/29	3/29–4/23
		11/4–11/28	11/28–12/22	12/22–1/16/80	
10/30–11/24	11/24–12/18	12/18–1/11/81			1/16–2/9
8/18–9/12	9/12–10/9	10/9–11/5	1/11–2/4	2/4–2/28	2/28–3/24
			11/5–12/8	12/8–1/23/82	
10/2–10/26	10/26–11/18	11/18–12/12	1/23–3/2	3/2–4/6	4/6–5/4
			12/12–1/5/83		
11/9–12/6	12/6–1/1/84			1/5–1/29	1/29–2/22
9/1–9/25	9/25–10/20	1/1–1/25	1/25–2/19	2/19–3/14	3/14–4/7
		10/20–11/13	11/13–12/9	12/10–1/4	
10/16–11/9	11/9–12/3	12/3–12/27	12/28–1/19		1/4–2/2
8/7–9/7	9/7–1/7			1/20–2/13	2/13–3/9
9/16–10/10	10/10–11/3	1/7–2/5	2/5–3/3	3/3–3/28	3/28–4/22
		11/3–11/28	11/28–12/22	12/22–1/15	
10/29–11/23	11/23–12/17	12/17–1/10			1/15–2/9
8/18–9/12	9/12–10/8	10/8–11/5	1/10–2/3	2/3–2/27	2/27–3/23
			11/5–12/10	12/10–1/16/90	
10/1–10/25	10/25–11/18	11/18–12/12	1/16–3/3	3/3–4/6	4/6–5/4
			12/12–1/5		
11/9–12/6	12/6–12/31	12/31–1/25/92		1/5–1/29	1/29–2/22
8/31–9/25	9/25–10/19	10/19–11/13	1/25–2/18	2/18–3/13	3/13–4/7
			11/13–12/8	12/8–1/3/93	
10/16–11/9	11/9–12/2	12/2–12/26	12/26–1/19		1/3–2/2
8/7–9/7	9/7–1/7			1/19–2/12	2/12–3/8
9/16–10/10	10/10–11/13	1/7–2/4	2/4–3/2	3/2–3/28	3/28–4/22
		11/3–11/27	11/27–12/21	12/21–1/15	
10/29–11/23	11/23–12/17	12/17–1/10/97			1/15–2/9
8/17–9/12	9/12–10/8	10/8–11/5	1/10–2/3	2/3–2/27	2/27–3/23
			11/5–12/12	12/12–1/9	
9/30–10/24	10/24–11/17	11/17–12/11	1/9–3/4	3/4–4/6	4/6–5/3
11/9–12/5	12/5–12/31	12/31–1/24		1/4–1/28	1/28–2/21
8/31–9/24	9/24–10/19	10/19–11/13	1/24–2/18	2/18–3/12	3/13–4/6
			11/13–12/8	12/8	
10/15–11/8	11/8–12/2	12/2–12/26	12/26/01–	12/8/00–	1/3–2/2
			1/19/02	1/3/01	
8/7–9/7	9/7–1/7/03		1/26/01–1/18	1/18–2/11	2/11–3/7

75

How to Use the Mars, Jupiter, and Saturn Tables

Find the year of your birth on the left side of each column. The dates when the planet entered each sign are listed on the right side of each column. (Signs are abbreviated to three letters.) Your birthday should fall on or between each date listed, and your planetary placement should correspond to the earlier sign of that period.

MARS SIGNS 1901–2002

Year	Month	Day	Sign		Year	Month	Day	Sign
1901	MAR	1	Leo		1905	JAN	13	Scp
	MAY	11	Vir			AUG	21	Sag
	JUL	13	Lib			OCT	8	Cap
	AUG	31	Scp			NOV	18	Aqu
	OCT	14	Sag			DEC	27	Pic
	NOV	24	Cap		1906	FEB	4	Ari
1902	JAN	1	Aqu			MAR	17	Tau
	FEB	8	Pic			APR	28	Gem
	MAR	19	Ari			JUN	11	Can
	APR	27	Tau			JUL	27	Leo
	JUN	7	Gem			SEP	12	Vir
	JUL	20	Can			OCT	30	Lib
	SEP	4	Leo			DEC	17	Scp
	OCT	23	Vir		1907	FEB	5	Sag
	DEC	20	Lib			APR	1	Cap
1903	APR	19	Vir			OCT	13	Aqu
	MAY	30	Lib			NOV	29	Pic
	AUG	6	Scp		1908	JAN	11	Ari
	SEP	22	Sag			FEB	23	Tau
	NOV	3	Cap			APR	7	Gem
	DEC	12	Aqu			MAY	22	Can
1904	JAN	19	Pic			JUL	8	Leo
	FEB	27	Ari			AUG	24	Vir
	APR	6	Tau			OCT	10	Lib
	MAY	18	Gem			NOV	25	Scp
	JUN	30	Can		1909	JAN	10	Sag
	AUG	15	Leo			FEB	24	Cap
	OCT	1	Vir			APR	9	Aqu
	NOV	20	Lib			MAY	25	Pic

	JUL	21	Ari		AUG	19	Can
	SEP	26	Pic		OCT	7	Leo
	NOV	20	Ari	1916	MAY	28	Vir
1910	JAN	23	Tau		JUL	23	Lib
	MAR	14	Gem		SEP	8	Scp
	MAY	1	Can		OCT	22	Sag
	JUN	19	Leo		DEC	1	Cap
	AUG	6	Vir	1917	JAN	9	Aqu
	SEP	22	Lib		FEB	16	Pic
	NOV	6	Scp		MAR	26	Ari
	DEC	20	Sag		MAY	4	Tau
1911	JAN	31	Cap		JUN	14	Gem
	MAR	14	Aqu		JUL	28	Can
	APR	23	Pic		SEP	12	Leo
	JUN	2	Ari		NOV	2	Vir
	JUL	15	Tau	1918	JAN	11	Lib
	SEP	5	Gem		FEB	25	Vir
	NOV	30	Tau		JUN	23	Lib
1912	JAN	30	Gem		AUG	17	Scp
	APR	5	Can		OCT	1	Sag
	MAY	28	Leo		NOV	11	Cap
	JUL	17	Vir		DEC	20	Aqu
	SEP	2	Lib	1919	JAN	27	Pic
	OCT	18	Scp		MAR	6	Ari
	NOV	30	Sag		APR	15	Tau
1913	JAN	10	Cap		MAY	26	Gem
	FEB	19	Aqu		JUL	8	Can
	MAR	30	Pic		AUG	23	Leo
	MAY	8	Ari		OCT	10	Vir
	JUN	17	Tau		NOV	30	Lib
	JUL	29	Gem	1920	JAN	31	Scp
	SEP	15	Can		APR	23	Lib
1914	MAY	1	Leo		JUL	10	Scp
	JUN	26	Vir		SEP	4	Sag
	AUG	14	Lib		OCT	18	Cap
	SEP	29	Scp		NOV	27	Aqu
	NOV	11	Sag	1921	JAN	5	Pic
	DEC	22	Cap		FEB	13	Ari
1915	JAN	30	Aqu		MAR	25	Tau
	MAR	9	Pic		MAY	6	Gem
	APR	16	Ari		JUN	18	Can
	MAY	26	Tau		AUG	3	Leo
	JUL	6	Gem		SEP	19	Vir

	NOV	6	Lib		APR	7	Pic
	DEC	26	Scp		MAY	16	Ari
1922	FEB	18	Sag		JUN	26	Tau
	SEP	13	Cap		AUG	9	Gem
	OCT	30	Aqu		OCT	3	Can
	DEC	11	Pic		DEC	20	Gem
1923	JAN	21	Ari	1929	MAR	10	Can
	MAR	4	Tau		MAY	13	Leo
	APR	16	Gem		JUL	4	Vir
	MAY	30	Can		AUG	21	Lib
	JUL	16	Leo		OCT	6	Scp
	SEP	1	Vir		NOV	18	Sag
	OCT	18	Lib		DEC	29	Cap
	DEC	4	Scp	1930	FEB	6	Aqu
1924	JAN	19	Sag		MAR	17	Pic
	MAR	6	Cap		APR	24	Ari
	APR	24	Aqu		JUN	3	Tau
	JUN	24	Pic		JUL	14	Gem
	AUG	24	Aqu		AUG	28	Can
	OCT	19	Pic		OCT	20	Leo
	DEC	19	Ari	1931	FEB	16	Can
1925	FEB	5	Tau		MAR	30	Leo
	MAR	24	Gem		JUN	10	Vir
	MAY	9	Can		AUG	1	Lib
	JUN	26	Leo		SEP	17	Scp
	AUG	12	Vir		OCT	30	Sag
	SEP	28	Lib		DEC	10	Cap
	NOV	13	Scp	1932	JAN	18	Aqu
	DEC	28	Sag		FEB	25	Pic
1926	FEB	9	Cap		APR	3	Ari
	MAR	23	Aqu		MAY	12	Tau
	MAY	3	Pic		JUN	22	Gem
	JUN	15	Ari		AUG	4	Can
	AUG	1	Tau		SEP	20	Leo
1927	FEB	22	Gem		NOV	13	Vir
	APR	17	Can	1933	JUL	6	Lib
	JUN	6	Leo		AUG	26	Scp
	JUL	25	Vir		OCT	9	Sag
	SEP	10	Lib		NOV	19	Cap
	OCT	26	Scp		DEC	28	Aqu
	DEC	8	Sag	1934	FEB	4	Pic
1928	JAN	19	Cap		MAR	14	Ari
	FEB	28	Aqu		APR	22	Tau

	JUN	2	Gem		AUG	19	Vir
	JUL	15	Can		OCT	5	Lib
	AUG	30	Leo		NOV	20	Scp
	OCT	18	Vir	1941	JAN	4	Sag
	DEC	11	Lib		FEB	17	Cap
1935	JUL	29	Scp		APR	2	Aqu
	SEP	16	Sag		MAY	16	Pic
	OCT	28	Cap		JUL	2	Ari
	DEC	7	Aqu	1942	JAN	11	Tau
1936	JAN	14	Pic		MAR	7	Gem
	FEB	22	Ari		APR	26	Can
	APR	1	Tau		JUN	14	Leo
	MAY	13	Gem		AUG	1	Vir
	JUN	25	Can		SEP	17	Lib
	AUG	10	Leo		NOV	1	Scp
	SEP	26	Vir		DEC	15	Sag
	NOV	14	Lib	1943	JAN	26	Cap
1937	JAN	5	Scp		MAR	8	Aqu
	MAR	13	Sag		APR	17	Pic
	MAY	14	Scp		MAY	27	Ari
	AUG	8	Sag		JUL	7	Tau
	SEP	30	Cap		AUG	23	Gem
	NOV	11	Aqu	1944	MAR	28	Can
	DEC	21	Pic		MAY	22	Leo
1938	JAN	30	Ari		JUL	12	Vir
	MAR	12	Tau		AUG	29	Lib
	APR	23	Gem		OCT	13	Scp
	JUN	7	Can		NOV	25	Sag
	JUL	22	Leo	1945	JAN	5	Cap
	SEP	7	Vir		FEB	14	Aqu
	OCT	25	Lib		MAR	25	Pic
	DEC	11	Scp		MAY	2	Ari
1939	JAN	29	Sag		JUN	11	Tau
	MAR	21	Cap		JUL	23	Gem
	MAY	25	Aqu		SEP	7	Can
	JUL	21	Cap		NOV	11	Leo
	SEP	24	Aqu		DEC	26	Can
	NOV	19	Pic	1946	APR	22	Leo
1940	JAN	4	Ari		JUN	20	Vir
	FEB	17	Tau		AUG	9	Lib
	APR	1	Gem		SEP	24	Scp
	MAY	17	Can		NOV	6	Sag
	JUL	3	Leo		DEC	17	Cap

1947	JAN	25	Aqu		MAR	20	Tau
	MAR	4	Pic		MAY	1	Gem
	APR	11	Ari		JUN	14	Can
	MAY	21	Tau		JUL	29	Leo
	JUL	1	Gem		SEP	14	Vir
	AUG	13	Can		NOV	1	Lib
	OCT	1	Leo		DEC	20	Scp
	DEC	1	Vir	1954	FEB	9	Sag
1948	FEB	12	Leo		APR	12	Cap
	MAY	18	Vir		JUL	3	Sag
	JUL	17	Lib		AUG	24	Cap
	SEP	3	Scp		OCT	21	Aqu
	OCT	17	Sag		DEC	4	Pic
	NOV	26	Cap	1955	JAN	15	Ari
1949	JAN	4	Aqu		FEB	26	Tau
	FEB	11	Pic		APR	10	Gem
	MAR	21	Ari		MAY	26	Can
	APR	30	Tau		JUL	11	Leo
	JUN	10	Gem		AUG	27	Vir
	JUL	23	Can		OCT	13	Lib
	SEP	7	Leo		NOV	29	Scp
	OCT	27	Vir	1956	JAN	14	Sag
	DEC	26	Lib		FEB	28	Cap
1950	MAR	28	Vir		APR	14	Aqu
	JUN	11	Lib		JUN	3	Pic
	AUG	10	Scp		DEC	6	Ari
	SEP	25	Sag	1957	JAN	28	Tau
	NOV	6	Cap		MAR	17	Gem
	DEC	15	Aqu		MAY	4	Can
1951	JAN	22	Pic		JUN	21	Leo
	MAR	1	Ari		AUG	8	Vir
	APR	10	Tau		SEP	24	Lib
	MAY	21	Gem		NOV	8	Scp
	JUL	3	Can		DEC	23	Sag
	AUG	18	Leo	1958	FEB	3	Cap
	OCT	5	Vir		MAR	17	Aqu
	NOV	24	Lib		APR	27	Pic
1952	JAN	20	Scp		JUN	7	Ari
	AUG	27	Sag		JUL	21	Tau
	OCT	12	Cap		SEP	21	Gem
	NOV	21	Aqu		OCT	29	Tau
	DEC	30	Pic	1959	FEB	10	Gem
1953	FEB	8	Ari		APR	10	Can

	JUN	1	Leo		NOV	14	Cap
	JUL	20	Vir		DEC	23	Aqu
	SEP	5	Lib	1966	JAN	30	Pic
	OCT	21	Scp		MAR	9	Ari
	DEC	3	Sag		APR	17	Tau
1960	JAN	14	Cap		MAY	28	Gem
	FEB	23	Aqu		JUL	11	Can
	APR	2	Pic		AUG	25	Leo
	MAY	11	Ari		OCT	12	Vir
	JUN	20	Tau		DEC	4	Lib
	AUG	2	Gem	1967	FEB	12	Scp
	SEP	21	Can		MAR	31	Lib
1961	FEB	5	Gem		JUL	19	Scp
	FEB	7	Can		SEP	10	Sag
	MAY	6	Leo		OCT	23	Cap
	JUN	28	Vir		DEC	1	Aqu
	AUG	17	Lib	1968	JAN	9	Pic
	OCT	1	Scp		FEB	17	Ari
	NOV	13	Sag		MAR	27	Tau
	DEC	24	Cap		MAY	8	Gem
1962	FEB	1	Aqu		JUN	21	Can
	MAR	12	Pic		AUG	5	Leo
	APR	19	Ari		SEP	21	Vir
	MAY	28	Tau		NOV	9	Lib
	JUL	9	Gem		DEC	29	Scp
	AUG	22	Can	1969	FEB	25	Sag
	OCT	11	Leo		SEP	21	Cap
1963	JUN	3	Vir		NOV	4	Aqu
	JUL	27	Lib		DEC	15	Pic
	SEP	12	Scp	1970	JAN	24	Ari
	OCT	25	Sag		MAR	7	Tau
	DEC	5	Cap		APR	18	Gem
1964	JAN	13	Aqu		JUN	2	Can
	FEB	20	Pic		JUL	18	Leo
	MAR	29	Ari		SEP	3	Vir
	MAY	7	Tau		OCT	20	Lib
	JUN	17	Gem		DEC	6	Scp
	JUL	30	Can	1971	JAN	23	Sag
	SEP	15	Leo		MAR	12	Cap
	NOV	6	Vir		MAY	3	Aqu
1965	JUN	29	Lib		NOV	6	Pic
	AUG	20	Scp		DEC	26	Ari
	OCT	4	Sag	1972	FEB	10	Tau

	MAR	27	Gem	1978	JAN	26	Can
	MAY	12	Can		APR	10	Leo
	JUN	28	Leo		JUN	14	Vir
	AUG	15	Vir		AUG	4	Lib
	SEP	30	Lib		SEP	19	Scp
	NOV	15	Scp		NOV	2	Sag
	DEC	30	Sag		DEC	12	Cap
1973	FEB	12	Cap	1979	JAN	20	Aqu
	MAR	26	Aqu		FEB	27	Pic
	MAY	8	Pic		APR	7	Ari
	JUN	20	Ari		MAY	16	Tau
	AUG	12	Tau		JUN	26	Gem
	OCT	29	Ari		AUG	8	Can
	DEC	24	Tau		SEP	24	Leo
1974	FEB	27	Gem		NOV	19	Vir
	APR	20	Can	1980	MAR	11	Leo
	JUN	9	Leo		MAY	4	Vir
	JUL	27	Vir		JUL	10	Lib
	SEP	12	Lib		AUG	29	Scp
	OCT	28	Scp		OCT	12	Sag
	DEC	10	Sag		NOV	22	Cap
1975	JAN	21	Cap		DEC	30	Aqu
	MAR	3	Aqu	1981	FEB	6	Pic
	APR	11	Pic		MAR	17	Ari
	MAY	21	Ari		APR	25	Tau
	JUL	1	Tau		JUN	5	Gem
	AUG	14	Gem		JUL	18	Can
	OCT	17	Can		SEP	2	Leo
	NOV	25	Gem		OCT	21	Vir
1976	MAR	18	Can		DEC	16	Lib
	MAY	16	Leo	1982	AUG	3	Scp
	JUL	6	Vir		SEP	20	Sag
	AUG	24	Lib		OCT	31	Cap
	OCT	8	Scp		DEC	10	Aqu
	NOV	20	Sag	1983	JAN	17	Pic
1977	JAN	1	Cap		FEB	25	Ari
	FEB	9	Aqu		APR	5	Tau
	MAR	20	Pic		MAY	16	Gem
	APR	27	Ari		JUN	29	Can
	JUN	6	Tau		AUG	13	Leo
	JUL	17	Gem		SEP	30	Vir
	SEP	1	Can		NOV	18	Lib
	OCT	26	Leo	1984	JAN	11	Scp

	AUG	17	Sag		JUL	12	Tau
	OCT	5	Cap		AUG	31	Gem
	NOV	15	Aqu		DEC	14	Tau
	DEC	25	Pic	1991	JAN	21	Gem
1985	FEB	2	Ari		APR	3	Can
	MAR	15	Tau		MAY	26	Leo
	APR	26	Gem		JUL	15	Vir
	JUN	9	Can		SEP	1	Lib
	JUL	25	Leo		OCT	16	Scp
	SEP	10	Vir		NOV	29	Sag
	OCT	27	Lib	1992	JAN	9	Cap
	DEC	14	Scp		FEB	18	Aqu
1986	FEB	2	Sag		MAR	28	Pic
	MAR	28	Cap		MAY	5	Ari
	OCT	9	Aqu		JUN	14	Tau
	NOV	26	Pic		JUL	26	Gem
1987	JAN	8	Ari		SEP	12	Can
	FEB	20	Tau	1993	APR	27	Leo
	APR	5	Gem		JUN	23	Vir
	MAY	21	Can		AUG	12	Lib
	JUL	6	Leo		SEP	27	Scp
	AUG	22	Vir		NOV	9	Sag
	OCT	8	Lib		DEC	20	Cap
	NOV	24	Scp	1994	JAN	28	Aqu
1988	JAN	8	Sag		MAR	7	Pic
	FEB	22	Cap		APR	14	Ari
	APR	6	Aqu		MAY	23	Tau
	MAY	22	Pic		JUL	3	Gem
	JUL	13	Ari		AUG	16	Can
	OCT	23	Pic		OCT	4	Leo
	NOV	1	Ari		DEC	12	Vir
1989	JAN	19	Tau	1995	JAN	22	Leo
	MAR	11	Gem		MAY	25	Vir
	APR	29	Can		JUL	21	Lib
	JUN	16	Leo		SEP	7	Scp
	AUG	3	Vir		OCT	20	Sag
	SEP	19	Lib		NOV	30	Cap
	NOV	4	Scp	1996	JAN	8	Aqu
	DEC	18	Sag		FEB	15	Pic
1990	JAN	29	Cap		MAR	24	Ari
	MAR	11	Aqu		MAY	2	Tau
	APR	20	Pic		JUN	12	Gem
	MAY	31	Ari		JUL	25	Can

	SEP	9	Leo		NOV	26	Aqu
	OCT	30	Vir	2000	JAN	4	Pic
1997	JAN	3	Lib		FEB	12	Ari
	MAR	8	Vir		MAR	23	Tau
	JUN	19	Lib		MAY	3	Gem
	AUG	14	Scp		JUN	16	Can
	SEP	28	Sag		AUG	1	Leo
	NOV	9	Cap		SEP	17	Vir
	DEC	18	Aqu		NOV	4	Lib
1998	JAN	25	Pic		DEC	23	Scp
	MAR	4	Ari	2001	FEB	14	Sag
	APR	13	Tau		SEP	8	Cap
	MAY	24	Gem		OCT	27	Aqu
	JUL	6	Can		DEC	8	Pic
	AUG	20	Leo	2002	JAN	18	Ari
	OCT	7	Vir		MAR	1	Tau
	NOV	27	Lib		APR	13	Gem
1999	JAN	26	Scp		MAY	28	Can
	MAY	5	Lib		JUL	13	Leo
	JUL	5	Scp		AUG	29	Vir
	SEP	2	Sag		OCT	15	Lib
	OCT	17	Cap		DEC	1	Scp

JUPITER SIGNS 1901–2002

1901	JAN	19	Cap	1911	DEC	10	Sag
1902	FEB	6	Aqu	1913	JAN	2	Cap
1903	FEB	20	Pic	1914	JAN	21	Aqu
1904	MAR	1	Ari	1915	FEB	4	Pic
	AUG	8	Tau	1916	FEB	12	Ari
	AUG	31	Ari		JUN	26	Tau
1905	MAR	7	Tau		OCT	26	Ari
	JUL	21	Gem	1917	FEB	12	Tau
	DEC	4	Tau		JUN	29	Gem
1906	MAR	9	Gem	1918	JUL	13	Can
	JUL	30	Can	1919	AUG	2	Leo
1907	AUG	18	Leo	1920	AUG	27	Vir
1908	SEP	12	Vir	1921	SEP	25	Lib
1909	OCT	11	Lib	1922	OCT	26	Scp
1910	NOV	11	Scp	1923	NOV	24	Sag

1924	DEC	18	Cap
1926	JAN	6	Aqu
1927	JAN	18	Pic
	JUN	6	Ari
	SEP	11	Pic
1928	JAN	23	Ari
	JUN	4	Tau
1929	JUN	12	Gem
1930	JUN	26	Can
1931	JUL	17	Leo
1932	AUG	11	Vir
1933	SEP	10	Lib
1934	OCT	11	Scp
1935	NOV	9	Sag
1936	DEC	2	Cap
1937	DEC	20	Aqu
1938	MAY	14	Pic
	JUL	30	Aqu
	DEC	29	Pic
1939	MAY	11	Ari
	OCT	30	Pic
	DEC	20	Ari
1940	MAY	16	Tau
1941	MAY	26	Gem
1942	JUN	10	Can
1943	JUN	30	Leo
1944	JUL	26	Vir
1945	AUG	25	Lib
1946	SEP	25	Scp
1947	OCT	24	Sag
1948	NOV	15	Cap
1949	APR	12	Aqu
	JUN	27	Cap
	NOV	30	Aqu
1950	APR	15	Pic
	SEP	15	Aqu
	DEC	1	Pic
1951	APR	21	Ari
1952	APR	28	Tau
1953	MAY	9	Gem
1954	MAY	24	Can

1955	JUN	13	Leo
	NOV	17	Vir
1956	JAN	18	Leo
	JUL	7	Vir
	DEC	13	Lib
1957	FEB	19	Vir
	AUG	7	Lib
1958	JAN	13	Scp
	MAR	20	Lib
	SEP	7	Scp
1959	FEB	10	Sag
	APR	24	Scp
	OCT	5	Sag
1960	MAR	1	Cap
	JUN	10	Sag
	OCT	26	Cap
1961	MAR	15	Aqu
	AUG	12	Cap
	NOV	4	Aqu
1962	MAR	25	Pic
1963	APR	4	Ari
1964	APR	12	Tau
1965	APR	22	Gem
	SEP	21	Can
	NOV	17	Gem
1966	MAY	5	Can
	SEP	27	Leo
1967	JAN	16	Can
	MAY	23	Leo
	OCT	19	Vir
1968	FEB	27	Leo
	JUN	15	Vir
	NOV	15	Lib
1969	MAR	30	Vir
	JUL	15	Lib
	DEC	16	Scp
1970	APR	30	Lib
	AUG	15	Scp
1971	JAN	14	Sag
	JUN	5	Scp
	SEP	11	Sag

1972	FEB	6	Cap	1986	FEB	20	Pic
	JUL	24	Sag	1987	MAR	2	Ari
	SEP	25	Cap	1988	MAR	8	Tau
1973	FEB	23	Aqu		JUL	22	Gem
1974	MAR	8	Pic		NOV	30	Tau
1975	MAR	18	Ari	1989	MAR	11	Gem
1976	MAR	26	Tau		JUL	30	Can
	AUG	23	Gem	1990	AUG	18	Leo
	OCT	16	Tau	1991	SEP	12	Vir
1977	APR	3	Gem	1992	OCT	10	Lib
	AUG	20	Can	1993	NOV	10	Scp
	DEC	30	Gem	1994	DEC	9	Sag
1978	APR	12	Can	1996	JAN	3	Cap
	SEP	5	Leo	1997	JAN	21	Aqu
1979	FEB	28	Can	1998	FEB	4	Pic
	APR	20	Leo	1999	FEB	13	Ari
	SEP	29	Vir		JUN	28	Tau
1980	OCT	27	Lib		OCT	23	Ari
1981	NOV	27	Scp	2000	FEB	14	Tau
1982	DEC	26	Sag		JUN	30	Gem
1984	JAN	19	Cap	2001	JUL	14	Can
1985	FEB	6	Aqu				

SATURN SIGNS 1903–2002

1903	JAN	19	Aqu	1916	OCT	17	Leo
1905	APR	13	Pic		DEC	7	Can
	AUG	17	Aqu	1917	JUN	24	Leo
1906	JAN	8	Pic	1919	AUG	12	Vir
1908	MAR	19	Ari	1921	OCT	7	Lib
1910	MAY	17	Tau	1923	DEC	20	Scp
	DEC	14	Ari	1924	APR	6	Lib
1911	JAN	20	Tau		SEP	13	Scp
1912	JUL	7	Gem	1926	DEC	2	Sag
	NOV	30	Tau	1929	MAR	15	Cap
1913	MAR	26	Gem		MAY	5	Sag
1914	AUG	24	Can		NOV	30	Cap
	DEC	7	Gem	1932	FEB	24	Aqu
1915	MAY	11	Can		AUG	13	Cap

	NOV	20	Aqu		FEB	21	Gem
1935	FEB	14	Pic	1973	AUG	1	Can
1937	APR	25	Ari	1974	JAN	7	Gem
	OCT	18	Pic		APR	18	Can
1938	JAN	14	Ari	1975	SEP	17	Leo
1939	JUL	6	Tau	1976	JAN	14	Can
	SEP	22	Ari				
1940	MAR	20	Tau		JUN	5	Leo
1942	MAY	8	Gem	1977	NOV	17	Vir
1944	JUN	20	Can	1978	JAN	5	Leo
1946	AUG	2	Leo		JUL	26	Vir
1948	SEP	19	Vir	1980	SEP	21	Lib
1949	APR	3	Leo	1982	NOV	29	Scp
	MAY	29	Vir	1983	MAY	6	Lib
1950	NOV	20	Lib		AUG	24	Scp
1951	MAR	7	Vir	1985	NOV	17	Sag
	AUG	13	Lib	1988	FEB	13	Cap
1953	OCT	22	Scp		JUN	10	Sag
1956	JAN	12	Sag		NOV	12	Cap
	MAY	14	Scp	1991	FEB	6	Aqu
	OCT	10	Sag	1993	MAY	21	Pic
1959	JAN	5	Cap		JUN	30	Aqu
1962	JAN	3	Aqu	1994	JAN	28	Pic
1964	MAR	24	Pic	1996	APR	7	Ari
	SEP	16	Aqu	1998	JUN	9	Tau
	DEC	16	Pic		OCT	25	Ari
1967	MAR	3	Ari	1999	MAR	1	Tau
1969	APR	29	Tau	2000	AUG	10	Gem
1971	JUN	18	Gem		OCT	16	Tau
1972	JAN	10	Tau	2001	APR	21	Gem

CHAPTER 4

Crack the Astrology Code— Decipher Those Mysterious Glyphs on Your Chart

The first time you look at a horoscope, you'll realize that astrology has a code all its own, written in strange-looking characters which represent the planets and signs. These symbols, or *glyphs,* are used by astrologers worldwide and by computer astrology programs. So, if you want to progress in astrology enough to read a horoscope, there's no way around it . . . you've got to know the meaning of the glyphs.

Besides enabling you to read a horoscope chart, learning the astrology code can help you interpret the meaning of the signs and planets, because each glyph contains a minilesson in what its planet or sign represents. And since there are only twelve signs and ten planets (not counting a few asteroids and other space creatures some astrologers use), they're a lot easier to learn than, say, Chinese!

Here's a code cracker for the glyphs, beginning with the glyphs for the planets. To those who already know their glyphs, don't just skim over the chapter! There are hidden meanings to discover, so test your glyphese.

The Glyphs for the Planets

The glyphs for the planets are easy to learn. They're simple combinations of the most basic visual elements: the circle, the semicircle or arc, and the cross. However, each component of a glyph has a special meaning in relation to the others, which adds up to create the total meaning of the symbol.

The circle, which has no beginning or end, is one of the oldest symbols of spirit or spiritual forces. All of the early diagrams of the heavens—spiritual territory—are shown in circular form. The never-ending line of the circle is the perfect symbol for eternity. The semicircle or arc is an incomplete circle, symbolizing the receptive, finite soul, which contains spiritual potential in the curving line.

The vertical line of the cross symbolizes movement from heaven to earth. The horizontal line describes temporal movement, here and now, in time and space. Combined in a cross, the vertical and horizontal planes symbolize manifestation in the material world.

The Sun Glyph ☉

The sun is always shown by this powerful solar symbol, a circle with a point in the center. The center point is you, your spiritual center, and the symbol represents your infinite personality incarnating (the point) into the finite cycles of birth and death.

The sun has been represented by a circle or disk since ancient Egyptian times, when the solar disk represented the sun god, Ra. Some archaeologists believe the great stone circles found in England were centers of sun worship. This particular version of the symbol was brought into common use in the sixteenth century, after German occultist and scholar Cornelius Agrippa (1486–1535) wrote a book called *Die Occulta Philosophia,* which became accepted as the standard work in its field. Agrippa collected many medieval astrological and magical symbols in this book, which have been used by astrologers since then.

The Moon Glyph ☽

The moon glyph is the most recognizable symbol on a chart, a left-facing arc stylized into the crescent moon. As part of a circle, the arc symbolizes the potential fulfillment of the entire circle, the life force that is still incomplete. Therefore, it is the ideal representation of the reactive, receptive, emotional nature of the moon.

The Mercury Glyph ☿

Mercury contains all three elemental symbols, the crescent, the circle, and the cross in vertical order. This is the "Venus with a hat" glyph (compare with the symbol of Venus). With another stretch of the imagination, can't you see the winged cap of Mercury the messenger? Think of the upturned crescent as antennae that tune in and transmit messages from the sun, reminding you that Mercury is the way you communicate, the way your mind works. The upturned arc is receiving energy into the spirit or solar circle, which will later be translated into action on the material plane, symbolized by the cross. All the elements are equally sized because Mercury is neutral; it doesn't play favorites! This planet symbolizes objective, detached, unemotional thinking.

The Venus Glyph ♀

Here the relationship is between two components, the circle or spirit and the cross of matter. Spirit is elevated over matter, pulling it upward. Venus asks, "What is beautiful? What do you like best? What do you love to have done to you?" Consequently,

Venus determines both your ideal of beauty and what feels good sensually. It governs your own allure and power to attract, as well as what attracts and pleases you.

The Mars Glyph ♂

In this glyph, the cross of matter is stylized into an arrowhead pointed up and outward, propelled by the circle of spirit. With a little imagination, you can visualize it as the shield and spear of Mars, the ancient god of war. You can deduce that Mars embodies your spiritual energy projected into the outer world. It's your assertiveness, your initiative, your aggressive drive, what you like to do to others, your temper. If you know someone's Mars, you know whether they'll blow up when angry or do a slow burn. Your task is to use your outgoing Mars energy wisely and well.

The Jupiter Glyph ♃

Jupiter is the basic cross of matter, with a large stylized crescent perched on the left side of the horizontal, temporal plane. You might think of the crescent as an open hand, because one meaning of Jupiter is "luck," what's handed to you. You don't work for what you get from Jupiter; it comes to you, if you're open to it.

The Jupiter glyph might also remind you of a jumbo jet plane with a huge tail fin, about to take off. This is the planet of travel, mental and spiritual, of expanding your horizons via new ideas, new spiritual dimensions, and new places. Jupiter embodies the optimism and enthusiasm of the traveler about to embark on an exciting adventure.

The Saturn Glyph ♄

Flip Jupiter over and you've got Saturn. (This might not be immediately apparent, because Saturn is usually stylized into an "h" form like the one shown here.) The principle it expresses is the opposite of Jupiter's expansive tendencies. Saturn pulls you back to earth—the receptive arc is pushed down underneath the cross of matter. Before there are any rewards or expansion, the duties and obligations of the material world must be considered. Saturn says, "Stop, wait, finish your chores before you take off!"

Saturn's glyph also resembles the scythe of old "Father Time." Saturn was first known as Chronos, the Greek god of time, for time brings all matter to an end. When it was the most distant planet (before the discovery of Uranus), Saturn was believed to be the place where time stopped. After the soul departed from Earth, it journeyed back to the outer reaches of the universe and finally stopped at Saturn, or at "the end of time."

The Uranus Glyph ♅

The glyph for Uranus is often stylized to form a capital "H" after Sir William Herschel, who discovered the planet. But the more esoteric version curves the two pillars of the H into crescent antennae, or "ears," like satellite disks receiving signals from space. These are perched on the horizontal material line of the cross (matter) and pushed from below by the circle of the spirit. To many sci-fi fans, Uranus looks like an orbiting satellite.

Uranus channels the highest energy of all, the white electrical light of the universal spiritual force which holds the cosmos together. This pure electrical energy is gathered from all over the universe. Because Uranian energy doesn't follow any ordinary celestial drumbeat, it can't be controlled or predicted (which is also true of those who are strongly influenced by this eccentric planet). In the symbol, this energy is manifested through the balance of polarities (the two opposite arms of the glyph) like the two polarized wires of a light bulb.

The Neptune Glyph ♆

Neptune's glyph is usually stylized to look like a trident, the weapon of the Roman god Neptune. However, on a more esoteric level, it shows the large, upturned crescent of the soul pierced through by the cross of matter. Neptune nails down, or materializes, soul energy, bringing impulses from the soul level into manifestation. That is why Neptune is associated with imagination or "imagining in," making an image of the soul. Neptune works through feeling, sensitivity, and a mystical capacity to bring the divine into the earthly realm.

The Pluto Glyph ♇

Pluto is written two ways. One is a composite of the letters PL, the first two letters of the word "Pluto" and coincidentally the initials of Percival Lowell, one of the planet's discoverers. The other, more esoteric symbol is a small circle above a large open crescent which surmounts the cross of matter. This depicts Pluto's power to regenerate—imagine a new little spirit emerging from the sheltering cup of the soul. Pluto rules the forces of life and death—after this planet has passed a sensitive point in your chart, you are transformed, reborn in some way.

Sci-fi fans might visualize this glyph as a small satellite (the circle) being launched. It was shortly after Pluto's discovery that we learned how to harness the nuclear forces that made space exploration possible. Pluto rules the transformative power of atomic energy, which totally changed our lives and from which there is no turning back.

The Glyphs for the Signs

On an astrological chart, the glyph for the sign will appear after that of the planet. For example, when you see the moon glyph followed first by a number and then by another glyph representing the sign, this means that the moon was passing over a certain degree of that astrological sign at the time of the chart. On the dividing lines between the segments or "houses" on your chart, you'll find the symbol for the sign that rules the house.

Because sun sign symbols do not contain the same basic geometric components of the planetary glyphs, we must look elsewhere for clues to their meanings. Many have been passed down from ancient Egyptian and Chaldean civilizations with few modifications. Others have been adapted over the centuries. In deciphering many of the glyphs, you'll often find that the symbols reveal a dual nature of the sign, which is not always apparent in the usual sun sign descriptions. For instance, the Gemini glyph is similar to the Roman numeral for two, and reveals this sign's longing to discover a twin soul. The Cancer glyph may be interpreted as resembling either the nurturing breasts or the self-protective claws of the crab, both symbols associated with the contrasting qualities of this sign. Libra's glyph embodies the duality of the spirit balanced with material reality. The Sagittarius glyph shows that the aspirant must also carry along the earthly animal nature in his quest. The Capricorn sea goat is another symbol with dual emphasis. The goat climbs high, yet is always pulled back by the deep waters of the unconscious. Aquarius embodies the double waves of mental detachment, balanced by the desire for connection with others in a friendly way. And finally, the two fishes of Pisces, which are forever tied together, show the duality of the soul and the spirit that must be reconciled.

The Aries Glyph ♈

Since the symbol for Aries is the ram, this glyph is obviously associated with a ram's horns, which characterize one aspect of the Aries personality—an aggressive, me-first, leaping-headfirst attitude. But the symbol can be interpreted in other ways as well. Some astrologers liken it to a fountain of energy, which Aries people also embody. The first sign of the zodiac bursts on the scene eagerly, ready to go. Another analogy is to the eyebrows and nose of the human head, which Aries rules, and the thinking power that is initiated in the brain.

One theory of this symbol links it to the Egyptian god Amun, represented by a ram in ancient times. As Amun-Ra, this god was believed to embody the creator of the universe, the leader of all the other gods. This relates easily to the position of Aries as the leader (or first sign) of the zodiac, which begins at the spring equinox, a time of the year when nature is renewed.

The Taurus Glyph ♉

This is another easy glyph to draw and identify. It takes little imagination to decipher the bull's head with long curving horns. Like the bull, the archetypal Taurus is slow to anger, but ferocious when provoked, as well as stubborn, steady, and sensual. Another association is the larynx (and thyroid) of the throat area (ruled by Taurus) and the eustachian tubes running up to the ears, which coincide with the relationship of Taurus to the voice, song, and music. Many famous singers, musicians, and composers have prominent Taurus influences.

Many ancient religions involved a bull as the central figure in fertility rites or initiations, usually symbolizing the victory of man over his animal nature. Another possible origin is in the sacred bull of Egypt, who embodied the incarnate form of Osiris, god of death and resurrection. In early Christian imagery, the Taurean bull represented St. Luke.

The Gemini Glyph ♊

The standard glyph immediately calls to mind the Roman numeral II and the "twins" symbol for Gemini. In almost all drawings and images used for this sign, the relationship between two persons is emphasized. Usually one twin will be touching the other, which signifies communication, human contact, and the desire to share.

The top line of the Gemini glyph indicates mental communication, while the bottom line indicates shared physical space.

The most famous Gemini legend is that of the twin sons, Castor and Pollux, one of whom had a mortal father, while the other was the son of Zeus, king of the gods. When it came time for the mortal twin to die, his grief-stricken brother pleaded with Zeus, who agreed to let them spend half the year on earth in mortal form and half in immortal life, with the gods on Mt. Olympus. This reflects a basic duality of humankind, which possesses an immortal soul, yet is also subject to the limits of mortality.

The Cancer Glyph ♋

Two convenient images relate to the Cancer glyph. It is easiest to decode the curving claws of the Cancer symbol, the crab. Like the crab, Cancer's element is water. This sensitive sign also has a hard protective shell to protect its tender interior. The crab must be wily to escape predators, scampering sideways and hiding under rocks. The crab also responds to the cycles of the moon, as do all shellfish. The other image is that of two female breasts, which Cancer rules, showing that this is a sign that nurtures and protects others as well as itself.

In ancient Egypt, Cancer was also represented by

the scarab beetle, a symbol of regeneration and eternal life.

The Leo Glyph ♌

Notice that the Leo glyph seems to be an extension of Cancer's glyph, with a significant difference. In the Cancer glyph, the lines curve inward protectively, while the Leo glyph expresses energy outwardly and there is no duality in the symbol (or in Leo).

Lions have belonged to the sign of Leo since earliest times, and it is not difficult to imagine the king of beasts with his sweeping mane and curling tail from this glyph. The upward sweep of the glyph easily describes the positive energy of Leos: the flourishing tail, their flamboyant qualities. Another analogy, which is a stretch of the imagination, is that of a heart leaping up with joy and enthusiasm, very typical of Leo, which also rules the heart. In early Christian imagery, the Leo lion represented St. Mark.

The Virgo Glyph ♍

You can read much into this mysterious glyph. For instance, it could represent the initials of "Mary Virgin," or a young woman holding a stalk of wheat, or stylized female genitalia, all common interpretations. The "M" shape might also remind you that Virgo is ruled by Mercury. The cross beneath the symbol reveals the grounded, practical nature of this earth sign.

The earliest zodiacs link Virgo with the Egyptian goddess Isis, who gave birth to the god Horus after her husband Osiris had been killed, in the archetype of a miraculous conception. There are many ancient statues of Isis nursing her baby son, which are reminiscent of medieval Virgin and Child motifs. This sign has also been associated with the image of the Holy

Grail, when the Virgo symbol was substituted with a chalice.

The Libra Glyph ♎

It is not difficult to read the standard image for Libra, the scales, into this glyph. There is another meaning, however, that is equally relevant: the setting sun as it descends over the horizon. Libra's natural position on the zodiac wheel is the descendant or sunset position (as Aries's natural position is the ascendant, or rising sign). Both images relate to Libra's personality. Libra is always weighing pros and cons for a balanced decision. In the sunset image, the sun (male) hovers over the horizontal Earth (female) before setting. Libra is the space between these lines, harmonizing yin and yang, spiritual and material, male and female, ideal and real worlds. The glyph has also been linked to the kidneys, which are ruled by Libra.

The Scorpio Glyph ♏

With its barbed tail, this glyph is easy to identify with the sign of the Scorpion. It also represents the male sexual parts, over which the sign rules. However, some earlier Egyptian symbols for Scorpio represent it as an erect serpent. You can also draw the conclusion that Mars was once its ruler by the arrowhead.

Another image for Scorpio, which is not identifiable in this glyph, is the eagle. Scorpios can go to extremes, either soaring like the eagle or self-destructing like the scorpion. In early Christian imagery, which often used zodiacal symbols, the Scorpio eagle was chosen to symbolize the intense apostle St. John the Evangelist.

The Sagittarius Glyph ♐

This glyph is one of the easiest to spot and draw—an upward pointing arrow lifting up a cross. The arrow is pointing skyward, while the cross represents the four elements of the material world, which the arrow must convey. Elevating materiality into spirituality is an important Sagittarius quality, which explains why this sign is associated with higher learning, religion, philosophy, and travel—the aspiring professions. Sagittarians can also send barbed arrows of frankness in their pursuit of truth. (This is also the sign of the super-salesman.)

Sagittarius is symbolically represented by the centaur, a mythological creature who is half man, half horse, aiming his arrow toward the skies. Though Sagittarius is motivated by spiritual aspiration, it also must balance the powerful appetites of the animal nature. The centaur Chiron, a figure in Greek mythology, became a wise teacher who, after many adventures and world travels, was killed by a poisoned arrow.

The Capricorn Glyph ♑

One of the most difficult symbols to draw, this glyph may take some practice. It is a representation of the sea goat: a mythical animal that is a goat with a curving fish's tail. The goat part of Capricorn wants to leave the waters of the emotions and climb to the elevated areas of life. But the fish tail is the unconscious, the deep chaotic psychic level that draws the goat back. Capricorn is often trying to escape the deep, feeling part of life by submerging himself in work, steadily ascending to the top. To some people, the glyph represents a seated figure with a bent knee, a reminder that Capricorn governs the knee area of the body.

An interesting aspect of this glyph is the contrast of the sharp pointed horns of the symbol, which represent the penetrating, shrewd, conscious side of Capricorn, with the swishing tail, which represents its serpentine, unconscious, emotional force. One Capricorn legend, which dates from Roman times, tells of the earthy fertility god, Pan, who tried to save himself from uncontrollable sexual desires by jumping into the Nile. His upper body then turned into a goat, while the lower part became a fish. Later, Jupiter gave him a safe haven in the skies, as a constellation.

The Aquarius Glyph ♒

This ancient water symbol can be traced back to an Egyptian hieroglyph representing streams of life force. Symbolized by the water bearer, Aquarius is distributor of the waters of life—the magic liquid of regeneration. The two waves can also be linked to the positive and negative charges of the electrical energy that Aquarius rules, a sort of universal wavelength. Aquarius is tuned in intuitively to higher forces via this electrical force. The duality of the glyph could also refer to the dual nature of Aquarius, a sign that runs hot and cold, is friendly but also detached in the mental world of air signs.

In Greek legends, Aquarius is represented by Ganymede, who was carried to heaven by an eagle in order to become the cup bearer of Zeus and to supervise the annual flooding of the Nile. The sign later became associated with aviation and notions of flight.

The Pisces Glyph ♓

Here is an abstraction of the familiar image of Pisces, two fishes swimming in opposite directions, yet bound together by a cord. The fishes represent the spirit, which yearns for the freedom of heaven, and the soul, which remains attached to the desires of the temporal world. During life on Earth, the spirit and the soul are bound together. When they complement each other, instead of pulling in opposite directions they facilitate the Pisces creativity. The ancient version of this glyph, taken from the Egyptians, had no connecting line, which was added in the fourteenth century.

In another interpretation, it is said that the left fish

indicates the direction of involution or the beginning of a cycle, while the right fish signifies the direction of evolution, the way to completion of a cycle. It's an appropriate grand finale for Pisces, the last sign of the zodiac.

CHAPTER 5

How Your Rising Sign Personalizes Your Horoscope

Have you ever wondered what makes your horoscope unique, how your chart could be different from that of anyone else born on your birthday? Yes, other babies who may have been born later or earlier on the same day, in the same hospital, as you were, will be sure to have most planets in the same signs as you do. Most of your high school class, in fact, will have several planets in the same signs as your planets, especially the slow-moving planets (Uranus, Neptune, Pluto) and very possibly Jupiter and Saturn, which usually spend a year or more in each sign.

What makes a horoscope truly "yours" is the rising sign (or ascendant), the sign that was coming up over the eastern horizon at the moment you were born. This sign establishes the exact horoscope of your birth time. In astrology, this is called the *rising sign,* often referred to as the ascendant. As the earth moves, a different sign rises every two hours.

If you have read the chapter in this book on houses, you'll know that the houses are twelve stationary divisions of the horoscope, which represent areas of life. The sign which is moving over the house describes that area of life. The rising sign marks the border of the first house, which represents your first presentation to the world, your physical body, and how you come across to others. It has been called your "shop window," the first impression you give to others. After the rising sign is determined, then each "house" will be influenced by the signs which follow it.

Once the rising sign is established, it becomes possible to analyze a chart accurately because the astrologer knows in which area of life (house) the planets will operate. For instance, if Mars is in Gemini and your rising sign is Taurus, then Mars will most likely be active in the second or financial house of your chart. If you were born later in the day and your rising sign is Virgo, then Mars will be positioned at the top of your chart, energizing your tenth house or career. That is why many astrologers insist on knowing the exact time of a client's birth, before they analyze a chart. The more exact your birthtime, the more accurately an astrologer can position the planets in your chart. This is important, because if you were born when the midportion of a sign was rotating over the horizon and a key planet—let's say Saturn—was in the early degrees of that sign, then it would already be over the horizon, located in the twelfth house, rather than the first. So the interpretation of your horoscope would be quite different: you would not have the serious Saturn influence in the way you come across to others, which would be the case if you were born an hour earlier. If a planet is near the ascendant, sometimes even a few minutes can make a big difference.

Your rising sign has an important relationship with your sun sign. Some will complement the sun sign; others hide it under a totally different mask, as if playing an entirely different role, so it is often difficult to guess the person's sun sign from outer appearances. For example, a Leo with a conservative Capricorn ascendant would come across as much less flamboyant than a Leo with a fiery Aries or Sagittarius ascendant. The exception is when the sun sign is reinforced by other planets; then, with other planets on its side, the sun may assert its personality much more strongly, overcoming the image of a contradictory rising sign. For example, a Leo with Venus and Jupiter also in

Leo might counteract the conservative image of the Capricorn ascendant, in the above example. However, in most cases, the ascendant is the ingredient most strongly reflected in the first impression you make.

Rising signs change every two hours with the Earth's rotation. Those born early in the morning when the sun was on the horizon will be most likely to project the image of their sun sign. These people are often called a "double Aries" or a "double Virgo," because the same sun sign and ascendant reinforce each other.

Look up your rising sign on the chart at the end of this chapter. Since rising signs change every two hours, it is important to know your birth time as close to the minute as possible. Even a few minutes' difference could change the rising sign and therefore the setup of your chart. If you are unsure about the exact time, but know within a few hours, check the following descriptions to see which is most like the personality you project.

Aries Rising—Fiery Emotions

You are the most aggressive version of your sun sign, with boundless energy which can be used productively, if it's channeled in the right direction. Watch a tendency to overreact emotionally and blow your top. You come across as openly competitive, a positive asset in business or sports. Be on guard against impatience, which could lead to head injuries. Your walk and bearing could have the telltale head-forward Aries posture. You may wear more bright colors, especially red, than others of your sign. You may also have a tendency to drive your car faster.

Taurus Rising—The Earth Mother

You'll exude a protective nurturing quality, even if you're male, which draws those in need of TLC and support. You're slow-moving, with a beautiful (or distinctive) speaking or singing voice that can be especially soothing or melodious. You probably surround yourself with comfort, good food, luxurious surroundings and sensual pleasures, and prefer welcoming others into your home to gadding about. You may have a talent for business, especially in trading, appraising, and real estate. This ascendant gives a well-padded or curvaceous physique, which gains weight easily. Women with this ascendant are naturally sexy in a bodacious way.

Gemini Rising—Expressive Talents

You're naturally sociable, with lighter, more ethereal mannerisms than others of your sign, especially if you're female. You love to communicate with people and express your ideas and feelings easily. You may have writing or public speaking talent. Like Drew Barrymore, you may thrive on a constantly changing scenario with a varied cast of characters, though you may be far more sympathetic and caring than you project. You will probably travel widely, changing partners and jobs several times (or juggling two at once). Physically, you should cultivate a calm, tranquil atmosphere, because your nerves are quite sensitive.

Cancer Rising—Sensitive Antennae

Like billionaire Bill Gates, you are naturally acquisitive, possessive, private, a moneymaker. You easily pick up others' needs and feelings, a great gift in business, the arts, and personal relationships, but guard against overreacting or taking things too personally, especially during full moon periods. Find creative outlets for your natural nurturing gifts, such as helping the less fortunate, particularly children. Your insights would be useful in psychology, your desire to feed and care for others in the restaurant, hotel, or child care industry. You may be especially fond of wearing romantic old clothes, collecting antiques, and of course, good food. Since your body may retain fluids, pay attention to your diet. To relax, escape to places near water.

Leo Rising—The Scene Player

You may come across as more poised than you really feel; however, you play it to the hilt, projecting a proud royal presence. This ascendant gives you a natural flair for drama, like Marilyn Monroe. You'll also project a much more outgoing, optimistic, sunny personality than others of your sign. You take care to please your public by always projecting your best star quality, probably tossing a luxuriant mane of hair or, if you're female, dazzling with a spectacular jewelry collection. Since you may have a strong parental nature, you could well be the regal family matriarch or patriarch.

Virgo Rising—Cool and Calculating

Virgo rising masks your inner nature with a practical, analytical outer image. You seem neat, orderly, more particular than others of your sign. Others in your life may feel they must live up to your high standards. Though at times you may be openly critical, this masks a well-meaning desire to have only the best for loved ones. Your sharp eye for details could be used in the financial world, or your literary skills could draw you to teaching or publishing. The healing arts, health care, service-oriented professions attract many with this Virgo emphasis in their chart. Like Madonna, you're likely to take good care of yourself, with great attention to health, diet, and exercise. Physically, you may have a very sensitive digestive system.

Libra Rising—The Charmer

Libra rising makes you appear as a charmer, more of a social, public person than others of your sign. Your private life will extend beyond your home and family to include an active social life. You may tend to avoid confrontations in relationships, preferring to smooth the way or negotiate diplomatically, rather than give in to an emotional reaction. Because you are interested in all aspects of a situation, you may be slow to reach decisions. Physically, you'll have good proportions and pleasing symmetry. You're likely to have pleasing, if not beautiful, facial features. You move gracefully, and you have a winning smile and good taste in your clothes and home decor. Legal, diplomatic, or public relations professions could draw your interest. Men with Libra rising, like Bill Clinton and John F. Kennedy, have charming smiles and easy social manner that charms the ladies.

Scorpio Rising—Magnetic Power

Even when you're in the public eye, like Jacqueline Kennedy Onassis, you never lose your intriguing air of mystery and sense of underlying power. You can be a master manipulator, always in control and moving comfortably in the world of power. Your physical impression comes across as intense, and many of you have remarkable eyes, with a direct, penetrating gaze. But you'll never reveal your private agenda, and you tend to keep your true feelings under wraps (watch a tendency toward paranoia). You may have an interesting romantic history with secret love affairs. Many of you heighten your air of mystery by wearing black. You're happiest near water and should provide yourself with a seaside retreat.

Sagittarius Rising—The Wanderer

You travel with this ascendant. You may also be a more outdoor, sportive type, with an athletic, casual, outgoing air. Your moods are camouflaged with cheerful optimism or a philosophical attitude. Though you don't hesitate to speak your mind, you can also laugh at your troubles or crack a joke more easily than others of your sign, like Candice Bergen, who is best known for her comedy role as the outspoken "Murphy Brown." This ascendant can also draw you to the field of higher education or to spiritual life. You'll seem to have less attachment to things and people and may travel widely. Your strong, fast legs are a physical bonus.

Capricorn Rising—Serious Business

This rising sign makes you come across as serious, goal-oriented, disciplined, and careful with cash. You are not one of the zodiac's big spenders, though you might splurge occasionally on items with good investment value. You're the traditional, conservative type in dress and environment, and you might come across as quite formal and businesslike. You'll function well in a structured or corporate environment where you can climb to the top. (You are always aware of who's the boss.) In your personal life, you could be a loner or a single parent who is "father and mother" to your children. Like Paul Newman, you're likely to prefer a quiet private life to living in the spotlight.

Aquarius Rising—One of a Kind

You come across as less concerned about what others think and could even be a bit eccentric. Your appearance is sure to be unique and memorable. You're more at ease with groups of people than others in your sign, and may be attracted to public life. Your appearance may be unique, either unconventional or unimportant to you. Those with the sun in a water sign (Cancer, Scorpio, Pisces) may exercise your nurturing qualities with a large group, an extended family, or a day care or community center. Audrey Hepburn and Princess Diana, who had this rising sign, were known for their unique charisma and work on behalf of worthy causes.

Pisces Rising—Romantic Roles

Your creative, nurturing talents are heightened and so is your ability to project emotional drama. And your dreamy eyes and poetic air bring out the protective instinct in others. You could be attracted to the arts, especially theater, dance, film, or photography, or to psychology or spiritual or charity work. You are happiest when you are using your creative ability to help others, as Robert Redford has done. Since you are vulnerable to mood swings, it is especially important for you to find interesting, creative work where you can express your talents and boost your self-esteem. Accentuate the positive and be wary of escapist tendencies, particularly involving alcohol or drugs, to which you are supersensitive.

RISING SIGNS—A.M. BIRTHS

	1 AM	2 AM	3 AM	4 AM	5 AM	6 AM	7 AM	8 AM	9 AM	10 AM	11 AM	12 NOON
Jan 1	Lib	Sc	Sc	Sc	Sag	Sag	Cap	Cap	Aq	Aq	Pis	Ar
Jan 9	Lib	Sc	Sc	Sag	Sag	Sag	Cap	Cap	Aq	Pis	Ar	Tau
Jan 17	Sc	Sc	Sc	Sag	Sag	Cap	Cap	Aq	Aq	Pis	Ar	Tau
Jan 25	Sc	Sc	Sag	Sag	Sag	Cap	Cap	Aq	Pis	Ar	Tau	Tau
Feb 2	Sc	Sc	Sag	Sag	Cap	Cap	Aq	Pis	Pis	Ar	Tau	Gem
Feb 10	Sc	Sag	Sag	Sag	Cap	Cap	Aq	Pis	Ar	Tau	Tau	Gem
Feb 18	Sc	Sag	Sag	Cap	Cap	Aq	Pis	Pis	Ar	Tau	Gem	Gem
Feb 26	Sag	Sag	Sag	Cap	Aq	Aq	Pis	Ar	Tau	Tau	Gem	Gem
Mar 6	Sag	Sag	Cap	Cap	Aq	Pis	Pis	Ar	Tau	Gem	Gem	Can
Mar 14	Sag	Cap	Cap	Aq	Aq	Pis	Ar	Tau	Tau	Gem	Gem	Can
Mar 22	Sag	Cap	Cap	Aq	Pis	Ar	Ar	Tau	Gem	Gem	Can	Can
Mar 30	Cap	Cap	Aq	Pis	Pis	Ar	Tau	Tau	Gem	Can	Can	Can
Apr 7	Cap	Cap	Aq	Pis	Ar	Ar	Tau	Gem	Gem	Can	Can	Leo
Apr 14	Cap	Aq	Aq	Pis	Ar	Tau	Tau	Gem	Gem	Can	Can	Leo
Apr 22	Cap	Aq	Pis	Ar	Ar	Tau	Gem	Gem	Gem	Can	Leo	Leo
Apr 30	Aq	Aq	Pis	Ar	Tau	Tau	Gem	Can	Can	Can	Leo	Leo
May 8	Aq	Pis	Ar	Ar	Tau	Gem	Gem	Can	Can	Leo	Leo	Leo
May 16	Aq	Pis	Ar	Tau	Gem	Gem	Can	Can	Can	Leo	Leo	Vir
May 24	Pis	Ar	Ar	Tau	Gem	Gem	Can	Can	Leo	Leo	Leo	Vir
June 1	Pis	Ar	Tau	Gem	Gem	Can	Can	Can	Leo	Leo	Vir	Vir
June 9	Ar	Ar	Tau	Gem	Gem	Can	Can	Leo	Leo	Leo	Vir	Vir
June 17	Ar	Tau	Gem	Gem	Can	Can	Can	Leo	Leo	Vir	Vir	Vir
June 25	Tau	Tau	Gem	Gem	Can	Can	Leo	Leo	Leo	Vir	Vir	Lib
July 3	Tau	Gem	Gem	Can	Can	Can	Leo	Leo	Vir	Vir	Vir	Lib
July 11	Tau	Gem	Gem	Can	Can	Leo	Leo	Leo	Vir	Vir	Lib	Lib
July 18	Gem	Gem	Can	Can	Can	Leo	Leo	Vir	Vir	Vir	Lib	Lib
July 26	Gem	Gem	Can	Can	Leo	Leo	Vir	Vir	Vir	Lib	Lib	Lib
Aug 3	Gem	Can	Can	Can	Leo	Leo	Vir	Vir	Vir	Lib	Lib	Sc
Aug 11	Gem	Can	Can	Leo	Leo	Leo	Vir	Vir	Lib	Lib	Lib	Sc
Aug 18	Can	Can	Can	Leo	Leo	Vir	Vir	Vir	Lib	Lib	Sc	Sc
Aug 27	Can	Can	Leo	Leo	Leo	Vir	Vir	Lib	Lib	Lib	Sc	Sc
Sept 4	Can	Can	Leo	Leo	Leo	Vir	Vir	Vir	Lib	Lib	Sc	Sc
Sept 12	Can	Leo	Leo	Leo	Vir	Vir	Lib	Lib	Lib	Sc	Sc	Sag
Sept 20	Leo	Leo	Leo	Vir	Vir	Vir	Lib	Lib	Sc	Sc	Sc	Sag
Sept 28	Leo	Leo	Leo	Vir	Vir	Lib	Lib	Lib	Sc	Sc	Sag	Sag
Oct 6	Leo	Leo	Vir	Vir	Vir	Lib	Lib	Sc	Sc	Sc	Sag	Sag
Oct 14	Leo	Vir	Vir	Vir	Lib	Lib	Lib	Sc	Sc	Sag	Sag	Cap
Oct 22	Leo	Vir	Vir	Lib	Lib	Lib	Sc	Sc	Sc	Sag	Sag	Cap
Oct 30	Vir	Vir	Vir	Lib	Lib	Sc	Sc	Sc	Sag	Sag	Cap	Cap
Nov 7	Vir	Vir	Lib	Lib	Lib	Sc	Sc	Sc	Sag	Sag	Cap	Cap
Nov 15	Vir	Vir	Lib	Lib	Sc	Sc	Sc	Sag	Sag	Cap	Cap	Aq
Nov 23	Vir	Lib	Lib	Lib	Sc	Sc	Sag	Sag	Sag	Cap	Cap	Aq
Dec 1	Vir	Lib	Lib	Sc	Sc	Sc	Sag	Sag	Cap	Cap	Aq	Aq
Dec 9	Lib	Lib	Lib	Sc	Sc	Sag	Sag	Sag	Cap	Cap	Aq	Pis
Dec 18	Lib	Lib	Sc	Sc	Sc	Sag	Sag	Cap	Cap	Aq	Aq	Pis
Dec 28	Lib	Lib	Sc	Sc	Sag	Sag	Sag	Cap	Aq	Aq	Pis	Ar

RISING SIGNS—P.M. BIRTHS

	1 PM	2 PM	3 PM	4 PM	5 PM	6 PM	7 PM	8 PM	9 PM	10 PM	11 PM	12 MIDNIGHT
Jan 1	Tau	Gem	Gem	Can	Can	Can	Leo	Leo	Vir	Vir	Vir	Lib
Jan 9	Tau	Gem	Gem	Can	Can	Leo	Leo	Leo	Vir	Vir	Vir	Lib
Jan 17	Gem	Gem	Gem	Can	Can	Leo	Leo	Vir	Vir	Vir	Lib	Lib
Jan 25	Gem	Gem	Can	Can	Leo	Leo	Leo	Vir	Vir	Lib	Lib	Lib
Feb 2	Gem	Can	Can	Can	Leo	Leo	Vir	Vir	Vir	Lib	Lib	Sc
Feb 10	Gem	Can	Can	Leo	Leo	Leo	Vir	Vir	Lib	Lib	Lib	Sc
Feb 18	Can	Can	Can	Leo	Leo	Vir	Vir	Vir	Lib	Lib	Sc	Sc
Feb 26	Can	Can	Leo	Leo	Leo	Vir	Vir	Lib	Lib	Lib	Sc	Sc
Mar 6	Can	Leo	Leo	Leo	Vir	Vir	Vir	Lib	Lib	Sc	Sc	Sc
Mar 14	Can	Leo	Leo	Vir	Vir	Vir	Lib	Lib	Lib	Sc	Sc	Sag
Mar 22	Leo	Leo	Leo	Vir	Vir	Lib	Lib	Lib	Sc	Sc	Sc	Sag
Mar 30	Leo	Leo	Vir	Vir	Vir	Lib	Lib	Sc	Sc	Sc	Sag	Sag
Apr 7	Leo	Leo	Vir	Vir	Lib	Lib	Lib	Sc	Sc	Sc	Sag	Sag
Apr 14	Leo	Vir	Vir	Vir	Lib	Lib	Sc	Sc	Sc	Sag	Sag	Cap
Apr 22	Leo	Vir	Vir	Lib	Lib	Lib	Sc	Sc	Sc	Sag	Sag	Cap
Apr 30	Vir	Vir	Vir	Lib	Lib	Sc	Sc	Sc	Sag	Sag	Cap	Cap
May 8	Vir	Vir	Lib	Lib	Lib	Sc	Sc	Sag	Sag	Sag	Cap	Cap
May 16	Vir	Vir	Lib	Lib	Sc	Sc	Sc	Sag	Sag	Cap	Cap	Aq
May 24	Vir	Lib	Lib	Lib	Sc	Sc	Sag	Sag	Sag	Cap	Cap	Aq
June 1	Vir	Lib	Lib	Sc	Sc	Sc	Sag	Sag	Cap	Cap	Aq	Aq
June 9	Lib	Lib	Lib	Sc	Sc	Sag	Sag	Sag	Cap	Cap	Aq	Pis
June 17	Lib	Lib	Sc	Sc	Sc	Sag	Sag	Cap	Cap	Aq	Aq	Pis
June 25	Lib	Lib	Sc	Sc	Sag	Sag	Sag	Cap	Cap	Aq	Pis	Ar
July 3	Lib	Sc	Sc	Sc	Sag	Sag	Cap	Cap	Aq	Aq	Pis	Ar
July 11	Lib	Sc	Sc	Sag	Sag	Sag	Cap	Cap	Aq	Pis	Ar	Tau
July 18	Sc	Sc	Sc	Sag	Sag	Cap	Cap	Aq	Aq	Pis	Ar	Tau
July 26	Sc	Sc	Sag	Sag	Sag	Cap	Cap	Aq	Pis	Ar	Tau	Tau
Aug 3	Sc	Sc	Sag	Sag	Cap	Cap	Aq	Aq	Pis	Ar	Tau	Gem
Aug 11	Sc	Sag	Sag	Sag	Cap	Cap	Aq	Pis	Ar	Tau	Tau	Gem
Aug 18	Sc	Sag	Sag	Cap	Cap	Aq	Pis	Pis	Ar	Tau	Gem	Gem
Aug 27	Sag	Sag	Sag	Cap	Cap	Aq	Pis	Ar	Tau	Tau	Gem	Gem
Sept 4	Sag	Sag	Cap	Cap	Aq	Pis	Pis	Ar	Tau	Gem	Gem	Can
Sept 12	Sag	Sag	Cap	Aq	Aq	Pis	Ar	Tau	Tau	Gem	Gem	Can
Sept 20	Sag	Cap	Cap	Aq	Pis	Pis	Ar	Tau	Gem	Gem	Can	Can
Sept 28	Cap	Cap	Aq	Aq	Pis	Ar	Tau	Tau	Gem	Gem	Can	Can
Oct 6	Cap	Cap	Aq	Pis	Ar	Ar	Tau	Gem	Gem	Can	Can	Leo
Oct 14	Cap	Aq	Aq	Pis	Ar	Tau	Tau	Gem	Gem	Can	Can	Leo
Oct 22	Cap	Aq	Pis	Ar	Ar	Tau	Gem	Gem	Can	Can	Leo	Leo
Oct 30	Aq	Aq	Pis	Ar	Tau	Tau	Gem	Can	Can	Can	Leo	Leo
Nov 7	Aq	Aq	Pis	Ar	Tau	Tau	Gem	Can	Can	Leo	Leo	Leo
Nov 15	Aq	Pis	Ar	Tau	Gem	Gem	Can	Can	Can	Leo	Leo	Vir
Nov 23	Pis	Ar	Ar	Tau	Gem	Can	Can	Leo	Leo	Leo	Vir	Vir
Dec 1	Pis	Ar	Tau	Gem	Gem	Can	Can	Can	Leo	Leo	Vir	Vir
Dec 9	Ar	Tau	Tau	Gem	Gem	Can	Can	Leo	Leo	Leo	Vir	Vir
Dec 18	Ar	Tau	Gem	Gem	Can	Can	Can	Leo	Leo	Vir	Vir	Vir
Dec 28	Tau	Tau	Gem	Gem	Can	Can	Leo	Leo	Vir	Vir	Vir	Lib

CHAPTER 6

The Moon—Our Light Within

In some astrology-conscious lands, the moon is given as much importance in a horoscope as the sun. Astrologers often refer to these two bodies as the "lights," an apt term, since they shed the most light upon our personality in a horoscope reading. This also is a more technically appropriate description, since the sun and moon are not really planets, but a star and a satellite.

The most fascinating aspect of the moon is its connection with our emotional state. Our moods seem to wax and wane with the moon. Even the state of shellfish, animals, and planets is affected by the moon phase. Imagine what would happen if the moon were somehow caused to change its orbit, perhaps by a bombarding asteroid. What would happen to the tides, to ocean and plant life, which respond to the moon, or to our own bodies, which are mostly water? Life on earth would be impossible!

As the closest celestial body, the moon represents your receptive, reflective, female, nurturing self. And it reflects who you were nurtured by—the "mother" or mother figure in your chart. In a man's chart, the moon position also describes his receptive, emotional, "yin" side, as well as the woman in his life who will have the deepest effect, usually his mother. (Venus reveals the kind of woman who attracts him physically.)

The sign the moon was passing through at birth reveals much about your inner life, your needs and secrets, as well as those of people you'd like to know better. You can learn what appeals to a person subconsciously by knowing their moon sign, which reflects their instinctive, emotional nature.

It's well worth having an accurate chart cast to determine your moon sign. Since accurate moon tables are too extensive for this book, check through these descriptions to find the moon sign that feels most familiar.

The moon is more at home in some signs than others. It rules maternal Cancer and is exalted in Taurus—both comforting, home-loving signs where the natural emotional energies of the moon are easily and productively expressed. But when the moon is in the opposite signs—Capricorn or Scorpio—it leaves the comfortable nest and deals with emotional issues of power and achievement in the outside world. Those of you with the moon in these signs are more likely to find your emotional role more challenging in life.

Moon in Aries

You are an idealistic, impetuous person who falls in and out of love easily. This placement makes you both independent and ardent. You love a challenge, but could cool once your quarry is captured. You should cultivate patience and tolerance—or you might tend to gravitate toward those who treat you rough, just for the sake of challenge and excitement.

Moon in Taurus

You are a sentimental soul who is very fond of the good life and gravitates toward solid, secure relationships. You like displays of affection and creature comforts—all the tangible trappings of a cozy, safe, calm atmosphere. You are sensual and steady emotionally, but very stubborn and determined. You can't be pushed and tend to dislike changes. You should make an effort to broaden your horizons and to take a risk sometimes.

Moon in Gemini

You crave mental stimulation and variety in life, which you usually get through either an ever-varied social life, the excitement of flirtation, and/or multiple professional involvements. You may marry more than once and have a rather chaotic emotional life due to your difficulty with commitment and settling down. Be sure to find a partner who is as outgoing as you are. You will have to learn at some point to focus your energies because you tend to be somewhat fragmented—to do two things at once, to have two homes or even two lovers. If you can find a creative way to express your many-faceted nature, you'll be ahead of the game.

Moon in Cancer

This is the most powerful lunar position, which is sure to make a deep imprint on your character. Your needs are very much associated with your reaction to the needs of others. You are very sensitive and self-protective, though some of you may mask this with a hard shell. This placement also gives you an excellent memory, keen intuition, and an uncanny ability to perceive the needs of others. All of the lunar phases will affect you, especially full moons and eclipses, so you would do well to mark them on your calendar. Because you're happiest at home, you may work at home or turn your office into a second home, where you can nurture and comfort people. (You may tend to "mother the world.") With natural psychic, intuitive ability, you might be drawn to occult work in some way. Or you may get professionally involved with providing food and shelter to others.

Moon in Leo

This warm, passionate moon takes everything to heart. You are attracted to all that is noble, generous, and aristocratic in life (and may be a bit of a snob). You have an innate ability to take command emotionally, but you do need strong support, loyalty, and loud applause from those you love. You are possessive of your loved ones and your turf and will roar if anyone threatens to take over your territory.

Moon in Virgo

You are rather cool until you decide if others measure up. But once someone or something meets your ideal standards, you hold up your end of the arrangement perfectly. You may, in fact, drive yourself too hard to attain some notion of perfection. Try to be a bit easier on yourself and others. Don't always act the censor! You love to be the teacher and are drawn to situations where you can change others for the better, but sometimes you must learn to accept others for what they are—enjoy what you have!

Moon in Libra

A partnership-oriented moon—you may find it difficult to be alone or to do things alone. After you have learned emotional balance by leaning on yourself first, you can have excellent relationships. It is best for you to avoid extremes, however, which set your scales swinging and can make your love life precarious. You thrive in a rather conservative, traditional, romantic relationship, where you receive attention and flattery—but not possessiveness—from your partner. You'll be your most charming in an elegant, harmonious atmosphere.

Moon in Scorpio

This is a moon that enjoys and responds to intense, passionate feelings. You may go to extremes and have a very dramatic emotional life, full of ardor, suspicion, jealousy, and obsession. It would be much healthier to channel your need for power and control into meaningful work. This is a good position for anyone in the fields of medicine, police work, research, the occult, psychoanalysis, or intuitive work, because life-and-death situations don't faze you. However, you do take personal disappointments very hard.

Moon in Sagittarius

You take life's ups and downs with good humor and the proverbial grain of salt. You'll love 'em and leave 'em, taking off on a great adventure at a moment's notice. "Born free" could be your slogan. Attracted by the exotic, you have wanderlust mentally and physically. You may be too much in search of new mental and spiritual stimulation to ever settle down.

Moon in Capricorn

Are you ever accused of being too cool and calculating? You have an earthy side, but you take prestige and position very seriously. Your strong drive to succeed extends to your romantic life, where you will be devoted to improving your lifestyle, rising to the top. A structured situation where you can advance methodically makes you feel wonderfully secure. You may be attracted to someone older or very much younger or from a different social world. It may be difficult to look at the lighter side of emotional relationships; however, the "up" side of this moon in the sign of its detriment is that you tend to be very dutiful and responsible to those you care for.

Moon in Aquarius

You are a people collector with many friends of all backgrounds. You are happiest surrounded by people and may feel uneasy when left alone. Though you usually stay friends with lovers, intense emotions and demanding one-on-one relationships turn you off. You don't like anything to be too rigid or scheduled. Though tolerant and understanding, you can be emotionally unpredictable and may opt for an unconventional love life. With plenty of space, you will be able to sustain relationships with liberal, freedom-loving types.

Moon in Pisces

You are very responsive and empathetic to others, especially if they have problems or are the underdog. (Be on guard against attracting too many people with sob stories.) You'll be happiest if you can express your creative imagination in the arts or in the spiritual or healing professions. Because you may tend to escape in fantasies or overreact to the moods of others, you need an emotional anchor to help you keep a firm foothold in reality. Steer clear of too much escapism (especially in alcohol) or reclusiveness. Places near water soothe your moods. Working in a field that gives you emotional variety will also help you to be productive.

What Eclipses Do to Your Moods

In case we've been taking the moon for granted, the eclipse seasons, which occur about every six months, remind us how important the moon is for our survival. Perhaps that is why eclipses have always had an ominous reputation. Folklore all over the world blames eclipses for catastrophes such as birth defects, crop failures, and hurricanes. Villagers on the peninsula of Baja California paint their fruit trees red and wear red ribbons and underwear to deflect "evil rays." During the total eclipse of July 1991, everyone retreated safely indoors to follow the eclipse on television. In other native societies, people play drums and make loud noises to frighten off heavenly monsters believed to destroy the light of the sun and moon. Only the romantic Tahitians seem to have positive feelings about an eclipse. In this sensual tropical paradise, legend declares that the "lights" go out when the sun and moon make love and procreate the stars.

Ancient Chaldean astrologer-priests were the first to time eclipses accurately. They discovered that 6,585 days after an eclipse, another eclipse would happen. By counting ahead after all the eclipses in a given year, they could predict eclipses eighteen years into the future. This technique was practiced by navigators through the centuries, including Christopher Columbus, who used his knowledge of an upcoming lunar eclipse to extort food from the frightened inhabitants of Jamaica in 1504. In ancient Mexico, Mayan astronomer-priests also discovered that eclipses occur at regular intervals and recorded them with a hieroglyph of a serpent swallowing the sun.

What Causes an Eclipse?

A solar eclipse is the passage of the new moon directly across the face of the sun. It is a very exciting and awesome event, which causes the sky to darken suddenly. Though the effect lasts only a few minutes, it is enough to strike panic in the uninformed viewer.

A lunar eclipse happens when the full moon passes through the shadow of the Earth on the opposite side from the sun; as a result, the Earth blocks out the sun's light from reaching the moon. The moon must be in level alignment with the sun and Earth for a lunar eclipse to occur.

Conditions are ripe for an eclipse twice a year, when a full or a new moon is most likely to cross the path of the sun at two points known as the *nodes*.

What to Know About Nodes

To understand the nodes, visualize two rings, one inside the other. As you move the rings, you'll notice that the two circles intersect at opposite points. Now imagine one ring as the moon's orbit and the other as the sun's (as seen from Earth). The crossing points are called the moon's "nodes."

For an eclipse to happen, two conditions must be met. First, the path of the orbiting moon must be close enough to a node. Second, this must happen at a time when there is either a new or a full moon. (Not every new or full moon happens close enough to the nodes to create an eclipse.) The axis of the nodes is continually moving backward through the zodiac at the rate of about one and a half degrees per month; therefore, eclipses will eventually occur in every sign of the zodiac.

How Often Do Eclipses Occur?

Whenever the sun draws close to one of the nodes, any new or full moon happening near that time will create an eclipse. This "eclipse season" happens twice a year, approximately six months apart. There are at least four eclipses each year, and there can be as many as seven. In 2002, there will be five eclipses:

- Full Moon in Sagittarius (lunar eclipse)—May 26
- New Moon in Gemini (solar eclipse)—June 10
- Full Moon in Capricorn (lunar eclipse)—June 24

- Full Moon in Taurus (lunar eclipse)—November 19
- New Moon in Sagittarius (solar eclipse)—December 4

Eclipses Have Family Ties

One of the most interesting things about eclipses is that they have "families." Each eclipse is a member of a string of related eclipses that pop up regularly. As mentioned before, the ancient Chaldeans, who were the first great sky-watchers, discovered that eclipses recur in patterns, repeating themselves after approximately eighteen years plus nine to eleven days, in a cycle lasting a total of approximately 1,300 years. Much later, in the eleventh century A.D., these patterns became known as the "Saros Series." (In ancient Greek, "saros" means repetition.)

Because each Saros Series begins at a moment in time, the initial eclipse has a horoscope, and therefore a "personality" which goes through stages of development as the series of eclipses progresses over its 1,300-year lifetime. So as a Saros Series moves through your chart, it will produce an eclipse with a similar "personality" every eighteen years. In the interim, you'll experience eclipses belonging to other Saros Series, which will exhibit their own special family characteristics. Therefore, there can be no one generic interpretation for eclipses, since each affects your horoscope in a different way, according to the personality of its particular Saros Series.

What Is the Purpose of an Eclipse in My Life?

Eclipses can bring on milestone events in your life, if they aspect a key point in your horoscope. In general, they shake up the status quo, bringing hidden areas out into the open. During this time, problems you've been avoiding or have brushed aside can surface to demand your attention. A good coping strategy is to accept whatever comes up as a challenge. It could make a big difference in your life. And don't forget the power of your sense of humor. If you can laugh at something, you'll never be afraid of it.

Second-guessing the eclipses is easy if you have a copy of your horoscope calculated by a computer. (If you do not have a computer or an astrology program, there are several sites on the Internet which will calculate your chart free. See the listings in the resource chapter of this book.) This enables you to pinpoint the area of your life which will be affected. However, you can make an educated guess, by setting up a rough diagram on your own. If you'd like to find out which area of your life this year's eclipses are most likely to affect, follow these easy steps. First, you must know the time of day you were born and look up your rising sign listed in the tables in this book. Then set up an estimated horoscope by drawing a circle, then dividing it into four parts by making a cross directly through the center. Continue to divide each of the parts into thirds, as if you were dividing a cake, until you have twelve slices. Write your rising sign on the middle left-hand slice, which would be the 9 o'clock point, if you were looking at your watch. Then continue listing the signs counterclockwise, until you have listed all twelve signs of the zodiac on the "slices" of the chart.

You should now have a basic diagram of your horoscope chart (minus the planets, of course). Starting with your rising sign "slice," number each portion consecutively, working counterclockwise. Since this year's eclipses will fall in Gemini, Sagittarius, Taurus, and Capricorn, find the number of these slices or "houses" on the chart and read the following descriptions for the kinds of issues that are likely to be emphasized.

If an eclipse falls in your FIRST HOUSE—
Events cause you to examine the ways you are acting independently, pushing you to become more visible and to assert yourself. This is a time when you feel compelled to make your own decisions and do your own thing. There is an emphasis on how you are coming across to others. You may want to change your physical appearance, body image, or style of dress in some way. Under affliction, there might be illness or physical harm.

If an eclipse falls in your SECOND HOUSE—
This is the place where you consider all matters of security. You consolidate your resources, earn money, acquire property, and decide what you value and what you want to own. On a deeper level, this house reveals your sense of self-worth, the inner values that draw wealth in various forms.

If an eclipse falls in your THIRD HOUSE—
Here you communicate, reach out to others, express your ideas, and explore different courses of action. You may feel especially restless, and have confrontations with neighbors or siblings. In your search for more knowledge, you may decide to improve your skills, get more education, or sign up for a course that interests you, which could ultimately alter your lifestyle. Local transportation, especially your car, might be affected by an eclipse here.

If an eclipse falls in your FOURTH HOUSE—
Here is where you put down roots and establish your home base. You'll consider what home really means to you. Issues involving parents, the physical setup or location of your home, or your immediate family demand your attention. You may be especially concerned with parenting or relationships with your own mother. You may consider moving your home to a new location or leaving home, untying family ties.

If an eclipse falls in your FIFTH HOUSE—

Here is where you express yourself, either through your personal talents or through procreating children. You are interested in making your special talents visible. This is also the house of love affairs and the romantic aspect of life, where you flirt, have fun, and enjoy the excitement of love. Hobbies and crafts, the ways you explore the playful child within, fall in this area.

If an eclipse falls in your SIXTH HOUSE—

This is your care and maintenance department, where you take care of your health, organize your life, and set up a daily routine. It is also the place where you perfect your skills and add polish to your life. The chores you do every day, the skills you learn, and the techniques you use fall here. If something doesn't "work" in your life, an eclipse is sure to bring this to light. If you've been neglecting your health, diet, and fitness, you'll probably pay the consequences during an eclipse, Or you may be faced with work that requires much routine organization and steady effort, rather than creative ability. Or you may be required to perform services for others. (In ancient astrology, this was the place of slavery!)

If an eclipse falls in your SEVENTH HOUSE—

This is the area of committed relationships, of those which involve legal agreements, of working in a close relationship with another. Here you'll be dealing with how you relate and what you'll be willing to give up for the sake of a marriage or partnership. Eclipses here can put extra pressure on a relationship and, if it's not working, precipitate a breakup. Lawsuits and open enemies also reside here.

If an eclipse falls in your EIGHTH HOUSE—

This area is concerned with power and control. Consider what you are willing to give up in order that something might happen. Power struggles, intense relationships, and a desire to penetrate a deeper mystery belong here. Debts, loans, financial matters that involve another party, and wheeling and dealing also come into focus. So does sex, where you surrender your individual power to create a new life together. Matters involving birth and death are also involved here.

If an eclipse falls in your NINTH HOUSE—
Here is where you look at the Big Picture: how everything relates to form a pattern. You'll seek information that helps you find meaning in life: higher education, religion, travel, and global issues. Eclipses here can push you to get out of your rut, explore something you've never done before, and expand your horizons.

If an eclipse falls in your TENTH HOUSE—
This is the high-profile point in your chart. Here is where you consider how society looks at you, and what your position is in the outside world. You'll be concerned about whether you receive proper credit for your work and if you're recognized by higher-ups. Promotions, raises, and other forms of recognition can be given or denied. Your standing in your career or community can be challenged, or you'll get publicly acknowledged for achieving a goal. An eclipse here can make you famous . . . or burst your balloon if you've been too ambitious or neglecting other areas of your life.

If an eclipse falls in your ELEVENTH HOUSE—
Your relationship with groups of people comes under scrutiny during an eclipse—whom you are identified with, whom you socialize with, and how well you are accepted by other members of your team. Activities of clubs, political parties, networking, and social inter-

actions become important. You'll be concerned about what other people think: "Do they like me?" "Will I make the team, or win the election?"

If an eclipse falls in your TWELFTH HOUSE—
This is the time when the focus turns to your inner life. An especially favorable eclipse here might bring you great insight and inspiration. Or events may happen which cause you to retreat from public life. Here is where we go to be alone, or to do spiritual or reparative work in retreats, hospitals, religious institutions, or psychotherapy. Here is where you deliver selfless service, through charitable acts. Good aspects from an eclipse could promote an ability to go with the flow, to rise above the competition and find an inner, almost mystical strength that enables you to connect with the deepest needs of others.

What Is the Best Thing to Do During an Eclipse?

When the natural rhythms of the sun and moon are disturbed, it's best to postpone important activities. Be sure to mark eclipse days on your calendar, especially if the eclipse falls in your birth sign. This year, Gemini, Sagittarius, Taurus, and Capricorn should take special note of the conscious and unconscious feelings that arise or are suppressed. With lunar eclipses, some possibilities could be a break from attachments, or the healing of an illness or substance abuse which had been triggered by the subconscious. The temporary event could be a healing time, when you gain perspective. During solar eclipses, when you could be in a highly subjective state, pay attention to the hidden subconscious patterns that surface, the emotional truth that is revealed in your feelings at this time.

The effect of the eclipse can reverberate for some time, often months after the event. But it is especially important to stay cool and make no major moves during the period known as the shadow of the eclipse, which begins about a week before as the energy begins to crescendo and lasts until at least three days after the eclipse, when the emotional atmosphere simmers down. After three days, the daily rhythms should be back to normal and you can proceed with business as usual.

The most positive way to view eclipses is as very special times, when we can receive great insight through a changed perspective. By blocking out the emotional pressure of the full moon, a lunar eclipse could be a time of reason, rather than confusion, a time when we can take a break from our problems. A solar eclipse, when the new moon blocks out the sun (or ego), could be a time when the moon's most positive qualities are expressed, bringing us a feeling of oneness, nurturing, and compassion.

CHAPTER 7

Astro-Mating—An Element-ary Guide to Love

How many people turn to astrology for the light it can shed on their love life! Probably the question astrologers hear most is: What sign is best for me in love? Or: I'm a Taurus and my lover is a Gemini—what are our prospects? Each sun sign does have certain predictable characteristics in love, and by comparing the sun signs, you can reach a better understanding of the dynamics of the relationship. However, it is very easy to oversimplify. Just because someone's sun sign is said to be "incompatible" is no reason why the relationship can't work out. A true in-depth comparison involves far more than just the sun sign. An astrologer considers the interrelationships of all the planets and houses (where they fall in your respective horoscopes). There are several bonds between planets that can offset any difficulties between sun signs. It's worthwhile to analyze them to learn more about your relationship. You can do this by making a very simple chart which compares the moon, Mars, and Venus, as well as the sun signs of the partners in a relationship. You can find the signs for Mars and Venus in the tables in this book. Unfortunately the moon tables are too long for a book of this size—so it might be worth your while to consult an astrological ephemeris (a book of planetary tables) in your local library or to have a computer chart cast to find out the moon placement.

Simply look up the signs of Mars and Venus (and

the Moon, if possible) for each person and list them, with the sun sign, next to each other, then add the *element* of each sign. The Earth signs are Taurus, Virgo, Capricorn. The Air signs are Gemini, Libra, Aquarius. The Fire signs are Aries, Leo, Sagittarius. And the Water signs are Cancer, Scorpio, Pisces.

Example:

ROMEO'S PLANETS:

SUN	MOON	MARS	VENUS
Aries/Fire	Leo/Fire	Scorpio/Water	Taurus/Earth

JULIET'S PLANETS:

SUN	MOON	MARS	VENUS
Pisces/Water	Leo/Fire	Aries/Fire	Aquarius/Air

As a rule of thumb, signs of the *same element* or *complementary elements* (fire with air and earth with water) get along best. So, after comparing this couple's planets, you can see that this particular Romeo and Juliet could have some challenges ahead.

The Lunar Link—Here's the Person You *Need*

The planet in your chart which governs your emotions is the moon. (Note: the moon is not technically a planet, but is usually referred to as one by astrologers.) So you would naturally take this into consideration when evaluating a potential romantic partnership. If a person's moon is in a good relationship to your sun, moon, Venus, or Mars, preferably in the same sign or element, you should relate well on some emotional level. Your needs will be compatible: you'll understand each other's feelings without much effort. If the moon is in a compatible element, such as earth with water or fire with air, you may have a few adjustments, but you will be able to make them easily. With a water-fire or earth-air combination, you'll have to make a considerable effort to understand where the other is coming from emotionally.

It's worth having a computer chart done, just to find the position of your moon. (Since the moon changes signs every two days, the tables are too long to print in this book.)

The Venus Attraction—Here's the One You *Want*

Venus is what you respond to, so if you and your partner have a good Venus aspect, you should have much in common. You'll enjoy doing things together. The same type of lovemaking will turn you both on. You'll have no trouble pleasing each other.

Look up both partners' Venus placements in the charts on page 69. Your lover's Venus in the same sign or a sign of the *same element* as your own Venus, Mars, moon, or sun is best. Second best is a sign of a compatible element (earth with water, air with fire). Venus in water with air, or earth with fire means that you may have to make a special effort to understand what appeals to each other. And you'll have to give each other plenty of space to enjoy activities that don't particularly appeal to you. By the way, this chart can work not only for lovers, but for any relationship where compatibility of tastes is important to you.

The Mars Connection—This One Lights Your Fire!

Mars positions reveal your sexual energy . . . how often you like to make love, for instance. It also shows your temper . . . do you explode or do a slow burn? Here you'll find out if your partner is direct, aggressive, and hot-blooded or more likely to take the cool, mental approach. Mutually supportive partners have their Mars working together in the same or complementary elements. But *any* contacts between Mars and Venus in two charts can strike sexy sparks. Even the difficult aspects, such as your partner's Mars three or six signs away from your sun, Mars, or Venus, can be sexually stimulating. Who doesn't get turned on by a challenge from time to time? On the other hand, the easy-flowing Mars relationships can drift into soporific dullness.

The Solar Bond

The sun is the focus of our personality and therefore the most powerful component involved. Each pair of sun signs has special lessons to teach and learn from each other. There is a negative side to the most ideal couple and a positive side to the unlikeliest match. Each has an up- and a downside. You'll find a comparison of your sun sign with every other one in the "pairs" section of the individual sun sign chapters in this book. If the forecast for you and your beloved (or business associate) seems like an uphill struggle, take heart! Such legendary lovers as Juan and Eva Peron, Ronald and Nancy Reagan, Harry and Bess Truman, Julius Caesar and Cleopatra, Billy and Ruth Graham, and George and Martha Washington are among the many who have made successful partnerships between supposedly incompatible sun signs.

Try astro-mating these hot celebrity couples for practice. Look up their planets in the "planet" tables in this book and discover the secret of their cosmic attraction. (Some may not be an "item" by the time this is published. Maybe you can figure out what went wrong!)

ARIES Matthew Broderick (3/21/62) and ARIES
  Sarah Jessica Parker (3/24/65)
PISCES Tea Leoni (2/25/66) and LEO David Du-
  chovny (8/7/61)

ARIES Warren Beatty (3/30/37) and GEMINI Annette Bening (5/29/58)

ARIES Al Gore (3/31/48) and LEO Tipper Gore (8/19/48)

ARIES Alec Baldwin (4/3/58) and SAGITTARIUS Kim Basinger (12/8/53)

TAURUS Barbra Streisand (4/24/42) and CANCER James Brolin (7/18/40)

TAURUS Uma Thurman (4/29/70) and SCORPIO Ethan Hawke (11/6/70)

TAURUS Carmen Electra (4/20/72) and TAURUS Dennis Rodman (5/13/61)

GEMINI Liz Hurley (6/10/65) and VIRGO Hugh Grant (9/9/60)

GEMINI Angelina Jolie (6/4/75) and LEO Billy Bob Thornton (8/4/55)

GEMINI Nicole Kidman (6/21/67) and CANCER Tom Cruise (7/3/62)

LEO Jennifer Lopez (7/24/70) and SCORPIO Sean "Puffy" Combs (11/4/69)

LEO Arnold Schwarzenegger (7/30/47) and SCORPIO Maria Shriver (11/6/55)

LEO Whitney Houston (8/9/53) and AQUARIUS Bobby Brown (2/5/69)

LEO Melanie Griffith (8/9/57) and LEO Antonio Banderas (8/10/60)

LIBRA Michael Douglas (9/25/44) and LIBRA Catherine Zeta-Jones (9/25/69)

TAURUS Jessica Lange (4/20/49) and SCORPIO Sam Shepard (11/5/43)

SCORPIO Hillary Clinton (10/26/47) and LEO Bill Clinton (8/19/46)

PISCES Kurt Russell (3/17/51) and SCORPIO Goldie Hawn (11/21/45)

SCORPIO Prince Charles (11/14/48) and CANCER Camilla Parker Bowles (7/17/47)

SAGITTARIUS Brad Pitt (12/18/63) and AQUARIUS Jennifer Aniston (2/11/69)

CAPRICORN Diane Sawyer (12/22/45) and SCORPIO Mike Nichols (11/6/46)

AQUARIUS Oprah Winfrey (1/29/54) and PISCES
  Stedman Graham (3/6/51)

  Now it's time to do a bit of astro-mating of your own!
Do you have what it takes to seduce these celebrity hunks?
Check your sun, moon, Mars, and Venus with theirs!

Prince William (6/21/82)

SUN: Cancer (water)
MOON: Cancer (water)
MARS: Libra (air)
VENUS: Taurus (earth)

Russell Crowe (4/7/64)

SUN: Aries (fire)
MOON: Aquarius (air)
MARS: Aries (fire)
VENUS: Gemini (earth)

Jude Law (12/29/72)

SUN: Capricorn (earth)
MOON: Scorpio (water)
MARS: Scorpio (water)
VENUS: Sagittarius (fire)

Leonardo DiCaprio (11/11/74)

SUN: Scorpio (water)
MOON: Libra (air)
MARS: Scorpio (water)
VENUS: Scorpio (water)

Matt Damon (10/8/70)

SUN: Libra (air)
MOON: Gemini (air)
MARS: Aquarius (air)
VENUS: Libra (air)

George Clooney (5/6/61)

SUN: Taurus (earth)
MOON: Capricorn (earth)
MARS: Leo (fire)
VENUS: Aries (fire)

Richard Gere (8/31/49)

SUN: Virgo (earth)
MOON: Sagittarius (fire)
MARS: Cancer (water)
VENUS: Libra (air)

Hugh Grant (9/9/60)

SUN: Virgo (earth)
MOON: Taurus (earth)
MARS: Gemini (air)
VENUS: Libra (air)

Kevin Costner (1/18/55)

SUN: Capricorn (earth)
MOON: Sagittarius (fire)
MARS: Aries (fire)
VENUS: Sagittarius (fire)

Mel Gibson (1/3/56)

SUN: Capricorn (earth)
MOON: Virgo (earth)
MARS: Scorpio (water)
VENUS: Aquarius (air)

Fabio (3/15/61)

SUN: Pisces (water)
MOON: Pisces (water)
MARS: Cancer (water)
VENUS: Aries (fire)

Brad Pitt (12/18/63)

SUN: Sagittarius (fire)
MOON: Capricorn (earth)
MARS: Capricorn (earth)
VENUS: Capricorn (earth)

Johnny Depp (6/9/63)

SUN: Gemini (air)
MOON: Capricorn (earth)
MARS: Virgo (earth)
VENUS: Taurus (earth)

Keanu Reeves (9/2/64)

SUN: Virgo (earth)
MOON: Leo (fire)
MARS: Cancer (water)
VENUS: Cancer (water)

Joaquin Phoenix (10/28/74)

SUN: Scorpio (water)
MOON: Aries (fire)
MARS: Scorpio (water)
VENUS: Scorpio (water)

CHAPTER 8

Ask the Expert—Should You Have a Personal Reading?

Though you can learn much about yourself and others from studying astrology yourself, there comes a time when you might want the objective opinion of a professional astrologer. Done by a qualified astrologer, the personal reading can be an empowering experience if you want to reach your full potential, size up a lover or business situation, or find out what the future has in store. There are so many options for readings today, however, that sorting through them can be a daunting task. Besides face-to-face consultations, there are readings by mail, phone, tape, and Internet. There are astrologers who are specialists in certain areas, such as finance or medical astrology. And unfortunately, there are many questionable practitioners who range from streetwise gypsy fortunetellers to unscrupulous scam artists. The following basic guidelines can help you sort out your options to find the reading that's right for you.

The One-on-One Reading

Nothing compares to a one-on-one consultation with a professional astrologer who has analyzed thousands of charts and can pinpoint the potential in yours. During your reading, you can get your specific questions answered. For instance, how to get along better with your mate or coworker. There are many astrologers who now combine their skills with training in psychology and are well suited to help you examine your alternatives.

To give you an accurate reading, an astrologer needs certain information from you, such as the date, time, and place where you were born. (A horoscope can be cast about anyone or anything that has a specific time and place.) Most astrologers will then enter this information into a computer, which will calculate a chart in seconds. From the resulting chart, the astrologer will do an interpretation.

If you don't know your exact birth time, you can usually locate it at the Bureau of Vital Statistics at the city hall or county seat of the state where you were born. If you still have no success in getting your time of birth, some astrologers can estimate an approximate birth time by using past events in your life to determine the chart. This technique is called *rectification*.

How to Find a Good Astrologer

Your first priority should be to choose a qualified astrologer. Rather than relying on word of mouth or grandiose advertising claims, choose your astrologer with the same care as any trusted adviser such as a doctor, lawyer, or banker. Unfortunately, anyone can claim to be an astrologer—to date, there is no licensing of astrologers or established professional criteria. However, there are nationwide organizations of serious, committed astrologers that can help you in your search.

Good places to start your investigation are organizations such as the American Federation of Astrologers or the National Council for Geocosmic Research (NCGR), which offer a program of study and certification. If you live near a major city, there is sure to be an active NCGR chapter or astrology club in your area—many are listed in astrology magazines available at your local newsstand. In response to many requests for referrals, the NCGR has compiled a directory of professional astrologers, which includes a glossary of terms and an explanation of specialties within the astrological field. Contact the NCGR headquarters (see Chapter 10, "The Sydney Omarr Yellow Pages") for information.

Be Aware of When to Beware

As a potentially lucrative freelance business, astrology has always attracted self-styled experts who may not have the knowledge or the counseling experience to give a helpful reading. These astrologers can range from the well-meaning amateur to the charlatan or street-corner gypsy who has for many years given astrology a bad name. Be very wary of astrologers who claim to have occult powers or who make pretentious claims of celebrated clients or miraculous achievements. You can often tell from the initial phone conversation if the astrologer is legitimate. He or she should ask for your birthday time and place and conduct the conversation in a professional manner. Any astrologer who gives a reading based only on your sun sign is highly suspect.

When you arrive at the reading, the astrologer should be prepared. The consultation should be conducted in a private, quiet place. The astrologer should be interested in your problems of the moment. A good reading involves feedback on your part, so if the reading is not relating to your concerns, you should let the astrologer know. You should feel free to ask questions and get clarifications of technical terms. The more you actively participate, rather than expecting the astrologer to carry the reading or come forth with oracular predictions, the more meaningful your experience will be. An astrologer should help you validate your current experience and be frank about possible negative happenings, but suggest a positive course of action.

In their approach to a reading, some astrologers may be more literal, others more intuitive. Those who have had counseling training may take a more psychological approach. Though some astrologers may seem to have an almost psychic ability, extrasensory perception or any other parapsychological talent is not essential. A very accurate picture can be drawn from the data in your horoscope chart.

An astrologer may do several charts for each client, including one for the time of birth and a "progressed chart," showing the evolution from birth to the present time. According to your individual needs, there are many other possibilities, such as a chart for a different location, if you are contemplating a change of place. Relationships between any two people, things, or events can be interpreted with a chart which compares one partner's horoscope with the other's. A composite chart, which uses the midpoint between planets in two individual charts to describe the relationship, is another commonly used device.

An astrologer will be particularly interested in transits—times when planets will pass over the planets or sensitive points in your birth chart, which signal important events in your life.

Many astrologers offer tape-recorded readings, another option to consider. In this case, you'll be mailed a taped reading based on your birth chart. This type of reading is more personal than a computer printout and can give you valuable insights, though it is not equivalent to a live dialogue with the astrologer, when you can discuss your specific interests and issues of the moment.

Phone Readings—Real or Phony?

Telephone readings come in two varieties, a dial-in taped reading, usually recorded in advance by an astrologer or a live consultation with an "astrologer" on the other end of the line. The taped readings are general daily or weekly forecasts, applied to all members of your sign and charged by the minute. The quality depends on the astrologer. *One caution*: Be aware that these readings can run up quite a telephone bill, especially if you get into the habit of calling every day. Be sure that you are aware of the per-minute cost of each call beforehand.

Live telephone readings also vary with the expertise of the astrologer. Ideally, the astrologer at the other end of the line enters your birth data into a computer, which calculates your chart. This chart will then be referred to during the consultation. The advantage of a live telephone reading is that your individual chart is used and you can ask about a specific problem. However, before you invest in any reading, be sure that your astrologer is qualified and that you fully understand in advance how much you will be charged. There should be no unpleasant financial surprises later.

About Computer Readings

Companies which offer computer programs (such as ACS, Matrix, Astrolabe) also offer a variety of computer-generated horoscope readings. These can be quite comprehensive, offering a beautiful printout of the chart plus many pages of detailed information about each planet and aspect of the chart. You can then study it at your convenience. Of course, the interpretations will be general, since there is no personal input from you, and may not cover your immediate concerns. Since computer-generated horoscopes are much lower in cost than live consultations, you might consider them as either a supplement or preparation for an eventual live reading. You'll then be more familiar with your chart and able to plan specific questions in advance. They also make a terrific gift for astrology fans. There are several companies in our "Yellow Pages" chapter which offer computerized readings prepared by reputable astrologers.

Whichever option you decide to pursue, may your reading be an empowering one!

CHAPTER 9

The "In" Sites Online

If you're curious to see a copy of your chart (or someone else's), want to study astrology in depth, or chat with another astrology fan, log on to the Internet! There you'll find a whole new world of astrology waiting for a click of your mouse. Thousands of astrological sites offer you everything from chart services to chat rooms to individual readings. Even better, you'll find *free* software, *free* charts, and *free* articles to download. You can virtually get an education in astrology from your computer screen, share your insights with new astrology-minded pals in a chat room or on a mailing list, then later meet them in person at one of the hundreds of conferences around the world.

The following sites were chosen for general interest from vast numbers of astrology-oriented places on the Net. Many have their own selection of links to other sites for further exploration. *One caveat*: Though these sites were selected with longevity in mind, the Internet is a volatile place where sites can disappear or change without notice. Therefore, some of our sites may have changed addresses, names, or content by the time this book is published.

Free Charts

Astrolabe Software at *http://www.alabe.com* distributes some of the most creative and user-friendly programs now available, like "Solar Fire," a favorite of top astrologers. Visitors to their site are greeted with a chart of the time you log on. You can get your chart calculated, with a mini-interpretation, e-mailed to you.

For an instant chart, surf to this address: *http://www.astro.ch* and check into ASTRODIENST, one of the first and best astrology sites on the Internet. Its world atlas will give you the accurate longitude and latitude of your birthplace for setting up your horoscope. You can print out your chart in a range of easy-to-read formats. One handy feature for beginners: The planetary placement is listed in words, rather than glyphs, alongside the chart (a real help for those who haven't yet learned to read the astrology glyph).

There are many other attractions at this site, such as a list of your astro-twins (famous people born on your birthdate). The site even sorts the "twins" to feature those who also have your identical rising sign. You can then click on their names and get instant charts of your famous sign-mates.

Free Software

Software manufacturers on the Web are generous with free downloads of demo versions of their software. You may then calculate charts using their data. This makes sense if you're considering investing serious money in astrology software, and want to see how the program works in advance. You can preview ASTROLABE Software programs favored by many professional astrologers at *http://www.alabe.com*. Check out the latest demo of "Solar Fire," one of the most user-friendly astrology programs available—you'll be impressed.

For a Fully Functional
Astrology Program:

Walter Pullen's amazingly complete ASTROLOG program is offered absolutely free at this site: *http://www.magitech.com/~cruiser1/astrolog.htm.*

ASTROLOG is an ultrasophisticated program with all the features of much more expensive programs. It comes in versions for all formats—DOS, Windows, MAC, UNIX—and has some cool features such as a revolving globe and a constellation map. A "must" for those who want to get involved with astrology without paying big bucks for a professional-caliber program. Or for those who want to add ASTROLOG's unique features to their astrology software library. This program has it all!

Another good resource for software is Astro Computing Services. Their Web site has free demos of several excellent programs. Note especially their "Electronic Astrologer," one of the most effective and reasonably priced programs on the market. It's very easy to use, a bonus for nontechies. Go to *http://www.astrocom.com* for ACS software, books, readings, chart services, and software demos. At this writing, there are free new moon and full moon reports.

Surf to *http://www.astroscan.ca* for a free program called ASTROSCAN. Stunning graphics and ease of use make this a winner.

At Halloran Software's site, *http://www.halloran. com,* there are four levels of Windows astrology software from which to choose. The "Astrology for Windows" shareware program is available in unregistered demo form as a free download and in registered form for $26.50, at this writing. The calculations in this program may be all that an astrology hobbyist needs. The price for the full-service program is certainly reasonable.

Free Screen Saver and More

The Astrology Matrix offers a way to put your sign in view with a downloadable graphic screensaver. There are also many other diversions at this site, where you may consult the stars, the I Ching, the runes, and the tarot. Here's where to connect with news groups and online discussions. Their almanac helps you schedule the best day to sign on the dotted line, ask for a raise, or plant your rosebush. Address: *http://thenewage.com.*

Free Astrology Course

Schedule a long visit to *http://www.panplanet.com,* where you will find the Canopus Academy of Astrology, a site loaded with goodies. For the experienced astrologer, there is a collection of articles from top astrologers. They've done the work for you when it comes to picking the best astrology links on the Web, so be sure to check out those bestowed with the Canopus Award of Excellence.

Astrologer Linda Reid, an accomplished astrology teacher and author, offers a complete online curriculum for all levels of astrology study plus individual tutoring. To get your feet wet, Linda is offering an excellent beginners' course at this site, a terrific way to get off and running in astrology.

Visit an Astro-Mall

Surf to *http://www.astronet.com* for the Internet's equivalent of an Astrology Mall. ASTRONET offers interactive fun for everyone. At this writing, there's a special area for teenage astrology fans, access to popular astrology magazines like *American Astrology,* advice to the lovelorn, as well as a grab bag of horoscopes, featured guests, and a shopping area for books, reports, software, and even jewelry.

Swoon.com is another mall-like site aimed at dating, mating, and relating. It has fun features to spark up your love life, plenty of advice for the lovelorn, as well as links to all the popular fashion magazine astrology columns. Address: *http://www.swoon.com.*

Find An Astrologer Here

Metalog Directory of Astrology
http://www.astrologer.com

Looking for an astrologer in your local area? Perhaps you're planning a vacation in Australia or France and would like to meet astrologers or combine your activities with an astrology conference there? Go no further than this well-maintained resource. Here is an extensive worldwide list of astrologers and astrology sites. There is also an agenda of astrology conferences and seminars all over the world.

The A.F.A. Web Site
http://www.astrologers.com

This is the interesting Web site of the prestigious American Federation of Astrologers. The A.F.A. has a very similar address to the *Metalog Directory* and also has a directory of astrologers, restricted to those who meet their stringent requirements. Check out their correspondence course if you would like to study astrology in depth.

Tools Every Astrologer Needs Are Online

Internet Atlas
http://www.astro.ch/atlas

Find the geographic longitude and latitude and the correct time zone for any city worldwide. You'll need this information to calculate a chart.

The Exact Time, Anywhere in the World
http://www.timeticker.com

A fun site with fascinating graphics which give you the exact time anywhere in the world. Click on the world map and the correct time and zone for that place lights up.

Check the Weather Forecast
http://www.weathersage.com

More accurate than your local TV forecast is the Weathersage, which uses astrology to predict snowstorms and hurricanes. Get your long-range local forecast at this super site.

Celebrate the Queen's Birthday
http://www.zodiacal.com

A great jumping-off place for an astrology tour of the Internet, this site has a veritable Burke's Peerage of royal birthdays. There's a good selection of articles, plus tools such as a U.S. and world atlas and information on conferences, software, and tapes. The links at this site will send you off in the right direction.

Astrology World
http://astrology-world.com

Astrologer Deborah Houlding has gathered some of the finest European astrologers on this super Web site, as well as a comprehensive list of links and conferences.

Astrology Alive
http://www.astrologyalive.com

Barbara Schermer has one of the most innovative approaches to astrology. She was one of the first astrologers to go online, so there's always a "cutting edge" to this site. Great list of links.

National Council for Geocosmic Research (NCGR)
http://www.geocosmic.org

A key stop on any astrological tour of the Net. Here's where you can find local chapters in your area, get information on the NCGR testing and certification programs, and get a conference schedule. You can also order lecture tapes from their nationwide conferences, or get complete lists of conference topics to study at home. Good links to resources.

Where to Find Charts of the Famous

When the news is breaking, you can bet Lois Rodden will be the first to get accurate birthdays of the headline makers, and put up their charts on her Web site: *www.astrodatabank.com*. Rodden's research is astrology's most reliable source for data of the famous and infamous. Her Web site specializes in birthdays and charts of current newsmakers, political figures, and international celebrities. You can purchase her database program, a wonderful research tool, which gives you thousands of birthdays sorted into categories.

Another site with birthdays and charts of famous people to download is *http://www.astropro.com*.

You can get the sun and moon sign, plus a biography of the hottest new film stars here: *http://www.mrshowbiz. com*. Or go to *http://www.imdb.com* for a comprehensive list of film celebrities including bios, plus lists of famous couples from today and yesteryear.

Yet another good source for celebrity birthdates is *http://www.metamaze.com/bdays*. You can find some interesting offbeat newsmakers here.

For Astrology Books

National Clearinghouse for Astrology Books

A wide selection of books on all aspects of astrology, from basics to advanced. Many hard-to-find books. Surf to: *http://www.astroamerica.com*.

These addresses also have a good selection of astrology books, some which are unique to the site:
http://www.panplanet.com
http://thenewage.com
http://www.astrocom.com

Browse the huge astrology list of online bookstore Amazon.com at *http://www.amazon.com*.

Astrology Tapes at Pegasus Tapes
http://www.pegasustape.com

You can study at home with world-famous astrologers via audiocassette recordings from Pegasus Tapes. There's a great selection taped from conferences, classes, lectures, and seminars. An especially good source for astrologers who emphasize psychological and mythological themes.

For History and Mythology Buffs

Be sure to visit the astrology section of this gorgeous site, dedicated to the history and mythology of many traditions. One of the most beautifully designed sites we've seen. Address: *http://www.elore.com*.

The leading authority on the history of astrology, Robert Hand, has an excellent site which features his cutting-edge research. See what one of astrology's great teachers has to offer. Address: *http://www.robhand.com*.

The Project Hindsight group is devoted to restoring the astrology of the Hellenistic period (300 B.C. to about

600 A.D.), the primary source for all later Western astrology. Some fascinating articles for astrology fans. Address: *http://www.projecthindsight-tghp.com/index.html.*

C.U.R.A. is a European site for historical researchers. Address: *http://cura.free.fr.*

Readers interested in mythology should also check out *http://pantheon.org/mythical/* for stories of gods and goddesses.

Astrology Magazines

The Mountain Astrologer
http://www.mountainastrologer.com

A favorite magazine of astrology fans, *The Mountain Astrologer* has an interesting Web site featuring the latest news from an astrological point of view, plus feature articles from the magazine.

Financial Astrology

Find out how financial astrologers play the market. Here are hot picks, newsletters, specialized financial astrology software, and mutual funds run by astrology seers. Go to *www.afund.com* or *www.alphee.com* for tips and forecasts from two top financial astrologers.

CHAPTER 10

The Sydney Omarr
Yellow Pages

Enter the world of astrology! If you want to find an astrology program for your computer, connect with other astrology fans, study advanced techniques, or buy books and tapes, consider this chapter "Astrology Central." Here you'll find the latest products and services available, as well as the top astrology organizations which hold meetings and conferences in your area.

There are organized groups of astrologers all over the country who are dedicated to promoting the image of astrology in the most positive way. The National Council for Geocosmic Research (NCGR) is one nationwide group that is dedicated to bringing astrologers together, promoting fellowship and high-quality education. Their accredited course system promotes a systematized study of all the different facets of astrology. Whether you'd like to know more about such specialties as financial astrology or techniques for timing events, or if you'd prefer the psychological or mythological approach, you'll find the leading experts at NCGR conferences.

Your computer can be a terrific tool for connecting with other astrology fans at all levels of expertise, as we explored in the Internet chapter in this book. Even if you are using a "dinosaur" from the 1980s, there are still calculation and interpretation programs available for DOS and MAC formats. They may not have all the bells and whistles or the exciting graphics, but they'll get the job done!

Newcomers to astrology should learn some of the basics, including the glyphs (astrology's special shorthand language) before you invest in a complex computer program. Use the chapter in this book to help you learn the symbols easily, so you'll be able to read the charts without consulting the "help" section of your program every time. Several programs, such as Astrolabe's "Solar Fire," have pop-up definitions to help you decipher the meanings of planets and aspects. Just click your mouse on a glyph or an icon on the screen, and a window with an instant definition appears.

You don't have to spend a fortune to get a perfectly adequate astrology program. In fact, if you are connected to the Internet, you can download one free. Astrology software is available at all price levels, from a sophisticated free application like *Astrology,* which you can download from a Web site, to inexpensive programs for under $100 such as Halloran's "Astrology for Windows," to the more expensive astrology programs such as "Winstar," "Solar Fire," or "Io" (for the Mac), which are used by serious students and professionals. Before you make an investment, it's a good idea to download a sample from the company's Web site or order a demo disk.

If you're baffled by the variety of software available, most of the companies on our list will be happy to help you find the right application for your needs.

Students of astrology who live in out-of-the-way places or are unable to fit classes into your schedule have several options. There are online courses offered at astrology Web sites, such as *www.panplanet.com,* and at the NCGR and AFA Web sites. Some astrology teachers will send you a series of audiotapes or you can order audiotaped seminars of recent conferences; other teachers offer correspondence courses that use their workbooks or computer printouts.

The Yellow Pages

Nationwide Astrology Organizations and Conferences

Contact these organizations for information on conferences, workshops, local meetings, conference tapes, and referrals:

National Council for Geocosmic Research

Educational workshops, tapes, conferences, and a directory of professional astrologers are available from this nationwide organization devoted to promoting astrological education. For a $35 annual membership fee, you get their excellent publications and newsletters, plus the opportunity to network with other astrology buffs at local chapter events (there are chapters in twenty states).

For general information about NCGR, contact:

NCGR
P.O. Box 38866
Los Angeles, CA 90038
Phone: 818-705-1678

Or visit their Web page, *http://www.geocosmic.org,* for updates and local events.

American Federation of Astrologers (A.F.A.)

One of the oldest astrological organizations in the United States, established in 1938. Conferences, conventions, and a correspondence course. Will refer you to an accredited A.F.A. astrologer.

A.F.A.
P.O. Box 22040
Tempe, AZ 85382

Phone: 602-838-1751
Fax: 602-838-8293

A.F.A.N. (Association for Astrological Networking)

(Networking, Legal Issues)
Did you know that astrologers are still being arrested for practicing in some states? AFAN provides support and legal information, and works toward improving the public image of astrology. Here are the people who will go to bat for astrology when it is attacked in the media. Everyone who cares about astrology should join!

A.F.A.N.
8306 Wilshire Blvd., Suite 537
Beverly Hills, CA 90211

ARC Directory

(Listing of astrologers worldwide)
2920 E. Monte Vista
Tucson, AZ 85716
Phone: 602-321-1114

Pegasus Tapes

(Lectures, conference tapes)
P.O. Box 419
Santa Ysabel, CA 92070

International Society for Astrological Research

(Lectures, workshops, seminars)
P.O. Box 38613
Los Angeles, CA 90038

ISIS Institute

(Newsletter, conferences, astrology tapes, catalog)
P.O. Box 21222
El Sobrante, CA 94820-1222
Phone: 888-322-4747
Fax: 510-222-2202

Astrology Software

Astrolabe

Box 1750-R
Brewster, MA 02631
Phone: 800-843-6682

Check out the latest version of their powerful "Solar Fire" software for Windows—it's a breeze to use and will grow with your increasing knowledge of astrology to the most sophisticated levels. This company also markets a variety of programs for all levels of expertise, a wide selection of computer astrology readings, and Mac programs. A good resource for innovative software as well as applications for older computers.

Matrix Software

407 N. State Street
Big Rapids, MI 49307
Phone: 800-PLANETS

A wide variety of software in all price ranges, demo disks, student and advanced levels, and lots of interesting readings. Check out "Winstar," their powerful professional software, if you're planning to study astrology seriously.

Astro Communications Services

Dept. AF693, PO Box 34487
San Diego, CA 92163-4487
Phone: 800-888-9983

Books, software for MAC and IBM compatibles, individual charts, and telephone readings. Find technical astrology materials here, such as "The American Ephemeris." They will calculate charts for you if you do not have a computer.

Air Software

115 Caya Avenue
West Hartford, CT 06110
Phone: 800-659-1247

Powerful, creative astrology software, like their millennium "Star Trax 2000." For beginners, check out "Father Time," which finds your best days. Or "Nostradamus," which answers all your questions. Financial astrology programs for stock market traders are a specialty.

Time Cycles Research—For Mac Users!!!

375 Willets Avenue
Waterford, CT 06385
Fax: 869-442-0625
E-mail: *astrology@timecycles.com*
Internet: *http://www.timecycles.com*

Where MAC users can find astrology software that's as sophisticated as it gets. If you have Mac, you'll love their beautiful graphic "IO Series" programs.

Astro-Cartography

(Charts for location changes)
Astro-Numeric Service Box 336-B
Ashland, OR 97520
Phone: 800-MAPPING

Astro-cartography is a sophisticated technique which superimposes an astrology chart on a map of the world. A fascinating study for serious students of astrology.

Astrology Magazines

In addition to articles by top astrologers, most have listings of astrology conferences, events, and local happenings.

AMERICAN ASTROLOGY
Dept. 4
P.O. Box 2021
Marion, OH 43306-8121

DELL HOROSCOPE
P.O. Box 53352
Boulder, CO 89321-3342

THE MOUNTAIN ASTROLOGER
P.O. Box 970
Cedar Ridge, CA 95924

Astrology Schools

Though there are many correspondence courses available through private teachers and astrological organizations, up until now, there has never been an accredited college of astrology. That is why the following address is so important.

Kepler College of Astrological Arts and Sciences

Kepler College, the first institution of its kind to combine an accredited liberal arts education with extensive astrological studies, is now in operation, after many years in planning. A degree-granting college that is also a center of astrological studies has long been the dream of the astrological community and will be a giant step forward in providing credibility to the profession. The Kepler College faculty comprises some of the most creative leaders in the astrology community.

For more information, contact:

Kepler College of Astrological Arts and Sciences
Business Office
4630 200th St. SW
Suite L-1
Lynnwood, WA 98036
Phone: 435-673-4292
Fax: 425-673-4983
Internet: *www.kepler.edu*

Your Taurus Home Pages— All About Your Life, Friends, Family, Work, and Style!

If you're a typical Taurus, you're stubborn, stable, and strong-willed. You're the one who'll shrewdly wheel and deal, and later see a goal through to the end, sometimes reluctant to cut your losses on a losing battle. Like the bull, your symbol, you need to control your turf, and you're not too comfortable away from your familiar field. And as a fixed sign, you'll resist change, preferring to stick with what you know rather than follow a risky trend.

As the original material girl (or boy), no one appreciates good food, pretty things and people, heavenly smells, beautiful music, and tactile pleasures like Venus-ruled Taurus, the zodiac sensualist. You insist on the finest and can tell the difference between the real and the phony better than anyone. Of course, some of you may be thinking that this doesn't sound like you at all. There *are* flamboyant Tauruses like Cher whose fiery Mars and Pluto in Leo put her stage center. Much depends on where the ten other planets that make up your horoscope fall as well as what sign was on the horizon at the moment you were born. Lots of planets in fire signs, for instance, could make you more extravagant, for instance. The more Taurus planets you have, the more likely the following descriptions will sound familiar.

The decor, clothes, colors, and style you'll love best are sure to resonate with your sun sign. So let the stars be your heavenly guide to find out what (and who) you'll love that'll love you back.

CHAPTER 11

Are You True to Type?

The Taurus Man— Sensual and Sensible

What you see is what you get with a typical Taurus male. You are usually quite uncomplicated in your wants and needs, and take life literally, preferring to think in terms of what you can experience with your senses, rather than in abstract concepts. Not one for a Spartan lifestyle, you like to enjoy the fruits of your labors. You're susceptible to physical comfort, if not outright luxury—tables laden with delicious, substantial food; the smell of full-blown roses (or a simmering pot on the kitchen stove); beautiful fabrics (and females) that are nice to touch. Overall, the atmosphere of plenty appeals to Taurus most. (Even the most pared-down Taurus lifestyle has comfort, sensual texture, and carefully chosen objects.)

Because you love to be surrounded by comfort and beauty, you may overindulge in good food, or pile up collections of objets d'art. You love your home and devote much time and effort to making it as comforting and welcoming as possible. In fact, it may be very difficult to lure you away from your well-feathered nest. You prefer to entertain at home, remaining on your own secure, comfortable turf, where you can enjoy your treasures and pleasures to the fullest in

160

familiar surroundings, rather than venturing out to explore new territory.

Slow to commit and equally slow to let go, your physical and emotional endurance is an asset in business, where you are an excellent judge of lasting value. Your focused approach usually moves you steadily toward your goal, like the strong, silent hero portrayed by Gary Cooper, rather than the swashbuckling extrovert on the fast track. You stick to your guns, rarely changing horses in midstream. Once you're committed, no one robs you easily of your rightful possessions or position. Taurus has so much patience that it takes a lot of pushing to make you angry, though one sure way to turn you into a raging bull is to threaten your well-established territory or your material security.

In a Relationship

The physical side of a relationship is high priority for sensual Taurus men. You need to be touched, held, and hugged. You love to look at the beauty of the human form. Romantically, you'll tumble hard and fast for physical beauty, especially if combined with a voluptuous, well-sculpted body. The combination of sensuality and endurance makes Taurus one of the great lovers of the zodiac, though your outward appearance is more wholesome and easygoing, like the Taurus movie heroes of the thirties and forties: Jimmy Stewart, Bing Crosby, James Mason, and Gary Cooper, or heartthrob George Clooney.

Letting go of anything, whether it's a threadbare, once-beloved old sweater or your first love, is especially difficult for you. You can carry the torch for years after a romance has faded, sometimes staying in an unhappy or abusive relationship long after another sign would have departed, In the extreme, this becomes an obsession—Taurus never seems to forget, especially a promise that was broken.

You can be one of the most devoted husbands, once

you have established a loving, cozy, secure home base. You're happiest with a rather domestic, earth mother–type woman who is interested in providing these things and won't interfere in your equally comfortable work routines. Before that time, however, you experiment with different erotic adventures. Such is your fondness for beauty of all kinds that you could easily fall for a flirtatious charmer or an independent beauty. However, ultimately, you'd prefer having your wife nearby—a partner who is too independent and self-sufficient will either send you off to greener pastures or make you see red. Since you have such a long memory for discomfort or grief, you may let grievances accumulate until you are pushed too far, then end the relationship with an explosion. However, when you do find a compatible mate, you can be the stable, secure, and sensual husband of most women's dreams.

The Taurus Woman—Earth Angel

You are the earth mother of the zodiac, an unabashed, uninhibited sensualist who revels in beauty in all its earthly manifestations. An animal lover and green-thumbed gardener, you see divinity in nature and respond almost spiritually to physical beauty in all its forms. Nature-loving Taurus takes an especially protective attitude toward the environment and the welfare of animals (you're sure to have at least one beloved pet).

Your other pronounced trait is stubbornness. When a Taurus woman sets her mind to something, there is no stopping her. When you undertake something, you'll wait until your infallible instincts tell you the time is right to take action, but once on track, you won't be derailed by other options. With blinders on, you'll bulldoze ahead until you get what you want, disregarding public opinion or advice to the contrary.

Taurus is slow to make changes, even in a situation

that you know won't work out. This has advantages, however, when you stick to a particular style or an image that works for you and make it your own. That is why so many Taurus women in show business stand out for their special style, which many try to copy, but few can imitate. Think of Audrey Hepburn, Katharine Hepburn, Carol Burnett, Barbra Streisand, Cher, and Candice Bergen, who are unique, memorable, and much imitated. All these women have had amazing professional longevity. While other stars fade, talented Taureans go from strength to strength, only improving with age as they build on their previous experience.

Another of your greatest gifts is your common sense. You're a realist who brings ideas down to earth. Though you may be less gifted in judging the complexities of people, you understand functional relevance: what really works. You drive a hard bargain, and you're the least likely of any sign to fall for a puffed-up sales pitch.

You'll also hold other people to their commitments, having little respect for those who change their minds or promise what they cannot deliver. Therefore, fire signs (Aries, Sagittarius, Leo) and air signs (Gemini, Libra, Aquarius) who offer glamour and dash rather than reliability could present special difficulties for you, Taurus. Though you love the glamour, you're not always willing to grant the freedom and flexibility these signs demand, or to leave your comfortable abode to accompany them to more exciting places (many Tauruses have "fear of flying," of losing control of their environment). You'll also give short shrift to the playboy who changes his mind and his women frequently and to the loser who doesn't produce.

In a Relationship

You rarely marry on a whim, and many of you give special consideration to a man's ability to provide the lifestyle you dream of (or to create it with you). The most successful Taurus relationships are those where both partners have similar goals and a mutual appreciation of talent and luxury, such as the Taurus actress with the director who helps develop her talent, or the Taurus fashion designer with the entrepreneur who backs her in business or provides her with a beautiful home. You often make a particularly good partner for a sensitive, artistic man, who appreciates the warm, stable, nurturing atmosphere you provide.

You're usually a talented homemaker (though you may delegate some or most of the chores to others), who prizes your secure home turf and family life above all. Whether you stay rooted in the same place for decades or, like Cher, change homes on a whim, each nest will be beautifully and comfortably, if not luxuriously, appointed. You'll hold the fort, giving your partner a welcoming, pampering environment.

A wizard with money, you have a talent for budgeting, investing, and finding a bargain. You'll be a full-time mother, if necessary, preferring to devote time and attention to your brood (though you may run a little business from your home).

Taurus in the Family

The Taurus Parent

Taurus takes to parenting naturally, and is an especially effective parent for young children, who benefit most from your calm, patient, nurturing qualities. You provide a firm foundation of love and a stable family atmosphere. Your heart goes out to children who are growing up in difficult circumstances, and you can be a tireless charity worker on their behalf. A good example was Taurus Audrey Hepburn, who traveled the world on behalf of UNESCO, even though ill herself. Cher's work with disfigured children also comes to mind.

Your demonstrative, affectionate nature seems designed to give a child a sense of security. Later, as the child grows more independent, it may be difficult for you to let go. (You may find it especially difficult to deal with the rebellious teenager who has a stubborn streak to match yours.) Indeed, many children of Taurus remain in the family nest into adulthood. A Taurus mom is a tough act to follow, as many young wives have discovered! And there is no one as protective as a Taurus dad.

The song "There's No Place Like Home" was surely written by a Taurus. Images of Mother baking chocolate-chip cookies in the kitchen and Daddy comfortably lodged in his favorite chair with a big dog lounging at his feet are Taurus stereotypes. Though few Taureans can manage the Norman Rockwell fantasy in today's world, this ideal is close to their hearts, and rare is the Taurus who doesn't long for a place in the country with swings on the trees, fragrant rose bushes, and a well-stocked kitchen.

The Taurus Stepparent

Your steady, calm nature can be reassuring to step-children longing for a stable atmosphere. Patiently, you'll wait for the children to become accustomed to the new family structure. When they do, you'll be warm and affectionate. However, when you must assert your disciplinary authority, do so with calm control, understanding that others with strong wills may resent your position.

Stepchildren will teach you to develop flexibility and can expand your horizons if given the chance. Be open to an extended family situation that may not follow the traditional rules. Children will appreciate your allowing them time alone with their biological parent to share mutual interests and strengthen bonds.

The Taurus Grandparent

In spirit, Taurus grandparents are picture-book elders of Norman Rockwell paintings, even if they look as glamorous as Candice Bergen. By this time, you've established a warm, comfortable home and are contented to gather all the family 'round. The Taurus grandma is the archetypal matriarch with a large brood to nurture, whether they are your own or other children in need. You'll provide the home where all the family gathers for holiday feasts, the garden of prize-winning flowers and fresh vegetables, and the special recipes no one else can quite duplicate. You'll be concerned about the children's future and may provide a trust fund or nest egg to finance their education. As the years go by, you'll strengthen family ties by planning celebrations, sending thoughtful notes, and making frequent phone calls. Your grandchildren will remember gratefully how you taught them the true meaning of family traditions by providing them with a strong sense of their own roots.

CHAPTER 12

"In Style" the Taurus Way

Just as your sign of the zodiac can illuminate your personality, it can also help you determine your most suitable style. The key to looking and feeling your best is to go with the specific colors, surroundings, and attitudes that resonate with your sun sign. Follow these tips to maximize your own Taurus star quality.

The Comforts of Home

Take cues from Mother Nature to create the Taurus decor that makes you feel most at home. Think "country" and you'll be right on target. The luxurious look of English or French country houses or the comfortable warmth of a cozy farmhouse suits you well. If you must live in the city, try to live near a park, use floral prints (or gutsy earthy colors), and fill your windows with plants (even indoor trees) to bring nature indoors, especially if you are looking out on a brick wall. Flowers spilling from antique containers are another wonderful Taurus touch.

Your furniture should be roomy and comfortable, upholstered in a feel-good fabric. Collections of pottery or delicate porcelain, artworks, sculpture, records, jewelry, and antiques vie for attention in your environment. Be sure there are enough shelves to display your treasures beautifully. Since you love good food and entertain at home, you'll want a large, well-equipped kitchen. Your animal companions should be considered also, with spaces to roam and places to roost.

Sensual Taurus Sounds

One of the most musical signs, you respond to rich, sensual sounds of all kinds, especially vocal music, because Taurus is associated with the voice. Perhaps you have a well-tuned piano or guitar for at-home musical entertainment. Since you are sensitive to the slightest distortion in tone, invest in an excellent sound system. You may collect the great vocalists like Barbra Streisand, Cher, Willie Nelson, and Ella Fitzgerald. Or rock to Janet Jackson, Stevie Wonder, and David Byrne. Taurus songwriters like Burt Bacharach, Oscar Hammerstein, and Irving Berlin created sensuous sounds that glorify the human voice.

Taurus Travels

Taureans generally prefer to stay in their own comfortable nest, so look for a "home away from home" when you travel. A comfortable hotel with a good restaurant where the owners know your preferences would be best. A luxurious cruise ship, or a pampering spa with a spectacular view or fragrant gardens, will soothe you when you are away from familiar turf.

After taking care of the amenities, there's Taurus's favorite pastime . . . shopping. Give yourself plenty of time to explore the local markets, sample the typical dishes of the country, and explore art museums. If you are booking a tour, let it be one that also explores the fine cuisine and antiques marketplaces of each region. You might also enjoy a vacation apprenticeship with a famous French or Italian chef.

Minimize travel discomforts by packing a tiny inflatable pillow and a lightweight Pashmina shawl, for instant warmth. Since food on the run is never your style, get a small insulated bag to carry your own favorite gourmet goodies and comfort foods, rather than relying on airline or train meals. A portable stereo with your favorite sounds relaxes you on the trip and blots out unwelcome noise. Bring along a scented candle for instant ambiance in your hotel room, as well as a few photos of loved ones to remind you of home.

Cancer and Pisces are wonderful traveling companions to share sunsets and moonlit walks along the shore. Scorpio and Capricorn will help you combine business with pleasure (and help you find a way to write off that trip as a tax deduction). Libra and Leo share your love of beauty and luxury (but will also want to travel first-class all the way) and will know all the finest shops.

A collapsible bag that can be packed inside your suitcase is a "must" for all those souvenirs you can't resist.

The Color of Taurus

You'll respond to the soft floral pastels of eighteenth-century painters or the woody, natural earth tones. Too many dark colors may depress you, and vibrant brights may disturb your tranquillity. You'd prefer the lush romantic shades of an English garden or the mossy neutrals of a woodland glade.

Taurus Style Setters

Taurus women have an especially lovely neck and throat, so be sure to emphasize it with beautiful necklaces, as Barbra Streisand does (you probably have an impressive jewelry collection), and off-the-shoulder styles. Stick to simple styles in luxurious fabrics, and you won't go wrong. Avoid anything fussy, especially if you've overindulged your Taurus appetite for good food.

Once Taurus finds your special "look," stick with it, whether it's as elegant and classic as Fred Astaire, Audrey Hepburn, and Candice Bergen or as trendy as Cher. Aim to be distinctively and consistently "you." Create your own styles, rather than latch on to a look for the sake of being In. Be sure to play up your femininity with perfume (all three of the above ladies at one time had their own signature scent).

Let the Taurus Fashion Leaders Inspire You

The late, great designer Halston epitomized Taurus style, with luxurious fabrics and simple, sensuous lines. Christian Lacroix has been inspired by the costumes of the French countryside to create whimsical, yet very luxurious, clothes. Jean-Paul Gaultier shows the sexy side of Taurus in his avant-garde clothes for rock stars such as Madonna. Michelle Pfeiffer, Janet Jackson, Cate Blanchett, and Uma Thurman are classic Taurus beauties whose looks will inspire you to make the most of yours.

Taurus models who lead the parade are Linda Evangelista and James King.

Taurus Gourmets

Taurus is one of the zodiac's gourmets (and gourmands). Never a picky eater, you can consume food in megaportions. Often you'll obsess about one type of food—one flavor of ice cream, for instance—and secretly gorge on it.

You derive so much pleasure from delicious food

that you could easily feel deprived on a strict diet. Then you'll overcompensate by bingeing and undoing your diet. A program that helps you form a long-range, health-promoting relationship with food is a better alternative. If problems send you running to the refrigerator, find a weight-watching group to give you support and encouragement, as well as a sensible diet program.

On the positive side, you especially appreciate food that is of premium quality and beautifully presented. Find an organic or farmers' market to provide your vegetables— you'll notice the difference—and learn to love fresh fruits and vegetables more than hearty meat and potatoes with sour cream and ice cream for dessert. A natural foods or macrobiotic cooking course could show you how to incorporate healthful recipes into your life.

CHAPTER 13

The Healthy Taurus

Though Taurus is a hardy sign with great stamina and endurance, you can become sluggish if you're overweight or if there is a thyroid problem. So if you can barely drag yourself off the couch, check your thyroid, since Taurus rules the neck and throat area, which includes the thyroid glands and vocal cords. If you're not getting enough sleep, try changing your pillow to one specially designed to support your neck area. Neck massages are a sybaritic way to release tension in the neck area and promote a more restful sleep.

Taurus is one of the signs that finds it extremely difficult to diet. The enjoyment of food is a major pleasure, and you don't like to be deprived of delicious sensations of any kind. Since you tend to like sweet and rich foods, the pounds pile on. You're sure to know the best bakery in your area. Though some Taureans, like Cher or the late Audrey Hepburn, remain slim, they usually do so with great effort and determination. Shift your pleasure from heavy foods and sweet confections to finding the freshest, most perfect produce. Search out vegetable recipes and shop at local farmers' markets. And be sure there are always plenty of low-calorie treats available when you feel the urge to raid the refrigerator.

You need a pleasant place to work out, and what could be more pleasant than a scenic natural park. Explore the woodlands and seashore in your area with long nature hikes. Or plant an extensive garden that requires lots of maintenance. Working with animals can also be a joy for Taurus. Try to hide your exercise within pleasurable activities. Walk or bicycle to work, dance or rock-climb, or work out to your favorite music.

CHAPTER 14

Taurus at Work!

Taurus needs a career with staying power. Long-term gains are your major interest, so you'll usually stick to one career direction. In the riskier professions, Taurus often succeeds because you hang in there the longest. The downside is that you may vegetate in a job that has no challenge, because you value the steady income. Taurus does not like change, especially sudden changes, so look for an initial job that offers strong growth potential. A company that promotes from within would be ideal.

Since Taurus is the sign of buying, appraising, and accumulating, you thrive in careers such as retailing, trading of any sort, auctions, dealing in art or collectibles, banking, or real estate. You might do very well in the new online auction field, especially if you have access to antiques or collectibles. Your love of nature could lead you into farming, landscape gardening, horticulture, or animal breeding. Taurus is a natural builder, so consider architecture, construction, or engineering. Your sensual side could gravitate to careers in the culinary arts, fashion, photography, or jewelry design, or to the fragrance or music industry.

Taurus in Charge

You like to have control, which can make you either a steady, wise leader, a benevolent dictator, or a tyrant. You will demand to have the last word on each aspect of your business, rarely changing your mind once you have made a decision. You'll be very nurturing of underlings, but you may hesitate to give them the independence they need to grow by trial and error. You tend to promote from within, working with people you have known for some time. You attitude is to build a solid structure for your organization, and you'll value that structure rather than flashy ideas or flash-in-the-pan products. Try to be more flexible and open to new ideas, however. Though you can be demanding, you are usually even-tempered and patient, and you value loyalty.

Taurus Teamwork

The Taurus worker is slow, steady, deliberate, and thorough. You are the one who comes through in a pinch; you are oriented toward seeing results, rather than speculating. Once you are comfortable, you'll stay in a position; therefore, you may not be the most ambitious employee. But you are much less likely to job-hop, preferring to stay in the same spot for years and steadily rise through the ranks.

You work best in surroundings that are pleasant and physically comfortable. And you like to handle money so that you can see it grow, so you'll always keep your eye on the bottom line. You have an innate sense of value, of being able to determine the truth worth of something, as well as the best price it can get on the market.

To Get Ahead Fast

Pick a company with potential that promotes from within. Then play up your best Taurus attributes.

- Loyalty
- Thoroughness
- Financial savvy
- Patience and perseverance
- Reliability
- Steadiness
- Evaluation and appraisal skills
- Practicality
- Negotiation skills

Taurus Career Role Models

Study the success stories of these Taurus entrepreneurs. You might get some useful tips for moving ahead on the fast track.

William Randolph Hearst (newspapers)
Dr. Benjamin Spock
Cornelius Vanderbilt
Aaron Spelling (TV producer and creator of *Beverly Hills 90210*, among other hits)
David O. Selznick (Hollywood tycoon)
George Lucas (*Star Wars*)
Ross Hunter
Barbra Streisand

Taurus Rich and Famous!

We're fascinated by reading tabloids and gossip items about the rich, famous, and infamous in the post-Millennium, but astrology can tell you more about your heroes than most magazine articles. Like what really turns them on (check their Venus). Or what makes them insecure (scope their Saturn). Compare similarities and differences between the celebrities who embody the typical Taurus sun sign traits (Jay Leno, Andie McDowell) and those who seem more eccentric (Cher, Dennis Rodman). Then look up other planets in the horoscope of your favorites, using the charts in this book, to see how other planets influence the horoscope. It's a fun way to get your education in astrology.

Jessica Lange (4/20/49)
Ryan O'Neal (4/20/41)
Luther Vandross (4/20/51)
Tony Danza (4/21/51)
Queen Elizabeth II (4/21/26)
Patti Lupone (4/21/49)
Charles Grodin (4/21/35)
Andie McDowell (4/21/58)
Anthony Quinn (4/21/15)
Peter Frampton (4/22/50)
Aaron Spelling (4/22/28)
Jack Nicholson (4/22/37)

Valerie Bertinelli (4/23/60)
David Birney (4/23/39)
Sandra Dee (4/23/42)
Lee Majors (4/23/39)
Eric Bogosian (4/24/53)
Barbra Streisand (4/24/42)
Shirley MacLaine (4/24/34)
Al Pacino (4/25/39)
Talia Shire (4/25/46)
Carol Burnett (4/26/33)
Anouk Aimee (4/27/34)
Coretta Scott King (4/27/27)
Sheena Easton (4/27/59)
Ann-Margret (4/28/41)
Jay Leno (4/28/50)
Andre Agassi (4/29/70)
Daniel Day-Lewis (4/29/57)
Michelle Pfeiffer (4/29/57)
Uma Thurman (4/29/70)
Jerry Seinfeld (4/29/55)
Chynna Phillips (4/29/68)
Carnie Wilson (4/29/68)
Cloris Leachman (4/30/30)
Willie Nelson (4/30/33)
Ian Zierling (4/30/64)
Jill Clayburgh (4/30/44)
Pierre Teilhard de Chardin (5/1/1881)
Kate Smith (5/1/09)
Jon Bon Jovi (5/2/62)
Bianca Jagger (5/2/45)
Christine Baranski (5/2/52)
Bing Crosby (5/2/04)
Doug Henning (5/3/47)
Wynonna Judd (5/3/64)
Audrey Hepburn (5/4/29)
Randy Travis (5/4/59)
Pia Zadora (5/4/56)
Ann B. Davis (5/5/20)
Lori Singer (5/6/62)

Darren McGavin (5/7/22)
Robert Browning (5/7/1812)
Rick Nelson (5/8/40)
Melissa Gilbert (5/8/64)
Candice Bergen (5/9/46)
Bono (5/10/60)
Linda Evangelista (5/10/65)
Louis Farrakhan (5/11/33)
Valentino (5/11/32)
Martha Graham (5/11/1894)
Natasha Richardson (5/11/63)
Gabriel Byrne (5/12/50)
Stephen Baldwin (5/12/66)
Bea Arthur (5/13/26)
Dennis Rodman (5/13/61)
Peter Gabriel (5/13/50)
Cate Blanchett (5/13/69)
David Byrne (5/14/52)
Jasper Johns (5/15/30)
Chazz Palminteri (5/15/51)
Pierce Brosnan (5/16/52)
Muktananda (5/16/08)
Tori Spelling (5/16/73)
Perry Como (5/18/12)
Janet Jackson (5/18/66)
Margot Fonteyn (5/18/19)
Nora Ephron (5/19/41)
David Hartman (5/19/35)
Cher (5/20/46)
Adela Rogers St. Johns (5/20/1894)
Jimmy Stewart (5/20/08)

CHAPTER 16

Taurus Pairs—How You Get Along with Every Other Sign

Are you thinking about teaming up with someone either romantically or professionally? Here are the pluses and minuses of every combination, so you'll know what to expect before you commit.

Taurus/Aries

PLUSES:
Aries gets slow-moving Taurus up and at 'em, waving a red flag before the bull. Taurus is excited and ready to charge. Aries gets direction, follow-through, and solid backup support, as well as a warm, loving, sensual companion who is devoted and loyal.

MINUSES:
Adapting to each other's pace calls for compromise, as Aries learns that you cannot be pushed, and you learn that Aries wants everything *now*. You could lock horns over short-term vs. long-term goals. You'll prefer comfortable, luxurious surroundings, while Aries happily sacrifices comfort for adventure. Separate vacations might be the only solution.

Taurus/Taurus

PLUSES:
Loyalty and emotions run deep with these sign mates. Here is the cozy, familiar, comfortable kind of love, spiced by strong sensuality. In this solid, secure relationship, you could be so contented, you never leave home!

MINUSES:
Disagreements, if they occur, can be devastating. You two lock horns and never let go. Or there's a permanent standoff. The other possibility is you'll bore—rather than gore—each other to death, or look for stimulation elsewhere.

Taurus/Gemini

PLUSES:
Next-door signs may be best friends as well as lovers. In this case, Gemini gets you out of the house and into the social life, adding laughter to love. Taurus has a soothing, stabilizing quality that can make nervous Gemini bloom.

MINUSES:
Homebody Taurus usually loves one-on-one relationships, while social Gemini loves to flirt with a crowd. Gemini will have to curb roving eyes and bodies. Infidelity can be serious business with Taurus—but taken lightly by Gemini. The balance scales between freedom and license swing and sway here.

Taurus/Cancer

PLUSES:
In theory, this should be one of the best combinations. Taurus can't get too much affection and TLC, which

Cancer happily provides. And Taurus protects Cancer from the cold world, with solid secure assets. Both are home-loving, emotional and sensual.

MINUSES:
Cancer's dark moods plus Taurus's stubbornness could create some muddy moments. Both partners should look for constructive ways to let off steam rather than brood and sulk over grievances.

Taurus/Leo

PLUSES:
Leo passion meets Taurus sensuality and there's a volcanic physical attraction, as you test each other's strength. Both lovers of beauty and comfort, you also have high ideas, fidelity, and a love of good food and music going for you. Taurus's money management could provide Leo with a royal lifestyle.

MINUSES:
Tensions between these two fixed signs are inevitable. Leo plays dangerous games here, such as denying affection or sex. Focus on building emotional security and avoiding no-win emotional showdowns. Leo's extravagance and Taurus's possessiveness could be bones of contention.

Taurus/Virgo

PLUSES:
Taurus admires Virgo's analytical mind, while Virgo admires Taurean concentration and goal orientation and feels secure with predictable Taurus. You enjoy taking care of each other. Relaxed, soothing Taurus

brings out Virgo's sensuality. Virgo brings the world of ideas home to Taurus.

MINUSES:
Virgo's nagging can cause Taurus self-doubt, which can show up in bullheaded stubbornness. Taurus's slow pace and ideal of deep-rooted comfort could feel like constraint to Virgo, who needs the stimulation of diversity and lively communication.

Taurus/Libra

PLUSES:
Both Venus-ruled signs, who are turned on by beauty and luxury, are happy to indulge each other. Libra brings intellectual sparkle and social savvy to Taurus. Taurus gives Libra financial stability and adoration. And Libra profits from Taurus's strong sense of direction and decisiveness.

MINUSES:
Taurus is possessive and enjoys staying at home. Libra loves social life and flirting. Watch out for jealousy, Taurus, because Libra's flirtations are rarely serious. Libra can be extravagant, while Taurus sticks to a budget and loves to see the money pile up in the bank—another cause for resentment.

Taurus/Scorpio

PLUSES:
Many marriages happen when these opposites attract. Taurus has a calming effect on Scorpio's innate paranoia. And Taurus responds to Scorpio's intensity and fascinating air of mystery. Together, these signs have the perfect complement of sensuality and sexuality.

MINUSES:
Problems of control are inevitable when you both want to run the show. Avoid long and bitter battles or silent standoffs by drawing territorial lines from the start. Then stick to them!

Taurus/Sagittarius

PLUSES:
Sagittarius energizes Taurus and gets this sign to take calculated risks and dare to think big. Taurus provides the solid support and steady income which can make Sagittarian ideas happen. Sagittarius will be challenged to produce, Taurus to stretch and grow.

MINUSES:
You are very different types who are not especially sympathetic to each other's needs. Taurus believes in hard work, Sagittarius in luck and seizing the moment of opportunity. Sagittarius is a rolling stone; Taurus is a quiet meadow. Sagittarius appreciates freedom; Taurus appreciates substance.

Taurus/Capricorn

PLUSES:
Your similar traditional values can make communication easy. This is a combination that works well on all levels. You find it easy to set goals, organize, and support each other. There's earthy passion and instinctive understanding.

MINUSES:
There may be too much "earth" here; the relationship can become too dutiful, practical, and unromantic. You both need to expand your horizons occasionally

and may look for stimulation elsewhere. Taurus may resent Capricorn's devotion to career, since home and family are top priority.

Taurus/Aquarius

PLUSES:
This is an uncomfortable, but stimulating, partnership between the conventional Taurus and the rule-breaking Aquarius. Taurus takes care of the practical, while Aquarius provides the inspiration and social involvement which shakes Taurus out of a rut.

MINUSES:
Resolution of conflicts can wear this one out. Taurus is predictable. Aquarius is unpredictable. Taurus loves privacy; Aquarius is a "people person." Taurus wants to settle down. Aquarius needs "space." Taurus is possessive; Aquarius is detached.

Taurus/Pisces

PLUSES:
This could be your dream lover. You both love the good things in life and can indulge each other sensually and sexually. Taurus's focus adds stability and direction to Pisces, while Piscean creativity is lovingly encouraged by Taurus.

MINUSES:
Taurus wants Pisces to produce, not just dream, and will try to corral the slippery fish into steady employment. Not a good idea. Pisces can't be bossed or caged, and will swim off, leaving Taurus with the dotted line unsigned!

CHAPTER 17

Astrological Outlook for Taurus in 2002

February and November will be your most memorable months of the year 2002. Saturn no longer is in Taurus, so you feel as if a weight has been lifted from your shoulders. What kept you from traveling will no longer be an impediment.

The numerical cycle indicates a possible change of residence or marital status. Attention revolves around domestic issues, the necessity for being diplomatic, and the tendency to forget resolutions concerning health. It's important to remember promises made to yourself about exercise, diet, and nutrition. Follow some basic rules, and you'll be healthier and happier as result.

Librans and other Taurus individuals will play major roles in your life this year. Your voice will change, no matter what your age. People comment, "Do you know that you sound different?" Do plenty of talking and singing, and utilize persuasive powers to get what you want.

Your lucky numbers will be 2, 6, and 4.

With Libra, it will be a matter of your Venus and the Libra Venus—it could be too much of a good thing. Libra will be encountering you in the eighth house, which means Libra becomes more aware of accounting procedures and interested in philosophical subjects and questions concerning life after death. You have a profound influence on Libra!

With Libra, it will be your sixth house that is most affected. Thus, with Libra, you'll be more active with coworkers and made more aware of your general health and what to do about it. Your diet will have a lot to do with keeping yourself strong and virile.

With another Taurus, forces tend to be scattered. You both have a "good time," but nothing serious results. You travel, become social, and buy clothes. Somehow it seems you save very little money. Leave the other Taurus for somebody else!

In the following pages, you will find your day-to-day guides. Heed them and you will be responding to the natural rhythm of your cycle. This will be a year which emphasizes marriage, income, and the purchase of luxury items. You will be very romantic, and this alone could make you happy.

Turn now to the pages that follow for information containing lucky lottery numbers, profitable days at the racetrack, and for your life, love, and immediate future.

CHAPTER 18

Eighteen Months of Day-by-Day Predictions—July 2001 to December 2002

JULY 2001

Sunday, July 1 (Moon in Scorpio to Sagittarius 11:13 p.m.)   On this Sunday, join forces with your partner or spouse. The major purpose is to outline plans and ideas for the upcoming holiday. Plan to make this July 4th meaningful, possibly by including the recitation of Thomas Jefferson's Declaration of Independence. Blend patriotism with innovation. Tonight Scorpio is involved.

Monday, July 2 (Moon in Sagittarius)   This will not be just another workday. People are active and expect you to be on time. You will be praised for past efforts, receiving credit long overdue. The emphasis is on reading, writing, and disseminating information. Flirt!

Tuesday, July 3 (Moon in Sagittarius)   News from your family relates to a possible inheritance. Dig deep for information; reject rumors and superficial reports. If you are thorough, you win admiration. The emphasis is on where you live, your marital status, and your income potential. Another Taurus plays a role.

Wednesday, July 4 (Moon in Sagittarius to Capricorn 8:21 a.m.)   Enjoy the holiday, but avoid unnecessary accidents, especially involving a swimming pool. What seems safe could be deceptive—obviously, playing with firecrackers could be an invitation to danger. Make the holiday meaningful for young people, encouraging them to be aware of its importance.

Thursday, July 5—Lunar Eclipse (Moon in Capricorn) The full moon, lunar eclipse, falls in Capricorn. It's not wise to travel. Have emergency tools available. Someone who preaches the gospel could be caught off guard, creating a possible scandal. Maintain your high standards, dealing gingerly with Cancer and Capricorn.

Friday, July 6 (Moon in Capricorn to Aquarius 7:32 p.m.)   On this Friday, a decision is reached concerning a project or relationship. The subject of marriage looms large. Follow your intuition and your heart. Special: Avoid heavy lifting! A long-distance call vindicates your judgment. Aries will play an exciting role.

Saturday, July 7 (Moon in Aquarius)   Hot Saturday! The sun keynote blends with your Venus. The sun is hot and Venus is love, adding up to "hot love"! Make a fresh start, highlighting original thinking. Be daring, confident, and up to date in connection with fashion. Lucky lottery: 1, 4, 6, 7, 10, 51.

Sunday, July 8 (Moon in Aquarius)   A family member helps resolve a computer error. Imprint your own style. Make a decision about your future direction, motivation, or marital status. A Cancer will invite you to participate in a royal swordfish dinner. Your obligation: Bring the best bottle of wine!

Monday, July 9 (Moon in Aquarius to Pisces 8:04 a.m.)   Emphasize diversity, giving full play to your intellectual curiosity. By this time tomorrow, the moon will be in your eleventh house, which is very favorable for winning friends and influencing important people. Good fortune is indicated in areas of finance and romance.

Tuesday, July 10 (Moon in Pisces)   Details tend to pile up if neglected. The Pluto keynote today enables you to be finished with trivial matters. Accent major issues as you tear down in order to rebuild on a solid structure. Leo, Scorpio, and another Taurus will play featured roles.

Wednesday, July 11 (Moon in Pisces to Aries 8:34 p.m.)   For racing luck, try these selections at all tracks: post position special—number 5 p.p. in this fifth race. Pick six: 3, 2, 1, 4, 5, 3. Watch for these letters in the names of potential winning horses or jockeys—E, N, W. Hot daily doubles: 3 and 2, 5 and 5, 6 and 8. Speed horses that get out in front will win and pay long-shot prices.

Thursday, July 12 (Moon in Aries)   A bonanza is received in connection with family affairs. The emphasis is on style, beautifying your surroundings, music, and the acquisition of an art object. Another Taurus talks about luxury items, food, fun, and frolic. Keep recent resolutions about exercise, diet, and nutrition.

Friday, July 13 (Moon in Aries)   You will be lucky unless you close your ears to opposing suggestions and ideas. A neighbor will confide, "My home life is in shambles!" Be helpful without becoming inextricably involved in a situation that does not directly concern you. Your fortunate number is 7.

Saturday, July 14 (Moon in Aries to Taurus 7:12 a.m.)   Lucky lottery: 7, 9, 12, 18, 27, 50. Accept an overtime assignment, for this could be the start of something big. You'll be among the high and mighty. You prove once again that, when pressure is on, you are up to it. Capricorn plays a key role.

Sunday, July 15 (Moon in Taurus) On this Sunday, you will feel a glow of satisfaction. A burden you should not have carried in the first place will be removed. A green light shines for travel plans, perhaps overseas. Provide time for the study of the language and customs of people in other lands.

Monday, July 16 (Moon in Taurus to Gemini 2:23 p.m.) Your personal cycle is high, so trust your judgment and intuition. Don't be told what to do. Designate where the action will be, even though this attracts envy and a possible enemy. Protect yourself at close quarters. Don't be bullied by someone who has little or nothing to offer. Leo is represented.

Tuesday, July 17 (Moon in Gemini) You have two choices—to trod along the same road or to create your own new traditions. A Cancer-born family member suggests, "Let me mix you a martini and cook a fine dinner and then you'll make the right decision!" Your lucky number is 2.

Wednesday, July 18 (Moon in Gemini to Cancer 5:55 p.m.) This could be your big money day. The moon in Gemini represents the location of lost articles, and indicates your participation in a profitable financial arrangement. Your cycle continues high, so you will be at the right place at a special moment almost effortlessly. A Sagittarian plays a role. Your lucky number is 3.

Thursday, July 19 (Moon in Cancer) A challenge is made to order for you! Almost by a lucky chance, you make the right moves and meet the right people. Doors previously shut tight will be opened almost as if by magic. Some people ask unreasonable questions, so aim your answers at people who appear always to be stupid.

Friday, July 20 (Moon in Cancer to Leo 6:42 p.m.)   The new moon in Cancer represents relatives, trips and visits, and the need to be especially careful in traffic. An aura of confusion exists, but some good will result. Test, experiment, and challenge those who are in love with the status quo. Gemini and Virgo will play astounding roles.

Saturday, July 21 (Moon in Leo)   Be with your family, if possible. The moon in Leo suggests entertaining at home. Discussions revolve around who loves whom, and whether or not marriage is a result. Call your travel agency, requesting specific information about Paris. Lucky lottery: 1, 5, 7, 8, 12, 16.

Sunday, July 22 (Moon in Leo to Virgo 6:28 p.m.)   The emphasis is on meditation, blending idealism with showmanship. Learn more about architecture, structure, and security and protection relating to loved ones. Define your terms, avoiding self-deception and seeing relationships as they actually exist, not merely as you wish they were.

Monday, July 23 (Moon in Virgo)   Your power day! The lunar position highlights creativity, style, responsibility, and a physical attraction. The Saturn keynote emphasizes successful investments and meeting and beating a deadline. Capricorn and Cancer will play fascinating roles, and have these letters in their names—H, Q, Z.

Tuesday, July 24 (Moon in Virgo to Libra 7:07 p.m.)   You'll be interested in a variety of subjects. Your attention span shows marked improvement. Let go of a burden you had no right to carry in the first place. An Aries confides an intimate problem. Confirm agreements with an agent handling your product overseas.

Wednesday, July 25 (Moon in Libra)   Lucky lottery: 1, 5, 6, 7, 14, 50. Make a fresh start; your intuitive intellect is honed to razor sharpness—so be aware of it and respond accordingly. A new family member is on the scene, commanding the spotlight. Leo and Aquarius play enticing games.

Thursday, July 26 (Moon in Libra to Scorpio 10:17 p.m.)   The Libra moon relates to sixth-house matters—health, work, and special services. Music plays a role. It's important to dance to your tune. Once again, the question of marriage will loom large. Your appetite for a gourmet dinner is sharp, despite a minor digestive problem.

Friday, July 27 (Moon in Scorpio)   A plan for the weekend features entertainment, exploration, and creative games. A Sagittarian who once played an important role in your life makes a dramatic reappearance, coinciding with elements of luck. It might be said by a hip person—"Play it cool, dude!"

Saturday, July 28 (Moon in Scorpio to Sagittarius 4:44 a.m.)   The Scorpio moon relates to your public image, legal rights, special permits, and partnership and marriage. Today's scenario features excitement, drama, and sex appeal—look and do your best and all will be well! In matters of speculation, stick with these numbers: 4 and 8.

Sunday, July 29 (Moon in Sagittarius)   A sure bet is that conditions will change—suddenly. Obstacles are removed and roadblocks will be transformed into stepping-stones toward your ultimate goal. A member of the opposite sex provides inspiration and creates controversy. Gemini, Virgo, and Sagittarius have leading roles.

Monday, July 30 (Moon in Sagittarius)   Use diplomacy calling on someone you did a tremendous favor for in the past. Remember: "Pride goes before a fall!" So don't be afraid to ask for help when needed. The scenario features design, remodeling, and making peace with a Libra and another Taurus. Expect to have luck with the number 6.

Tuesday, July 31 (Moon in Sagittarius to Capricorn 2:16 p.m.)   Insist on a solid structure and durable goods. Sweet whispered promises will not hold up in court! Neptune is involved with your Venus, which creates a beautiful illusion, but will not pay the rent! If married, there will be an addition to your family in the not-too-distant future. Pisces figures prominently.

AUGUST 2001

Wednesday, August 1 (Moon in Capricorn)   Add up things, checking for accounting errors. On this Wednesday, you have a feeling that you're going to win a lot of money! Leo, Scorpio, and another Taurus, who play leading roles, could have these letters in their names—D, M, V. Your fortunate number is 4.

Thursday, August 2 (Moon in Capricorn)   Review lessons, including reading, writing, arithmetic, and spelling. Watch for change, travel, and variety. A flirtation tonight gets things going. The focus is also on a domestic adjustment that will include a possible change of residence or marital status.

Friday, August 3 (Moon in Capricorn to Aquarius 1:52 a.m.)   This Friday will provide time for you to prepare in connection with fashion, special appearance, and enhancing an aura of drama. A visitor who makes a surprise appearance wants to remain close to home. Pay close attention to your psychic impressions. Pisces is in the picture.

Saturday, August 4 (Moon in Aquarius) The full moon in Aquarius represents participation in a community project and the need to accept a leadership role. The Saturn keynote symbolizes discipline, timing, and completing a project that currently might be in the throes of confusion and depression. Your lucky number is 8.

Sunday, August 5 (Moon in Aquarius to Pisces 2:29 p.m.) A memorable Sunday! Someone from another country communicates with an invitation, sincere and sincerely wanting to be a part of your team. Aries and Libra figure in this picture, representing a determination to finish what was started.

Monday, August 6 (Moon in Pisces) What a Monday! Your light shines bright, providing wisdom and entertainment for someone of the opposite sex. Passages that were dark will receive the benefit of more light. Leo and Aquarius, who play outstanding roles, will have these letters in their names—A, S, J.

Tuesday, August 7 (Moon in Pisces) An aura of mystery surrounds you. Remember that it is fun to be fooled, not to be deceived. The spotlight is on partnership, cooperative efforts, and marriage. The scenario obviously is crowded—take one step at a time! Cancer and Capricorn play dynamic roles.

Wednesday, August 8 (Moon in Pisces to Aries 3:03 a.m.) Within 24 hours, when the moon enters Aries, you can begin packing your bags. A long journey is in the stars. Focus on tradition, philosophy, and dealings in a foreign land. Entertain, write, publish, and laugh at your own foibles. Your lucky number is 3.

Thursday, August 9 (Moon in Aries)   Is your packing done? The latest indications are that the trip is on! Focus on universal appeal, receiving an offer that is glamorous but has little or no base to it. Leo, Scorpio, and another Taurus, who figure prominently, have these letters in their names—D, M, V.

Friday, August 10 (Moon in Aries to Taurus 2:21 p.m.)   What had been held back will be released—to your advantage. The Aries moon relates to your twelfth house, indicating that you will be visiting someone who is temporarily confined to hospital or home. Gemini, Virgo, and Sagittarius are in this picture.

Saturday, August 11 (Moon in Taurus)   You'll be enjoying the comforts of home. With the moon in your sign, by remaining in familiar quarters you will be doing the right thing at the right time. Opinions are divided among those close to you: Some insist you are a real genius, while others say you are determined and a stubborn critter.

Sunday, August 12 (Moon in Taurus to Gemini 10:56 p.m.)   Your spiritual values soar, for the moon in your sign means that your cycle is at a peak. You will be rescued at the last minute. Keep shooting for the moon—don't fall victim to the feeling that all is right and effort is futile. Neptune is involved, which presents an aura of mystery, intrigue, and possible deception.

Monday, August 13 (Moon in Gemini)   A powerful day! Your cash flow resumes. You will be at the right place at a special moment, almost effortlessly. Don't press issues. Be receptive and enthusiastic without being naive. Within 24 hours, you will be involved in obtaining funding, and you will also locate a valuable article or lost antique.

Tuesday, August 14 (Moon in Gemini)   Material is received from a foreign land, so study carefully, write questions, and send them off. Coming into your life will be a dynamic Aries who insists, "You are the right person for me." Your interest in plants and painting is emphasized.

Wednesday, August 15 (Moon in Gemini to Cancer 3:53 a.m.)   Lucky lottery: 1, 3, 9, 11, 18, 30. Be original. Choose a product that interests you and invest! Make personal appearances, wearing shades of yellow and gold. It's no day to be shy, so speak up, letting others know where you stand. A Leo will figure prominently.

Thursday, August 16 (Moon in Cancer)   Relatives are involved in planning a surprise party. Keep your eyes on the road, avoiding a tendency to take for granted that other drivers are intelligent. Capricorn and Cancer, who will play colorful roles, have these letters in their names—B, K, T.

Friday, August 17 (Moon in Cancer to Leo 5:24 a.m.) Highlight diversity, versatility, and the acquisition of an art object. A Cancer invites you to dine—delicious! Bide your time in connection with an upcoming deal. Some who are in a nasty mood will comment, "This had better be your night for good luck!"

Saturday, August 18 (Moon in Leo)   Don't put round pegs in square holes—give yourself time to recover from a recent automobile shake-up. Your cycle is interesting as a family member blurts out, "I love you and have always loved you!" Leo, Scorpio, and another Taurus will play outstanding roles.

Sunday, August 19 (Moon in Leo to Virgo 4:52 a.m.)   The new moon in Leo represents property value, long-term negotiations, home, the protection of your family, and a decision relating to your marital status. The spotlight is on a legal agreement not altogether favorable. A Leo will play a stunning role. Your lucky number is 5.

Monday, August 20 (Moon in Virgo)   For racing luck, try these selections at all tracks: post position special—number 2 p.p. in the fourth race. Pick six: 4, 8, 3, 2, 1, 7. Watch for these letters in the names of potential winning horses or jockeys—F, O, X. Hot daily doubles: 4 and 8, 3 and 6, 5 and 7. Local jockeys ride favorites and turn in sensational wins.

Tuesday, August 21 (Moon in Virgo to Libra 4:18 a.m.)   Critics abound, and racing writers are not shy about pointing out your faults. Theatrical experts follow suit. Some suggest you could use a few more lessons from a drama teacher. Work backstage; learn secrets of how to win audiences.

Wednesday, August 22 (Moon in Libra)   Lucky lottery: 8, 12, 14, 16, 39, 51. A relationship that had cooled will once again be hot, perhaps too hot not to cool down. Use elements of timing and surprise. Subjects will include your marital status, engineering, architecture, and the need to be on familiar ground.

Thursday, August 23 (Moon in Libra to Scorpio 5:49 a.m.)   On this Thursday, you get things done. People who come to watch will also become participants. Do your work, completing tasks with an aura of joy. Aries and Libra, who figure prominently, will have these letters in their names—I and R.

Friday, August 24 (Moon in Scorpio)   Very exciting! The Scorpio moon relates to cooperative efforts, publicity, legal rights, and your marital status. A lively disagreement attracts the attention of onlookers. Make an intelligent concession, remembering that pride goes before a fall! Leo is represented.

Saturday, August 25 (Moon in Scorpio to Sagittarius 10:59 a.m.)   The emphasis continues on cooperative efforts, partnership, sales ability and your marital status. A fiery presentation brings results. Show off your talents. Anecdotes are guaranteed to bring laughs. A Scorpio individual declares, "You have got what it takes and I am with you!"

Sunday, August 26 (Moon in Sagittarius)   This Sunday is made to order for you to entertain. The light touch wins—some complain, "This place reminds me of a jumble of confusion!" Shoot back: "Nobody is begging you to stay!" Pleasant news tonight brings forth love and laughter and a serious discussion of your future.

Monday, August 27 (Moon in Sagittarius to Capricorn 8:01 p.m.)   The Sagittarian moon relates to accounting, hidden wealth, physical attraction, and a display of your charming personality. People warn, "You are taking too much for granted; that Scorpio can be dangerous!" Another Taurus will play a dramatic role.

Tuesday, August 28 (Moon in Capricorn)   Lucky day! The numerical and astrological aspects point to winning selections. Someone who once found you only mildly interesting has a change of heart. You are in demand as both friend and lover. Gemini will play an astonishing role. Your fortunate number is 5.

Wednesday, August 29 (Moon in Capricorn)   Today's Venus keynote blends with your Venus signifier, making for too much of a good thing! Say, "No, thanks. Although I love the dessert, I must refuse!" Focus on exercise, diet, and nutrition. A gift received is an art object or a luxury item. Libra is involved.

Thursday, August 30 (Moon in Capricorn to Aquarius 7:47 a.m.) Define your terms; look beyond the immediate. The answers you seek will be found behind the scenes. A local hypnotist discusses his art, requesting your feature performance. You will learn a lot, especially the art of conversation. But make clear: "I don't think I want to be one of your audience volunteers!"

Friday, August 31 (Moon in Aquarius) On this last day of August, with the moon in Aquarius, you will participate in a public relations coup. You will also receive proposals concerning business, career, or marriage. An exciting Aquarian wants to be with you and says so. Cancer and Capricorn are also in this picture.

SEPTEMBER 2001

Saturday, September 1 (Moon in Aquarius to Pisces 8:31 p.m.) A pleasant evening at home—if you so desire! Music plays an integral role; Isaac Stern could be on television. One way or another, sounds will figure prominently. The focus is also on a family reunion, on dealings with another Taurus who sincerely desires to be a part of your life.

Sunday, September 2 (Moon in Pisces) Be quiet within. The full moon in your eleventh house coincides with the fulfillment of hopes and wishes. Romance will blend with meditation. Pisces and Virgo will play outstanding roles, and will have these letters in their names—G, P, Y.

Monday, September 3 (Moon in Pisces)   The emphasis is on organization and on being knowledgeable about elements of timing and surprise. You'll have more responsibility and a chance to hit the financial jackpot. An intense relationship could get too hot not to cool down. Capricorn is in this picture.

Tuesday, September 4 (Moon in Pisces to Aries 8:57 a.m.)   On this Tuesday, keep the lines of communication open. A long-distance call will play a major role. An impediment to the fulfillment of your goal will be erased. A Pisces says goodbye, but not forever. A minor incident could develop into a major theme.

Wednesday, September 5 (Moon in Aries)   The Aries moon relates to lost articles that will be discovered in a most unlikely place. When questioning people, be aggressive. A secret hiding place is discovered because of Aries persistence. Lucky lottery: 1, 11, 12, 22, 33, 45.

Thursday, September 6 (Moon in Aries to Taurus 8:16 p.m.)   One might say (one will declare) that dust settles. A confusing array of events finally falls into place—the puzzle could be solved. The spotlight falls on family, home, and the value of property. Libra and another Taurus will become your allies in settling a financial dilemma.

Friday, September 7 (Moon in Taurus)   Highlight versatility, get ready for what could become a very lively weekend—be up to date on fashion and news. Expect big doings soon, for the cycle is such that you will be at the right place at a crucial moment. A Sagittarius plays a role.

Saturday, September 8 (Moon in Taurus)   The moon in is your sign, indicating the high cycle for Taurus. You'll get valuable help that clears the path ahead. Your judgment and intuition are on target. The answer to a question is: "Affirmative." This is the time to make your move. Your lucky number is 4.

Sunday, September 9 (Moon in Taurus to Gemini 5:40 a.m.) Today, you should read, write, teach, publish, and advertise. Someone who was previously indifferent will say in so many words, "I am thrilled to observe your creative side at work!" Gemini, Virgo, and Sagittarius figure in this exciting scenario.

Monday, September 10 (Moon in Gemini) The lunar emphasis is on finding lost articles, improving your income potential, and learning the secrets of successful investing. You'll muse, "This may be Monday but it ain't blue!" Libra, Scorpio, and another Taurus, who play outstanding roles, have these letters in their names—F, O, X.

Tuesday, September 11 (Moon in Gemini to Cancer 12:07 p.m.) Your intuition steps up activities. Some people claim they know best how to live your life and suggest that you change your name. Pisces and Virgo figure in this dynamic scenario, and have these letters in their names—G, P, Y.

Wednesday, September 12 (Moon in Cancer) Elements of timing and luck ride with you. Keep your plans flexible. Welcome a visit from a relative who is in your cheering section. You may be knocked down, but you will rise before the count of ten. Cancer and Capricorn are in the front lines.

Thursday, September 13 (Moon in Cancer to Leo 3:14 p.m.) Your popularity increases. People of all political persuasions are drawn to you, seeking to convince, to attract, and perhaps even to fall in love. Aries and Libra could dominate this scenario, and will have these initials in their names—I and R.

Friday, September 14 (Moon in Leo)   For racing luck, try these selections at all tracks: post position special—number 7 p.p. in the third race. Pick six: 1, 2, 7, 4, 5, 5. Watch for these letters in the names of potential winning horses or jockeys: A, S, J. Hot daily doubles: 1 and 2, 6 and 4, 7 and 5. Leo jockeys give outstanding rides aboard long shots.

Saturday, September 15 (Moon in Leo to Virgo 3:38 p.m.)   Saturday night will be most unusual, including family and special events that might take place at home. Keep your resolutions about diet and nutrition. A Cancer will not be insulted if you say, "Everything is delicious, but I want to keep a promise to myself to eat less."

Sunday, September 16 (Moon in Virgo)   Some people will comment, "Plenty of wit and wisdom around this table—perhaps it should be renamed 'The Taurus Algonquin Table!' " Cancer, Capricorn, and Virgo will play exciting roles, and have these letters in their names—C, L, U. Your lucky number is 3.

Monday, September 17 (Moon in Virgo to Libra 2:59 p.m.)   The new moon in Virgo represents creativity, style, physical attraction, and possibly the beginning of a romance. On this Monday, you will muse, "I don't know why, but I feel revitalized!" Leo, Scorpio, and another Taurus play fascinating roles.

Tuesday, September 18 (Moon in Libra)   That good feeling remains. It got under way 24 hours ago; don't permit it to escape! You receive a gift representing true love. Get your original thoughts and ideas on paper. Virgo and Sagittarius figure prominently. Your lucky number is 5.

Wednesday, September 19 (Moon in Libra to Scorpio 3:27 p.m.)   Lucky lottery: 1, 19, 22, 24, 32, 33. On this Wednesday, expect an invitation to participate in a soirée. Libra moon relates to ability to fix things and to do repair work at home. Once again you are made aware of diet and nutrition that takes willpower—you are doing the right thing!

Thursday, September 20 (Moon in Scorpio)   The moon in your marriage house makes it obvious that legal arrangements are necessary. Focus also on public relations and on proposals that involve partnership and marriage. Define terms, refusing to fall victim to self-deception. Pisces figures prominently.

Friday, September 21 (Moon in Scorpio to Sagittarius 7:02 p.m.)   A powerful day for you to get things done. You receive backing from those in authority. The Scorpio moon continues to stir juices about controversial legalities and your marital status. Capricorn and Cancer figure in this exciting scenario, and could have these initials in their names—H, Q, Z.

Saturday, September 22 (Moon in Sagittarius)   You will be introduced to someone from a foreign country who modestly says, "I know so little about your country. Is it possible to show me around this Saturday night?" Aries and Libra enjoy a clash of ideas while you act as umpire.

Sunday, September 23 (Moon in Sagittarius)   Make a fresh start, digging deep for information. You might not find hidden wealth, but you could uncover treasure. A gift received features gold, and it will help beautify your surroundings and home. Leo and Aquarius figure prominently, and will prove entertaining, literate, and eager to please.

Monday, September 24 (Moon in Sagittarius to Capricorn 2:48 a.m.)   On this Monday, it will be necessary to take risks. Write the scenario as it takes place—the key is to choose direction and motivation, and finally to wake up in love. Food will figure prominently; you'll reciprocate by providing a marvelous wine. Capricorn is in the picture.

Tuesday, September 25 (Moon in Capricorn)   Spiritual matters command your attention. Look beyond the immediate, realizing once again that there are more things on heaven and earth than might fit your philosophy. Give a low bow to another Taurus, William Shakespeare. Gemini plays an exciting role.

Wednesday, September 26 (Moon in Capricorn to Aquarius 2:04 p.m.)   For racing luck, try these selections at all tracks: post position special—number 4 p.p. in the fourth race. Pick six: 1, 8, 2, 4, 6, 6. Watch for these letters in the names of potential winning horses or jockeys—D, M, V. Hot daily doubles: 1 and 8, 7 and 7, 6 and 4. Favorites win, but their time is disappointing. Taurus and Scorpio jockeys have excellent rides.

Thursday, September 27 (Moon in Aquarius)   Get ready for change, travel, variety, and additional duties that lead to promotion. Someone in authority comments, "We should have used your talents long ago!" The emphasis is on writing, reading, and disseminating information. A flirtation is more serious than you originally anticipated.

Friday, September 28 (Moon in Aquarius)   Entertain at home. Repay a favor. Present a special person with an unusual gift. The emphasis is on music, style, and dancing to your own rhythm. Libra, Scorpio, and another Taurus, who will play fascinating roles, have these letters in their names—F, O, X. Your lucky number is 6.

Saturday, September 29 (Moon in Aquarius to Pisces 2:49 a.m.)   The moon will be changing signs—to your advantage. Within 24 hours, people, places, and situations that seemed out of reach will become available. Whatever psychic capabilities you possess will surge forward. Pisces and Virgo are involved.

Sunday, September 30 (Moon in Pisces)   What a Sunday! The moon will be in your eleventh house, with a powerful Saturn keynoted. What you wished for will be obtained, with no strings attached! In matters of speculation, stick with the number 8. You'll have pleasant dealings with Cancer and Capricorn.

OCTOBER 2001

Monday, October 1 (Moon in Pisces to Aries 3:06 p.m.)   On this first day of October, you are sensitive to trends and cycles. A Pisces helps make your dream come true. Terms will be defined. Real estate figures prominently. You could be in love, for you are walking on air! Your lucky number is 7.

Tuesday, October 2 (Moon in Aries)   The full moon in Aries tells you something of importance is going on behind your back. A relative is involved. It finally dawns on you, "That's why the special message and the trip were necessary!" A long-distance communication relates to an overseas investment.

Wednesday, October 3 (Moon in Aries)   Lucky lottery: 1, 9, 10, 12, 14, 36. A fiery Aries demands, "I deserve the full story—the facts, not evasions!" Participate in a humanitarian project. A relative from now on will wear a helmet when riding a motorcycle.

Thursday, October 4 (Moon in Aries to Taurus 1:59 a.m.)   By making a fresh start, you rid yourself of debts and responsibilities belonging to another. Light shines in areas previously dark. Emphasize independence and the courage of your convictions. A Leo declares, "At times, I think you can work miracles!" Your lucky number is 1.

Friday, October 5 (Moon in Taurus)   For racing luck, try these selections at all tracks: post position special—number 2 p.p. in the second race. Pick six: 2, 2, 1, 8, 3, 8. Watch for these letters in the names of potential winning horses and jockeys—B, K, T. Hot daily doubles: 2 and 2, 4 and 4, 3 and 8. Favorites win; Cancer and Capricorn jockeys are up on strong horses.

Saturday, October 6 (Moon in Taurus to Gemini 11:10 a.m.)   Lucky lottery: 2, 3, 12, 15, 25, 40. A childhood friend makes a surprise appearance, with much to talk over. Your cycle is high, so the scenario features fun and games and a night of love and laughter. Too much food represents a lack of necessary discipline required for health.

Sunday, October 7 (Moon in Gemini)   The lunar position highlights wealth previously hidden. A family fortune becomes visible. The mood for celebration replaces resentment that you were not informed. Keep your plans flexible. Be willing to sign a waiver. Leo, Scorpio, and another Taurus figure in this dramatic scenario.

Monday, October 8 (Moon in Gemini to Cancer 6:18 p.m.)   A lively Monday! The puzzle pieces fall into place. Finally, you get the complete story. There are many complications, but your Taurus determination helps you survive, despite a minor crisis. Your hearing and speech are vulnerable. From now on, you will believe in vitamins!

Tuesday, October 9 (Moon in Cancer) All indications, both astrological and numerical, point to family, home, durability, and loyalty. You again discover the right direction. Tonight a home-cooked meal will please everyone. Cancer will be the star of the evening. Your lucky number is 6.

Wednesday, October 10 (Moon in Cancer to Leo 10:52 p.m.) Lucky lottery: 6, 7, 12, 14, 15, 22. Today you enjoy the performance of a magician and sensational illusions! Don't attempt to figure out the methods. Put logic aside, relaxing and being transported far from reality. Virgo will play an outstanding role.

Thursday, October 11 (Moon in Leo) Hanging on to the past is sentimental, but will not pay your obligations. A contract originally signed by Capricorn requires attention. Bring together people whose ideas and philosophies are opposites. A minor controversy erupts; you'll be dubbed the peacemaker.

Friday, October 12 (Moon in Leo) Luck rides with you! You could win substantial amounts and be placed in charge of valuable property. Gemini and Sagittarius figure in this scenario. You are asked to decide which one from a series of names. A romantic reunion provides stimulation and inspiration.

Saturday, October 13 (Moon in Leo to Virgo 12:56 a.m.) Let bygones be bygones! Be finished with trivia and go for the big time. You have paid your dues, so enjoy a period of euphoria, no matter what the length of time. Stress courage, originality, and romance. Leo will dominate the action. Your fortunate number is 1.

Sunday, October 14 (Moon in Virgo) Stick to tried-and-true methods. The moon position emphasizes style, creativity, and the stirring of ambition. It is fixed for you to win—don't disappoint people who have faith in your potential. What was lost will be retrieved. Express thanks without being obsequious.

Monday, October 15 (Moon in Virgo to Libra 1:25 a.m.) The lunar position symbolizes the stirring of creative juices. The Jupiter keynote blends with your Venus significator, so you'll be lucky when it comes to picking winners. Take note of your dreams. Gemini and Sagittarius play distinguished roles.

Tuesday, October 16 (Moon in Libra) It might be a case of the blind leading the blind. The Libra moon relates to work methods, basic issues, and repairs. You will hear music to your liking, so regain your personal rhythm and dance to your own tune. A Scorpio and another Taurus could be involved in a romance. Your lucky number is 4.

Wednesday, October 17 (Moon in Libra to Scorpio 2:02 a.m.) Get ready to examine written material. You'll hear this announcement: "I am a doctor of scripts, and you are well!" After receiving encouragement, go to it, but don't wait too long! A temperamental relative complains, "You never seem to have enough time for me!"

Thursday, October 18 (Moon in Scorpio) Marriage and domestic life are featured. Make room in your budget for decoration and remodeling. Count your blessings and money. A Libran says and means it, "Don't ever feel deserted while I am alive!" The emphasis is on diet, nutrition, and volunteering to help a family who is currently down on their luck.

Friday, October 19 (Moon in Scorpio to Sagittarius 4:46 a.m.) On this Friday you undergo a mystical experience. The Scorpio moon relates to special appearances before the public. The discovery of additional legal rights and proposals involves your career, business, or marriage. Pisces and Virgo, who figure in this scenario, have these letters in their names—G, P, Y.

Saturday, October 20 (Moon in Sagittarius) The results of recent agreements, contacts, and contracts come to light. A Scorpio, although aggressive, will insist on fair play, fighting for your rights to be in the minority. Capricorn and Cancer will side with you, encouraging you to remain. Your lucky number is 8.

Sunday, October 21 (Moon in Sagittarius to Capricorn 11:12 a.m.) Look beyond the immediate. Communicate with someone based overseas. A grand opportunity exists for distribution, publication, and promotion. Those who said it could not be done will tonight be eating crow. Aries and Libra, who will play outstanding roles, have these letters in their names— I and R.

Monday, October 22 (Moon in Capricorn) The green light flashes, so move ahead. Remember that climbing the mountain to success begins with one step. Accent style, liberty, freedom, and derring-do. Do not follow others; set the pace and move ahead in the face of temporary opposition. Leo and Aquarius help you to emerge victorious.

Tuesday, October 23 (Moon in Capricorn to Aquarius 9:26 p.m.) For a time, you'll be asking, "Could this be déjà vu?" Later, lights that were dimmed will be bright. Places and faces become distinguishable. The interest in philosophy and religions of the world will be much in evidence. There's a home-cooked meal tonight that hits the spot.

Wednesday, October 24 (Moon in Aquarius) Lucky lottery: 1, 4, 10, 11, 12, 36. Accept an invitation to attend a social affair aimed at getting volunteers for a political or charitable campaign. Be agreeable, not naive. Exchange ideas with a lively Gemini. A serious Capricorn relates a dream, some of which could be prophetic.

Thursday, October 25 (Moon in Aquarius) Patience truly will be a virtue—you are being observed by the personnel director. Obstacles will be cleared. Show the courage of your convictions. Locate the missing lock or key. Leo, Scorpio, and another Taurus, who play outstanding roles, have these letters in their names—D, M, V.

Friday, October 26 (Moon in Aquarius to Pisces 9:54 a.m.) Hang on to ideals, despite those who hoot and jeer. Someone of the opposite sex asserts, "I was first drawn to you because of your insistence on being truthful despite the consequences." Gemini, Virgo, and Sagittarius figure in this dynamic, unorthodox scenario.

Saturday, October 27 (Moon in Pisces) A family member cautions, "Don't tell everybody your business!" A scheme could be hatched aimed at throwing you off balance. Maintain an even keel, insisting on getting an explanation of what's been happening. Remember that what is given to you could also be taken away. A Libra figures prominently.

Sunday, October 28—Daylight Saving Time Ends (Moon in Pisces to Aries 9:13 p.m.) Play the waiting game! The moon in Pisces represents your eleventh house, that section of your horoscope that deals with winning friends and influencing people. It also represents the pleasure principle. People marvel at elements of luck and timing that ride with you. Pisces is represented.

211

Monday, October 29 (Moon in Aries)   Make it crystal clear that you are not a fly-by-night. Say it out loud: "I am here to perfect my techniques, to organize, and to be sure that policies and orders are recognized and acted on." Capricorn and Cancer, who will play adventurous roles, have these letters in their names— H, Q, Z.

Tuesday, October 30 (Moon in Aries)   More recognition comes to you today. This helps in the distribution and selling of your product. Solutions to health problems are profitable for you. Pay attention to blood pressure and to healing emotional wounds. Aries and Libra will play memorable roles.

Wednesday, October 31 (Moon in Aries to Taurus 7:46 a.m.)   In the spirit of Halloween, wear a costume featuring bright colors, including yellow and gold. You will be attracted to exotic characters, such as movie stars, sports heroes, or the male romantic lead in a hot movie. Remember: This also is National Magic Day, in memory of the great Houdini.

NOVEMBER 2001

Thursday, November 1 (Moon in Taurus)   The full moon in your sign, plus a Saturn keynote, makes this first day of November both trying and exhilarating, both challenging and productive. Capricorn and Cancer, who will play outstanding roles, have these letters in their names—H, Q, Z.

Friday, November 2 (Moon in Taurus to Gemini 4:11 p.m.)   Romance is in the air! A clash of ideas stimulates your creativity, style, and sexuality. With your Venus ruling planet, it should come as no surprise that unless there is love in your life, it might as well be "no life." Libra plays a role.

Saturday, November 3 (Moon in Gemini)   Make a fresh start, but count your change. The Gemini moon indicates that what was lost will be recovered. You'll have a reason to celebrate this Saturday night! Leo and Aquarius, who figure in an exciting scenario, have these letters in their names—A, S, J. Your lucky number is 1.

Sunday, November 4 (Moon in Gemini to Cancer 10:42 p.m.)   A family member displays skill as a psychic reader. Neither encourage nor discourage this skill, but permit this fascination with the occult to run its course. Expect a marvelous Sunday-night dinner— Cancer is in the role of chef.

Monday, November 5 (Moon in Cancer)   For racing luck, try these selections at all tracks: post position special—number 5 p.p. in the seventh race. Pick six: 3, 7, 5, 1, 2, 4. Watch for these letters in the names of potential winning horses or jockeys—C, L, U. Hot daily doubles: 3 and 7, 3 and 3, 6 and 4. Sagittarian jockeys are up on long shots and win by photo finishes.

Tuesday, November 6 (Moon in Cancer)   On this Tuesday, stick to your routine until the task is completed. Scorpio and another Taurus, who play sensational roles, have these letters in their names—D, M, V. Be aware of structure, design, and architecture in order to protect your home and family. You will have luck with the number 4.

Wednesday, November 7 (Moon in Cancer to Leo 3:32 a.m.)   Lucky lottery: 5, 7, 20, 25, 50, 51. Be on the move! Don't drive too fast in traffic, for people with nervous disorders, on the road, are dangerous! Be aware of your own weaknesses. The spotlight is on reading, writing, and flirting!

Thursday, November 8 (Moon in Leo)   Attention revolves around your domestic life, including where you live and your marital status. Stress harmony, realizing you cannot become accomplished overnight. Libra and another Taurus figure in an exciting scenario.

Friday, November 9 (Moon in Leo to Virgo 6:48 a.m.) Take time out to get to know someone. It's a different kind of Friday, so be quiet within, sharing private feelings with an understanding person. If there is opposition to your plans, realize that this is part of the territory. Virgo is involved.

Saturday, November 10 (Moon in Virgo)   A power Saturday night! The Virgo moon relates to fifth-house activities, including creativity, sensuality, personal magnetism, and sex appeal. Meet and beat a deadline. Listen carefully to questions and problems expressed by your children. Lucky lottery: 1, 4, 5, 18, 22, 32.

Sunday, November 11 (Moon in Virgo to Libra 8:52 a.m.)   Numerous puzzles are presented and you solve most of them—you'll be very lucky! Define your terms, outline your boundaries, and reply to a relative, "I don't know how I do it—it might be luck but I just do it!" Keep lines of communication open—you'll be speaking to someone who lives abroad.

Monday, November 12 (Moon in Libra)   Your judgment and intuition hit the bull's-eye. An aggressive Leo shows the way, displaying courage and talent. You'll receive encouragement, and even a possible financial backing. Scorpio and another Taurus revel in the antics of frustrated people.

Tuesday, November 13 (Moon in Libra to Scorpio 10:44 a.m.)   You could be pondering, "No matter what time I start, I seem to end up in the same place!" On this Tuesday, your appetite is sharp and you feel revitalized. Your main thought is, "I will do my best and stick to my original conclusion!" A Cancer is involved.

Wednesday, November 14 (Moon in Scorpio)   On this Wednesday, with the moon in your seventh house, attention revolves around your marital status, public relations, and legal affairs. Gemini and Sagittarius play fascinating roles and could have these letters in their names—C, L, U. You will have luck with the number 3.

Thursday, November 15 (Moon in Scorpio to Sagittarius 1:51 p.m.)   The new moon is in Scorpio, so attention continues to fall on legal rights, public appearances, and a decision about marriage. A lively Scorpio decides, "I will have things my way, no matter what!" You will learn that there is a difference between being generous and being extravagant.

Friday, November 16 (Moon in Sagittarius)   Focus on accounting and on learning more about tax and license requirements for a projected venture. Tear down in order to rebuild; decorate and remodel. Plumbing may require repair, so don't put it off too long! A flirtation is interesting, but could get dangerous.

Saturday, November 17 (Moon in Sagittarius to Capricorn 7:39 p.m.)   A Libra family member declares, "Everybody's nerves around here seem shot—I will stay until all of you are healed!" Music figures prominently. A domestic adjustment is featured. You will be adequately paid for special services. Your lucky number is 6.

Sunday, November 18 (Moon in Capricorn)   Within 24 hours, the moon will be in your house of entertainment, style, and travel. Philosophical concepts dominate, and you win major points with diplomacy. This could be a quiet Sunday, when discussions revolve around publishing, theology, and meditation. Pisces is involved.

Monday, November 19 (Moon in Capricorn) You will be rewarded for efforts that involve teaching, advertising, and publishing. You remove a hazard that could have gummed up the works. Cancer and Capricorn, who play outstanding roles, have these letters in their names—H, Q, Z.

Tuesday, November 20 (Moon in Capricorn to Aquarius 4:54 a.m.) Focus on distance, language, and the power of prayer. You were perhaps the world's most powerful cynic, but that was then and this is now. Reach beyond the immediate to discover that today you have the power of prophecy. Aries and Libra play exciting roles.

Wednesday, November 21 (Moon in Aquarius) Make a fresh start in a new direction. The lunar position highlights your career, business, promotion, and leadership. Leo and Aquarius, who will figure prominently, could have these initials in their names—A, S, J. The spotlight falls on special service, and on praise from someone who previously ignored you.

Thursday, November 22 (Moon in Aquarius to Pisces 4:51 p.m.) On this Thanksgiving, the moon will be in Aquarius, your tenth house, so you will be expected to play a leading role and to introduce various guests. Perhaps you will give a short talk on the meaning of the holiday. A Thanksgiving dinner may best be described as sumptuous.

Friday, November 23 (Moon in Pisces) On this Friday, a variety of emotions are featured. You will be both lighthearted and perhaps desperately serious. Spiritual values surge forth, for the Pisces moon relates to friendship and winning ways. Gemini and Sagittarius will liven up today's festivities.

Saturday, November 24 (Moon in Pisces)   Obstacles are removed. A path is cleared so that progress can continue with a unique project. Leo, Scorpio, and another Taurus, who figure prominently, will have these letters in their names—D, M, V. An Aquarian declares, "I have never enjoyed these holidays more than I have being with you!"

Sunday, November 25 (Moon in Pisces to Aries 5:20 a.m.)   Secrets will be revealed within 24 hours. Control a tendency to be aggressive. People planned to surprise you; that's why the secret. A clandestine relationship comes to light. Aries will be involved. You will be informed, "You seem to be invisible—it reminds me of 'the little man who wasn't there!' "

Monday, November 26 (Moon in Aries)   A family member declares, "Now that the secret is out, we hope you understand and if you were offended, please forgive us!" You will comprehend; it was a grand plan aimed at pleasing and surprising you. A Libra figures prominently.

Tuesday, November 27 (Moon in Aries to Taurus 4:04 p.m.)   A Tuesday surprise! You feared this would be a dull day; you said so out loud. It will turn out to be the opposite of dull! Pisces and Virgo play significant roles. In matters of speculation, stick with the number 7. A hiding place is discovered!

Wednesday, November 28 (Moon in Taurus)   The moon in your sign equates to your high cycle, and to your ability to be at the right place at a crucial moment. You exude an aura of sensuality and sex appeal, as a family member says, "You are perhaps the luckiest person I know!" Capricorn and Cancer could startle by revealing ideas the government might consider dangerous.

217

Thursday, November 29 (Moon in Taurus) High-light a universal outlook, reaching beyond the immediate. Take time to study the language and attitudes of people living in foreign lands. Separation from a loved one was painful, but an exciting reunion makes up for it. Aries and Libra are in the picture.

Friday, November 30 (Moon in Taurus to Gemini 12:02 a.m.) The pressure of a financial obligation will be removed. Emphasize originality, independence, and a fresh start in a new direction. Within 24 hours, you could hit the financial jackpot. A Gemini will play an outstanding role. A Leo fascinates with color coordination and showmanship.

DECEMBER 2001

Saturday, December 1 (Moon in Gemini) You will have luck with these numbers: 3, 6, 9. The spotlight is on money, payments, collections, and an uncanny ability to locate lost articles. Stay informed about foreign exchange rates. Deal with a travel agency in connection with a projected European tour.

Sunday, December 2 (Moon in Gemini to Cancer 5:29 a.m.) Make a fresh start in a new direction—within 24 hours, your financial pressure will be relieved. Your cash flow is due to resume, and you will be introduced to someone who might be destined to play a major role in your life. Leo and Aquarius, who figure prominently, have these initials in their names—A, S, J.

Monday, December 3 (Moon in Cancer) On this Monday, extend the hand of forgiveness to someone who said the wrong thing at the wrong time. The emphasis is on property, basic values, and a decision relating to your home, family, or marital status. Cancer and Capricorn, who are in the picture, have these initials in their names—B, K, T.

Tuesday, December 4 (Moon in Cancer to Leo 9:14 a.m.)   Fight your way through a maze of red tape as a Sagittarian becomes your valuable ally. You'll be told by a fascinating member of the opposite sex, "You are a blend of toughness, sensitivity, and romance." Your reply: "Those words are music to my ears!"

Wednesday, December 5 (Moon in Leo)   Lucky lottery: 4, 7, 8, 40, 48, 51. The moon in Leo represents the sale or purchase of property and acquisition of durable goods that apply to homemaking. Stick to your resolutions concerning exercise, diet, and nutrition. Scorpio plays a fantastic role!

Thursday, December 6 (Moon in Leo to Virgo 12:10 p.m.)   Watch for change, travel, and a variety of sensations and experiences. The answer to your question: Affirmative. A flirtation lends spice but carries with it responsibility. Don't hurt anyone while pursing your own happiness. Virgo plays a top role.

Friday, December 7 (Moon in Virgo)   Attention revolves around children, challenge, decorating, remodeling, and history. On this day in 1941, Pearl Harbor was attacked, starting the U.S. involvement in World War II. The emphasis on domestic life and on serious discussions among your family about "What is next for us?"

Saturday, December 8 (Moon in Virgo to Libra 2:56 p.m.)   On this Saturday, much soul searching takes place. A spiritual adviser proves helpful. Define your terms; outline your boundaries; see people and relationships in a realistic light. The moon position in your fifth house relates to creativity, physical attraction, and the stirring of creative juices.

Sunday, December 9 (Moon in Libra)   Balance will be achieved between feelings and thoughts. Obtain solid financial advice. Pounce on an opportunity, but keep a promise to yourself. Capricorn and Cancer will play roles in this scenario.

Monday, December 10 (Moon in Libra to Scorpio 6:08 p.m.)   Today you can get things done. Confront a Libran with this question: "Do you really think you can stand the hardship of starting over with no money?" The answer you receive depends upon the circumstances—either happy or sad. Aries is also involved.

Tuesday, December 11 (Moon in Scorpio)   A marriage contract is ready. The sun keynote blends with your Venus, bringing "hot love." Romance dominates, and you could hear these words, "You need tender, loving care!" Leo and Aquarius, who figure prominently, have these letters, initials in their names—A, S, J.

Wednesday, December 12 (Moon in Scorpio to Sagittarius 10:29 p.m.)   For racing luck, try these selections at all tracks: post position special—number 6 p.p. in the fifth race, Pick six; 2, 2, 5, 7, 6, 8. Watch for these letters in the names of potential winning horses or jockeys—B, K, T. Hot daily doubles; 2 and 2, 4 and 1, 4 and 4. Cancer jockeys lose in photo finishes.

Thursday, December 13 (Moon in Sagittarius)   Let these be your key words: "Don't give up the ship!" Within 24 hours, you will be more aware of who you are and why you are here, and you will learn about prospects for a business partnership or marriage. Focus on diversity as you satisfy your intellectual curiosity. Sagittarius is involved.

Friday, December 14—Solar Eclipse (Moon in Sagittarius)   The new moon, solar eclipse in Sagittarius, affects accounting procedures and a discovery bordering on the occult. A relationship that was close to marriage is all shook up! Leo, Scorpio, and another Taurus play fascinating roles.

Saturday, December 15 (Moon in Sagittarius to Capricorn 4:47 a.m.)   The financial status of someone who would be your partner is revealed, possibly in an embarrassing way. Ride with the tide; rough weather soon will subside. By digging deep for information, you will eventually reach the truth. A payment schedule is involved; you will receive your share. Your lucky number is 5.

Sunday, December 16 (Moon in Capricorn)   A family member who had been missing could make a surprise appearance. Domestic issues dominate, and music figures prominently. A Capricorn declares, "All is well; we have been through rougher weather and we will emerge safe and sound!"

Monday, December 17 (Moon in Capricorn to Aquarius 1:43 p.m.)   On this Monday, you can afford to pick and choose. Select the best, insisting on quality goods and overcoming a tendency toward self-deception. Be realistic in view of relationships involving the sale and purchase of property. Pisces and Virgo please in dramatic roles.

Tuesday, December 18 (Moon in Aquarius)   The emphasis is on prestige, conferences with community leaders, extra responsibility, and the chance for substantial rewards. You get lessons in survival—Capricorn and Cancer figure in this exciting scenario. Be sure your machinery is well oiled.

Wednesday, December 19 (Moon in Aquarius)   Lucky lottery: 3, 4, 8, 9, 11, 22. People compete to see who can wine and dine you—not bad at all! Your sales ability is heightened. On a personal level, be kind to someone whose heart might be broken. Aries and Cancer play instrumental roles.

Thursday, December 20 (Moon in Aquarius to Pisces 1:09 a.m.)   Clear aside emotional debris, stressing original thinking, the courage of your convictions, and inventiveness. A very sensitive Leo pulls manipulative strings. Respond: "I am no marionette; I will decide my own future and potential!" Get going on a project!

Friday, December 21 (Moon in Pisces)   A major wish comes true! The moon position emphasizes your ability to win friends and influence people among higher-ups. You'll have good fortune in finance and romance. For luck, stick with the number 2. Cancer and Capricorn will attempt a takeover.

Saturday, December 22 (Moon in Pisces to Aries 1:44 a.m.)   What a Saturday! The Pisces moon relates to your ability to cause others to be in a romantic mood. Forces scatter if you attempt to please everyone. Please yourself, then others will follow suit. Supersensitivity about your body image will be overcome. Your lucky number is 3.

Sunday, December 23 (Moon in Aries)   Don't equate delay with defeat. The Aries moon indicates that someone is trying to catch up with you! Secret meetings take place for various purposes. Leo, Scorpio, and another Taurus, who figure prominently, will have these letters in their names—D, M, V.

Monday, December 24 (Moon in Aries)   On this Christmas Eve, you receive gifts relating to books, writing, and communications. An Aries presents a most unusual gift involving a surprise party. You'll hear testimonials to your character, good looks, and generosity. Gemini, Virgo, and Sagittarius are also in the picture.

Tuesday, December 25 (Moon in Aries to Taurus 1:10 a.m.)   It's Christmas Day, so look for the restoration of domestic harmony. Music is involved and biographies are featured. You might be feeling, "I don't really think I should be put on such a pedestal!" A Scorpio persuades you to feel otherwise. Libra and another Taurus make this a most memorable Christmas.

Wednesday, December 26 (Moon in Taurus)   Lucky lottery: 2, 7, 16, 25, 39, 40. Don't give away secrets! A vengeful individual, very jealous, wants you to fall on your face. Resist! The element of deception is present—know it, protect yourself in clinches. Pisces is destined to appear at the right time.

Thursday, December 27 (Moon in Taurus to Gemini 9:37 a.m.)   Your power play day—this is one Thursday you will long remember! On a personal level, a romance could go haywire. Controversy and the law are involved—be aware of a mechanical obstruction relating to your automobile. People in top echelons understand your needs and will reward your talents and values.

Friday, December 28 (Moon in Gemini)   Predict your future and make it come true! Distance and language barriers figure prominently. People you thought were indifferent will display the fact that you are well liked. A love relationship gets back on track, but don't permit it to get so hot that it must cool down.

Saturday, December 29 (Moon in Gemini to Cancer 1:38 p.m.)   Let go of past grievances, freeing yourself of preconceived notions. Stress romance, creativity, and the courage of your convictions. Avoid heavy lifting. Wear bright colors and make personal appearances. Leo and Aquarius figure in this scenario. Your lucky number is 1.

Sunday, December 30 (Lunar Eclipse—Moon in Cancer) The full moon, lunar eclipse, falls in the area of your horoscope associated with relatives, trips and visits, postponements. A temperamental Cancer proves to have a one-track mind. Later, all will be well, so permit a complicated situation to iron itself out.

Monday, December 31 (Moon in Cancer to Leo 5:08 p.m.) New Year's Eve: Plenty of fun and frolic along with the need to be very careful in traffic. During a celebration, there will be minor mixups. You might be whispering to one person, but your words fall on the ears of someone else. All in all, however, there is sweetness and joy as you look forward to 2002.

HAPPY NEW YEAR!

JANUARY 2002

Tuesday, January 1 (Moon in Leo) The first day of the year will see you having more responsibility, perhaps the responsibility of helping some people accept the idea of new conditions and a new year. Capricorn and Cancer play major roles, and could have these letters or initials in their names: H, Q, Z.

Wednesday, January 2 (Moon in Leo to Virgo 6:33 p.m.) The idea hits home, "This is a new year, the second year of the 21st century. Today I can see the big picture, and I will be happy!" Aries and Libra play key roles, and could have these letters in their names: I and R. Lucky lottery: 9, 13, 36, 46, 50, 51.

Thursday, January 3 (Moon in Virgo) Make a fresh start in a new direction. Keep dental and medical appointments. People "bother" you with minor questions and problems. Remember, they are not minor to the people asking—give comfort where possible. Leo and Aquarius play memorable roles, and could have these initials in their names: A, S, J.

Friday, January 4 (Moon in Virgo to Libra 8:23 p.m.) Questions about cooperative efforts, public relations, partnership, and marriage will loom large. The moon will be in Virgo, your fifth house, and you will exude personal magnetism and an aura of sensuality and sex appeal. Cancer and Capricorn will play astounding roles.

Saturday, January 5 (Moon in Libra) Your numerical cycle is 3, which equates to Jupiter—this blends with your natal Venus and means you could be "lucky in love." What begins as lighthearted romance or flirtation could become more serious than you anticipated. Know when to say, "Enough is enough!"

Sunday, January 6 (Moon in Libra to Scorpio 11:41 p.m.) On this Sunday, you get good news about your income potential. You also receive a gift relating to jewelry or flowers or both. Be gracious and grateful but not obsequious. Leo, Scorpio, and another Taurus could be involved, and have these letters in their names: D, M, V.

Monday, January 7 (Moon in Scorpio) On this Monday, you feel alert, alive, and ready to pounce on opportunities. Gemini, Virgo, and Sagittarius will play memorable roles. Here is how you might know some of them: they could have these letters or initials in their names: E, N, W. Have luck with number 5.

Tuesday, January 8 (Moon in Scorpio) Lie low; play the waiting game. Today's emphasis is on public relations, legal matters, and your marital status. Both numerically and astrologically, you are destined to be active in a partnership. Focus on music, style, and the ability to dance to your own tune. Libra is in the picture.

Wednesday, January 9 (Moon in Scorpio to Sagittarius 4:57 a.m.)   A partnership is tested. Do not hang on to a losing proposition. Avoid self-deception. It's important to see people, places, and relationships as they are, not merely as you wish they could be. Pisces and Virgo play top roles, and could have these initials in their names—G, P, Y.

Thursday, January 10 (Moon in Sagittarius)   On this, the 10th day of the month, talk of travel could dominate. Costs figure prominently, but consultation with a financial adviser assures you, "It can be afforded!" Money, payments, collections, promotion, and production dominate this very powerful cycle.

Friday, January 11 (Moon in Sagittarius to Capricorn 12:18 p.m.)   Your intuitive intellect works overtime. You discern what you actually need; you learn more about the direction your life is taking and what you should do about it. Meditation will help, but brooding would hurt. Aries plays a fascinating role.

Saturday, January 12 (Moon in Capricorn)   Racing luck—all tracks: post position special—number 7 p.p. in the third race. Pick six: 1, 4, 7, 3, 8, 5. Watch for these letters or initials in the names of potential winning horses or jockeys: A, S, J. Hot daily doubles: 1 and 4, 6 and 6, 1 and 1. Leo jockeys will bring in long shots.

Sunday, January 13 (Moon in Capricorn to Aquarius 9:41 p.m.)   The new moon is in Capricorn, your house of travel, which means you face facts about costs and practicality. The numerical cycle 2 represents the moon and the zodiacal sign of Cancer. Stay close to familiar ground, settle domestic differences, and conserve energy and money.

Monday, January 14 (Moon in Aquarius)   On this Monday, you sense that "something good" is about to happen. Within 24 hours, when the Moon will be in Aquarius, some of your fondest hopes and wishes could come true. This will be no ordinary Monday. You could win a contest, and there will be other highlights.

Tuesday, January 15 (Moon in Aquarius)   With the moon in your tenth house, you make inroads toward your ultimate goal. It will be necessary, with the number 4 Pluto keynote, to tear down in order to rebuild. Some people warn, "You cannot do it that way!" Respond by doing it "that way."

Wednesday, January 16 (Moon in Aquarius to Pisces 9:01 a.m.)   Get ready for change, travel, and adventure. Realize that you will meet lively, vibrant people including Gemini, Virgo, and Sagittarius. This could be a day of advancement—read, write, and learn by teaching. Lucky lottery: 5, 12, 13, 17 18, 50.

Thursday, January 17 (Moon in Pisces)   Attention revolves around your home, family, and ability to beautify your surroundings. The Pisces moon represents your eleventh house, which means that many of your desires will be fulfilled. Your popularity is on the rise. Be near water if possible. Libra is represented.

Friday, January 18 (Moon in Pisces to Aries 9:34 p.m.)   Be discreet. You have a secret, and some would like to pry it from you. Don't tell. Maintain an aura of mystery and intrigue. You have power that you are not aware of. Tonight you become aware! Pisces and Virgo play dynamic roles, and could have these letters in their names: G, P, Y.

Saturday, January 19 (Moon in Aries)   A lively Saturday. Focus on power, authority, and promotion.

You'll have more responsibility in connection with your career and relationship. If married, you rediscover your mate in a positive way. If single, you'll have some questions to answer in connection with your marital status. Your lucky number is 8.

Sunday, January 20 (Moon in Aries)   The Aries moon represents a secret that could be "explosive." Strive for emotional equilibrium. Control your temper, despite the fact that you have the right to be angry. Visit a friend temporarily confined to home or hospital. An Aries helps you succeed in achieving your objective.

Monday, January 21 (Moon in Aries to Taurus 9:45 a.m.)   Make a fresh start. Stand tall in the face of those who want to drag you down to their level. You have the strength, but when it comes to romance, you could be very weak. Leo and Aquarius play dramatic roles, and have these initials in their names: A, S, J.

Tuesday, January 22 (Moon in Taurus)   Questions about partnership and marriage arise. Your cycle is high, so trust your judgment and intuition. The moon in your sign represents your high cycle—take the initiative in business, career, and romance. You exude personal magnetism and an aura of sensuality and sex appeal.

Wednesday, January 23 (Moon in Taurus to Gemini 7:26 p.m.)   Racing luck—all tracks: post position special—number 5 p.p. in the seventh race. Pick six: 5, 3, 7, 2, 1, 1. Watch for these letters or initials in the names of potential winning horses or jockeys: C, L, U. Hot daily doubles: 5 and 3, 4 and 7, 2 and 2. Speed horses get out in front and win, paying long-shot prices.

Thursday, January 24 (Moon in Gemini)   What had been lost will be recovered. You find it where you last left it. It might be kind of embarrassing, so you need not talk about it. Leo, Scorpio, and another Taurus play dynamic roles, and could have these letters or initials in their names—D, M. V.

Friday, January 25 (Moon in Gemini) Highlight versatility and an ability to locate bargains and to act on information. A salesperson talks fast. If you don't understand, ask him to repeat. Money is involved. Be sure to count your change. Gemini, Virgo, and Sagittarius play top roles. Have luck with number 5.

Saturday, January 26 (Moon in Gemini to Cancer 1:15 a.m.) Relatives play featured roles. A short trip is necessary in connection with a special visit. A favor is returned. You almost forgot that a relative owed you money—it could be paid today. Libra, Scorpio, and another Taurus figure in this scenario. A Cancer is also involved.

Sunday, January 27 (Moon in Cancer) On this Sunday, spiritual values surface. If you take time to meditate, you will be doing yourself a great favor. See people, places, and relationships in a realistic light— avoid self-deception. A Cancer relative is obsequious in thanking you for a past favor.

Monday, January 28 (Moon in Cancer to Leo 3:29 a.m.) On this Monday, there will be a full moon in Leo, that section of your horoscope representing land, real estate, and the sale or purchase of a home. A new kind of romantic spark enters the domestic situation, and applies to your mate. You feel invigorated.

Tuesday, January 29 (Moon in Leo) There will be much talk of travel, romance, and creativity. You'll be finished with an obligation which "weighed you down." You have more freedom to travel, to create, and to love. Aries and Libra play top roles, and have these initials in their names: I and R.

Wednesday, January 30 (Moon in Leo to Virgo 3:39 a.m.) The moon in Virgo today represents your fifth house, which relates to children, challenge, change, variety, and sexual attraction. Focus on independence, creativity, inventiveness, and a fresh start in a new direction. Lucky lottery: 1, 10, 12, 13, 18, 22.

Thursday, January 31 (Moon in Virgo) On this last day of January, you will be alive, alert, dynamic, and sexy. The fifth-house moon also equates to investigation, character analysis, reading, and writing. A reunion means an end to talk of "breaking up." Cancer and Capricorn will play outstanding roles.

FEBRUARY 2002

Friday, February 1 (Moon in Virgo to Libra 3:44 a.m.) On this first day of February, your workload becomes easier. Look beyond the immediate and explore the possibility of a journey overseas to look for a representative of your talent or product in a foreign nation. Aries and Libra will play outstanding roles.

Saturday, February 2 (Moon in Libra) Shake off preconceived notions. People who claimed you were not creative enough to change your mind will suffer embarrassment. Leo and Aquarius play important roles, and could have these letters in their names: A, S, J. Your lucky number is 1.

Sunday, February 3 (Moon in Libra to Scorpio 5:34 a.m.) Be with your family, and straighten out a financial dispute. A Cancer declares, "I'm with you all the way!" Imprint your style; avoid heavy lifting if possible. A Capricorn follows suit by declaring, "No matter what, I believe in you and will stand with you!"

Monday, February 4 (Moon in Scorpio)   The number 3 numerical cycle relates to Jupiter—it is Jupiter and your natal Venus. Elements of timing and luck ride with you—you receive an art object as a gift. Express appreciation, without being obsequious. Gemini and Sagittarius play exciting roles.

Tuesday, February 5 (Moon in Scorpio to Sagittarius 10:21 a.m.)   Scorpio plus the moon in Scorpio this morning means that questions concerning partnership and marriage will loom large. Review material, and get ready for a clash of ideas. Leo, Scorpio, and another Taurus play significant roles.

Wednesday, February 6 (Moon in Sagittarius)   Racing luck—all tracks: post position special—number 3 p.p. in the fifth race. Pick six: 4, 1, 3, 2, 3, 1. Watch for these letters or initials in the names of potential winning horses or jockeys: E, N, W. Hot daily doubles: 4 and 1, 6 and 5, 2 and 2. Speed horses win, and will pay long-shot prices.

Thursday, February 7 (Moon in Sagittarius to Capricorn 6:07 p.m.)   Keep plans flexible. The sudden need for a journey will be part of today's scenario. Beautify your surroundings. Pay heed to suggestions by Leo, Scorpio, and another Taurus. A family member says, "I wish you would pay more attention to me." Have luck with number 6.

Friday, February 8 (Moon in Capricorn)   The Capricorn moon represents your travel and philosophy sector. What appeared long ago and far away will suddenly be at your doorstep. See people, places, and relationships as they are, not merely as you wish they could be. Pisces and Virgo play dramatic roles.

Saturday, February 9 (Moon in Capricorn)   Lucky lottery: 1, 8, 10, 26, 40, 46. Spiritual values surface. Dig deep for information concerning philosophy, theology, and the cultures of other lands. Financial aid comes from a surprise source. Capricorn and Cancer will play significant roles.

Sunday, February 10 (Moon in Capricorn to Aquarius 4:14 a.m.) Within 24 hours, your popularity will be on the rise. You will be asked to participate in political-charitable campaigns. As the moon moves toward Aquarius, your tenth house, you'll have more authority and responsibility. Aries plays a role.

Monday, February 11 (Moon in Aquarius) You win friends and influence people. You attract those who can be of immense help in obtaining funding. Those who claimed it could not be done will be eating crow. This means you do what seemed impossible. Leo and Aquarius will be won over to your side.

Tuesday, February 12 (Moon in Aquarius to Pisces 3:52 p.m.) The new moon in Aquarius coincides with your ability to have others await your stamp of approval. People who offered stubborn resistance will make intelligent concessions. Your heroic efforts can open the doors of fame, fortune. House hunting is featured.

Wednesday, February 13 (Moon in Pisces) The Jupiter numerical cycle plus Pisces moon in a favorable aspect to your Venus promises a day of achievement and popularity. In personal affairs, you could fall in love—don't make promises you know cannot be kept. Lucky lottery: 3, 12, 17, 18, 28 30.

Thursday, February 14 (Moon in Pisces) You receive more Valentine cards than in previous years. Cupid does play a role; the arrow hits the mark and you could fall helplessly in love. If you are married, the spark that brought you together with your mate in the first place will reignite.

Friday, February 15 (Moon in Pisces to Aries 4:24 a.m.) Mercury blends with your Venus—your ideas and writings find favor with more people than you originally anticipated. You'll be urged to go on. People express a liking for your style. Key words will be change, travel, and a variety of sensations and experiences. Gemini is represented.

Saturday, February 16 (Moon in Aries) A family member helps in making a list of priorities. The Aries moon in your twelfth house equals secret information—remember, discretion is the better part of valor. Libra, Scorpio, and another Taurus play dramatic roles. A family outing would be constructive, and ultimately profitable.

Sunday, February 17 (Moon in Aries to Taurus 4:57 p.m.) Meditation is necessary if you are to avoid brooding about what should have been done. Define terms; outline boundaries. Concern with real estate will be part of this scenario. Be quiet within, and heed your intuitive intellect. Pisces figures in today's activities.

Monday, February 18 (Moon in Taurus) The number 8 numerical cycle equates to Saturn, which blends with your Venus natal ruler. Be realistic about romance and flirtation. Your cycle is high, so circumstances are turning in your favor even as you read these lines. Capricorn plays a top role.

Tuesday, February 19 (Moon in Taurus) Take the initiative. The indications are that you win a contest and the hearts of people. Focus on selectivity, and insist on quality. Complete a project. Let go of obligations that were not your own in the first place. People are drawn to you, and will confide their marital problems.

Wednesday, February 20 (Moon in Taurus to Gemini 3:48 a.m.) Lucky lottery: 5, 16, 21, 22, 23, 50. Make a fresh start in a new direction. Fulfill a promise made to a relative. Some people say you appear to be here, there, and everywhere. Be versatile, without scattering your forces. Leo plays an outstanding role.

Thursday, February 21 (Moon in Gemini)   The emphasis is on cooperative efforts, experimentation, investigation, and discovery. Maintain a sense of the ridiculous. Announce: "There are two ways of doing things, the right way and my way!" Capricorn and Cancer will play memorable roles.

Friday, February 22 (Moon in Gemini to Cancer 11:13 a.m.)   Racing luck—all tracks: post position special—number 7 p.p. in the third race. Pick six: 1, 5, 7, 6, 2, 8. Watch for these letters or initials in the names of potential winning horses or jockeys: C, L, U. Hot daily doubles: 1 and 5, 3 and 3, 4 and 6. Sagittarius jockeys win photo finishes—long-shots!

Saturday, February 23 (Moon in Cancer)   Review your accounting procedures. Check bank balances; count your change. Computers may be going haywire—don't permit this to do so at your expense. Leo, Scorpio, and another Taurus play roles you will long remember. Proofreading is necessary.

Sunday, February 24 (Moon in Cancer to Leo 2:34 p.m.)   Within 24 hours, your "sex appeal" will be at its height. Don't break too many hearts. At the very least, offer tea and sympathy. Gemini, Virgo, and Sagittarius figure in this scenario. Give full play to your intellectual curiosity. Expand mental-emotional horizons.

Monday, February 25 (Moon in Leo)   Plan ahead in connection with a journey—it will not be a final "goodbye." Be sure your house is in order; take steps to be sure pets and other dependents are provided for. Clear your conscience if you are to be at your best. Libra plays a role.

Tuesday, February 26 (Moon in Leo to Virgo 2:48 p.m.)   Your pace slows, and this is as it should be. Take time to reflect and to send "thank you" cards to those who proved of immense help. Remember: "Manners before morals!" Pisces and Virgo play important roles, and have these letters or initials in their names—G, P, Y.

Wednesday, February 27 (Moon in Virgo)   The full moon in your fifth house emphasizes the "flow of creative juices." Attention revolves around children, change, and a variety of sensations. Cancer and Capricorn will play memorable roles. Focus on promotion, production, extra responsibility, and financial rewards.

Thursday, February 28 (Moon in Virgo to Libra 1:46 p.m.)   A short month, but you complete a project. Someone of the opposite sex confides, "I suppose you have noticed that I can hardly keep my hands off you!" Open lines of communication. Give thought and study to another language. Aries and Libra play exciting roles.

MARCH 2002

Friday, March 1 (Moon in Libra)   As you get ready for a weekend of fun and frivolity, don't bypass necessary tasks and details. Leo and Aquarius play outstanding roles and will have these letters or initials in their names: A, S, J. Maintain emotional equilibrium. What appears to be love at first sight is likely only a strong attraction.

Saturday, March 2 (Moon in Libra to Scorpio 1:52 p.m.)   It might be the difference between fire and the firefly, as Mark Twain put it. You come close to finding the right words or the right actions in connection with your family, especially your mother. Your left eye may require attention. A Cancer is involved.

Sunday, March 3 (Moon in Scorpio) Diversify. Count your change. You don't have to be a big spender in order to be regarded as a "sport." The Scorpio moon relates to partnership, cooperative efforts, and your marital status. Watch your weight—keep resolutions about exercise, diet, and nutrition.

Monday, March 4 (Moon in Scorpio to Sagittarius 4:54 p.m.) On this Monday, you receive proposals of business and career, partnership and marriage. Maintain your standards, but be willing to make intelligent concessions. Scorpio and another Taurus play leading roles, and have these letters in their names—D, M, V.

Tuesday, March 5 (Moon in Sagittarius) The moon in Sagittarius relates to your work, basic issues, and health. You might combine business with a health resort—it turns out that you know many people who have tried the place and have gotten good results. Write that report!

Wednesday, March 6 (Moon in Sagittarius to Capricorn 11:48 p.m.) Attention revolves around your home, family, and protection against fire and other kinds of damage. There's music in your life tonight. A special member of your family sings, and you appreciate the quality. Beautify your surroundings. Tune the piano, if necessary. Your lucky number is 6.

Thursday, March 7 (Moon in Capricorn) What was considered an easy project could actually be on a "slippery slope." Be in training, so that you can be in the best possible condition. Pisces and Virgo play outstanding roles, and could have these letters or initials in their names—G, P, Y.

Friday, March 8 (Moon in Capricorn)   You get things done today—your way! Focus on leadership, responsibility, and possibly being "madly in love." You attract envy from mean-spirited people. Many will accuse you of being where you are because of favoritism. Capricorn figures in this scenario.

Saturday, March 9 (Moon in Capricorn to Aquarius 9:56 a.m.)   Highlight universal appeal. Look beyond the immediate; give study to language and the cultures of people in other countries. You are special, and by the time the moon takes over from the sun, you'll know it for sure. Have luck with number 9.

Sunday, March 10 (Moon in Aquarius)   On this Sunday, your energy returns, and spiritual values surface. You make a fresh start in a new direction. You wear brighter colors and make personal appearances. Some members of the opposite sex declare, "You never looked better!" Leo plays a fascinating role.

Monday, March 11 (Moon in Aquarius to Pisces 9:56 p.m.)   Your intuitive intellect is honed to razor-sharpness. Trust a hunch. Maintain your self-esteem. Do not bow down to demands. Set your own policy and follow it. Cancer and Capricorn play unique roles, and could have these letters or initials in their names—B, K, T.

Tuesday, March 12 (Moon in Pisces)   This could be considered an odd day to celebrate, being Tuesday. However, the numerical cycle 3 equates to Jupiter, the planet of good fortune. It blends with your Venus, and the Jupiter-Venus combination could be translated as luck in speculation and in love. Sagittarius is involved.

Wednesday, March 13 (Moon in Pisces) Lucky lottery: 4, 12 13, 18, 22, 48. Many of your affairs are in a confused state—you can use this Wednesday to unravel them. People admire you and will say so. One member of the opposite sex is so bold as to confide, "At times I find it difficult not to put my hands on you!"

Thursday, March 14 (Moon in Pisces to Aries 9:01 p.m.) Racing luck—all tracks: post position special—number 3 p.p. in the second race. Pick six: 2, 3, 5, 4, 3, 3. Be alert for these letters or initials in the names of potential winning horses or jockeys: E, N, W. Hot daily doubles: 2 and 3, 4 and 4, 6 and 2. Gemini, Virgo, and Sagittarius jockeys ride winners and pay good prices.

Friday, March 15 (Moon in Aries) The moon in your twelfth house reveals that what had been a secret will no longer be hidden from you. Write your views. A clever dream interpretation could be the guidepost to the future. Libra, Scorpio, and another Taurus play significant roles, and have these letters in their names: F, O, X.

Saturday, March 16 (Moon in Aries to Taurus 10:59 p.m.) This will be a "strange Saturday." Meditation is necessary if you are to find the truth of who you are, where you are going, and why. Pisces and Virgo play revealing roles in your life today, and could have these letters or initials in their names—G, P, Y.

Sunday, March 17 (Moon in Taurus) On this St. Patrick's Day, have fun, but remember resolutions about going easy on adult beverages. Your cycle is high, so be selective and choose quality as circumstances turn in your favor. Capricorn is in the picture.

Monday, March 18 (Moon in Taurus) The moon in your sign means your financial picture is brighter than you originally anticipated. You are held in high esteem by three people you thought did not care for you. You find out differently today. Aries and Libra play special roles, and have these letters in their names: I and R.

Tuesday, March 19 (Moon in Taurus to Gemini 10:18 a.m.)   You waited for this day—don't waste it! Your numerical and astrological aspects are at a peak—you will be knocking on the doors of fame and fortune. This time, the doors will open! Leo and Aquarius play fantastic and unusual roles. Your lucky number is 1.

Wednesday, March 20 (Moon in Gemini)   A lost article could be located. You could win money in a contest. Keep your plans flexible. Don't be afraid to change your mind; creative people do it all the time. Gemini, Cancer, and Capricorn are in the picture. Lucky lottery; 1, 12, 18, 19, 20, 50.

Thursday, March 21 (Moon in Gemini to Cancer 9:05 p.m.)   On this Thursday, you marvel at your own wit, wisdom, and intellectual curiosity. Don't hold back, no pulling of punches. Gemini and Sagittarius will be on your side, and will play meaningful roles. Experiment, explore, and discover. Your popularity is on the rise!

Friday, March 22 (Moon in Cancer)   Everything points to a "pileup" of details. Attention revolves around land, the buying and selling of a home, real estate, and getting involved in a decorating project. Cancer plays a memorable role, saying you are invaluable and should be thinking of yourself as such.

Saturday, March 23 (Moon in Cancer)   Success is indicated via written words. A Cancer-born relative talks about how far you can go if you put your mind to it. Be gracious, and say, "Thank you," without being obsequious. Virgo and Sagittarius get in the act, and could be your main supporters.

Sunday, March 24 (Moon in Cancer to Leo 12:10 a.m.)   Stick close to home; enjoy a clash of ideas with Leo. Real estate is involved, along with future profits. Art objects and luxury items will be part of today's scenario, under your direction. Libra and another Taurus are part of the action. Have luck with number 6.

Monday, March 25 (Moon in Leo)   On this Monday, protect yourself in emotional clinches. With the moon in Leo, you tend to be romantic and to toss logic aside. Safeguard your interests and make intelligent concessions, without abandoning your principles. Pisces and Virgo will play major roles.

Tuesday, March 26 (Moon in Leo to Virgo 1:42 a.m.) Everything seems to be going your way when it comes to career and business. Some of your social plans are subject to change. Don't be bitter about that possibility. Someone you thought you loved suddenly stands lower on your priority list. A Cancer is involved.

Wednesday, March 27 (Moon in Virgo)   Analyze the possibilities of promoting your talent or product overseas. A reunion tonight is romantic, but could lack "fire." In your mind, you can do anything for someone you once loved—except to love again. Aries and Libra play "mysterious" roles.

Thursday, March 28 (Moon in Virgo to Libra 1:03 a.m.)   The full moon in your sixth house represents your work methods, and a romantic friendship that involves a coworker. Make a fresh start. Stress independence. Highlight originality and your pioneering spirit. Avoid heavy lifting. Be sympathetic to someone who confides a marital problems.

Friday, March 29 (Moon in Libra)   Strive for balance between work and play. Maintain your emotional equilibrium. Seek justice for all—fight if the cause is right. Your voice is compelling tonight. People comment, "You could get anything by using your hypnotic voice!" Aquarius is involved.

Saturday, March 30 (Moon in Libra to Scorpio 12:21 a.m.)   Could be a meaningful Saturday night, with the emphasis on partnership, cooperative efforts, and marriage. People are drawn to you with their problems, some quite intimate. Do your best. As you help solve problems of others, your own dilemmas are diminished. Your lucky number is 3.

Sunday, March 31 (Moon in Scorpio)   On this last day of March, with the moon in Scorpio, you could find yourself entangled with someone who refuses to let go. It will be up to you to say these words, "Enough is enough!" The opposition is strong—a clash of ideas will be meaningful. Scorpio is in this picture.

APRIL 2002

Monday, April 1 (Moon in Scorpio to Sagittarius 1:49 a.m.)   You won't be easy for others to fool, but you could fall victim to self-deception. Family members have a surprise waiting, but it is well hidden. Cancer and Capricorn play exciting roles, and could have these letters or initials in their names: B, K, T.

Tuesday, April 2 (Moon in Sagittarius)   You will be celebrating the arrival of a relative who has been away for a long time. Investigate and discover—focus on intellectual curiosity. Keep recent resolutions about exercise, diet, and nutrition. Gemini and Sagittarius play leading roles. Your lucky number is 3.

Wednesday, April 3 (Moon in Sagittarius to Capricorn 6:58 a.m.)   The Sagittarius moon continues to promote advertising, publishing, and travel plans. Your interest in the occult is also fanned by the lunar position. Leo, Scorpio, and another Taurus figure prominently, and could have these letters and initials in their names: D, M, V. Lucky lottery: 14, 24, 37, 46, 48, 50.

Thursday, April 4 (Moon in Capricorn) Get ready for change and variety and give full play to your curiosity. The accent is on reading, writing, teaching, and a short trip aimed at recovering legal documents. Gemini, Virgo, and Sagittarius will play dramatic roles, and have these initials in names: E, N, W.

Friday, April 5 (Moon in Capricorn to Aquarius 4:06 p.m.) The lunar position emphasizes leadership and the ability to look ahead and perceive potential. There's music in your life. Libra and another Taurus will figure prominently. You will be tempted to break your diet resolutions—fight it! Have luck with number 6.

Saturday, April 6 (Moon in Aquarius) Racing luck—all tracks: post position special—number 1 p.p. in the sixth race. Pick six: 2, 6, 5, 1, 1, 1. Watch for these letters or initials in the names of potential winning horses or jockeys: G, P, Y. Hot daily doubles: 2 and 6, 1 and 5, 4 and 4. Horses usually slow could break track records—long-shot prices.

Sunday, April 7—Daylight Saving Time Begins (Moon in Aquarius) Although it is Sunday, you will be up and around. The numerical cycle 8 equates to Saturn, which blends with your Venus. This could be a day when you learn the truth concerning your career and romance. Capricorn and Cancer play mysterious roles, and have these initials in their names: H, Q, Z.

Monday, April 8 (Moon in Aquarius to Pisces 4:57 a.m.) On this Monday, what once appeared long ago and far away will come close. This could include travel to a foreign land and will also encompass publishing, advertising, and promotion. People will be drawn to you. The more you help others with their problems, the more your own dilemmas will dissolve.

Tuesday, April 9 (Moon in Pisces)   Make a fresh start in a new direction. With the Pisces moon in your eleventh house, you win friends and influence people. You will have luck in matters of speculation, especially if you stick with number 1. Leo and Aquarius play dynamic roles today.

Wednesday, April 10 (Moon in Pisces to Aries 5:39 p.m.)   Lucky lottery: 2, 7, 11, 12, 16, 22. Focus on partnership, marriage, and a visit to an institution or a hospital where a friend is confined. Circumstances are moving in your favor. If patient and persistent, you'll have your choice of the best quality. A Cancer plays a role.

Thursday, April 11 (Moon in Aries)   Within 24 hours, you might strike it rich! Meantime, give full play to your intellectual curiosity. Examine, discover, and add to your knowledge, general and otherwise. A joyous evening tonight! You will receive compliments on your appearance and entertainment.

Friday, April 12 (Moon in Aries to Taurus 5:54 a.m.)   The new moon in your twelfth house coincides with discovery and learning where your friend stands in connection with how many days he will remain in the institution. Check the details; count your change; do plenty of proofreading. Scorpio is in this picture.

Saturday, April 13 (Moon in Taurus)   Share knowledge. Realize that, even as you read these words, circumstances move in your favor. You will be attractive physically. A flirtation is hot and heavy. Written material plays an important role—your own material is especially significant.

Sunday, April 14 (Moon in Taurus)   Attention revolves around your home, art objects, music, and ways
to make your home more beautiful. Libra, Scorpio,
and another Taurus figure in this dynamic scenario.
Be firm, but diplomatic. A family member approaches
you on the subject of money for education.

*Monday, April 15 (Moon in Taurus to Gemini 4:55
p.m.)*   The moon in your sign represents your high
cycle—almost effortlessly, you'll be at the right place
at a crucial moment. Circumstances favor your efforts.
You'll know you are winning, and others dub you "the
big winner!" Pisces and Virgo play dominant roles.

Tuesday, April 16 (Moon in Gemini)   On this
Tuesday, you might feel as if you're on an escalator—
you take steps up, then you are once again down.
Strive for balance. You get what you want today. The
key is to obtain what you need. Capricorn and Cancer
figure in this scenario.

Wednesday, April 17 (Moon in Gemini)   Racing
luck—all tracks: post position special—number 8 p.p.
in the first race. Pick six: 8, 2, 1, 5, 3, 7. Watch for
these letters or initials in the names of potential winning horses or jockeys: I and R. Hot daily doubles: 8
and 2, 8 and 5, 3 and 7. Foreign horses or jockeys
from other lands will be in the money.

*Thursday, April 18 (Moon in Gemini to Cancer 1:59
a.m.)*   Time to settle differences within your family.
Get rid of preconceived notions. Make a fresh start in
a new direction. Focus on inventiveness, originality,
daring, and the courage of your convictions. Don't
hold back, or you will lose an opportunity. Leo will
play an important role.

Friday, April 19 (Moon in Cancer)   You could be
at the crossroads, either moving or remaining where

you are. There are close ties that hold; it will not be easy for you to decide to "break away." The moon in its own sign, Cancer, represents relatives who feel you owe them loyalty, if not money.

Saturday, April 20 (Moon in Cancer to Leo 8:19 a.m.)   On this Saturday, expect fun, frolic, games, and a glorious reunion with someone you once loved. Gemini and Sagittarius play leading roles, and could have these letters or initials in their names—C, L, U. Keep abreast of fashion news—you could have something of value to offer the pundits.

Sunday, April 21 (Moon in Leo)   On this Sunday, with the moon in your fourth house of Leo, there will be emotional fireworks at home. You'll be asked to perform certain duties which you will approach as annoyances. Turn on your Taurus charm; be diplomatic and agreeable.

Monday, April 22 (Moon in Leo to Virgo 11:33 a.m.)   The workweek begins with an aura of change and a variety of sensations. Gemini, Virgo, and Sagittarius play significant roles, and could have these letters or initials in their names: E, N, W. Try on bright, colorful clothing—emerge from any emotional shell.

Tuesday, April 23 (Moon in Virgo)   You will be subject to "loving criticism." A Virgo declares, "I would not say these things to you or make suggestions, unless I felt really close!" Focus on your home, family, financial security, and a design which could win you an award.

Wednesday, April 24 (Moon in Virgo to Libra 12:20 p.m.)   Lucky lottery: 6, 7, 13, 14, 18, 51. You exude an aura of sensuality, personal magnetism, and sex appeal. Don't break too many hearts! The numerical cycle 7 equates to Neptune—be careful of deception, self or otherwise. Pisces plays a role.

Thursday, April 25 (Moon in Libra) You get things done in your own way. That could be the key. Stick to your own style and methods. A reward is due; you get recognition that "escaped" you in previous attempts. Capricorn and Cancer will be at the forefront, making this one of your most productive days.

Friday, April 26 (Moon in Libra to Scorpio 12:15 p.m.) Your cycle is complete. You could be asked to go overseas in search for a representative for your talents or products. A relationship has progressed to the point of whether to begin anew or to end it. Aries and Libra figure in this dramatic scenario.

Saturday, April 27 (Moon in Scorpio) The full moon in your seventh house, Scorpio, relates to partnership, cooperative efforts, and having an argument before reaching terms. The emphasis is on marriage and promises that are shattered. The question of a fresh start in a new direction will be settled. Have luck with number 1.

Sunday, April 28 (Moon in Scorpio to Sagittarius 1:13 p.m.) What you felt had been long settled could again be open to question. A Cancer asserts, "I never really gave the question any serious thought, and it should be put up for grabs once again!" Capricorn also gets into the swing of things, declaring, "I'm willing to try again!"

Monday, April 29 (Moon in Sagittarius) Your interest in the occult results in criticism from those who feel you are playing with a stacked deck. This scenario features fun, frolic, and curiosity. This is the time to explore and discover—do it on your own, if necessary. Have luck with number 3.

Tuesday, April 30 (Moon in Sagittarius to Capricorn 5:02 p.m.) Check the details. Instructions could be garbled. Make sure they are clearly understood. Leo, Scorpio and another Taurus figure in this dramatic scenario. On this last day of April, do your best to clarify your position. A computer could be out of order—do something about it!

MAY 2002

Wednesday, May 1 (Moon in Capricorn)   You will have reason to celebrate tonight. With the moon in your ninth house, you will hear news about the possible representation of your product or talent overseas. You know what you want and need, so don't let others talk you out of it. Your lucky number is 3.

Thursday, May 2 (Moon in Capricorn)   The accent is on publishing reviews, and letting others know where you stand and why. Overcome distance and language barriers. A Scorpio who does not always agree could become your ally. If you are thorough when proofreading, embarrassing mistakes will be discovered, and you'll get credit for finding them.

Friday, May 3 (Moon in Capricorn to Aquarius 12:44 a.m.)   Within 24 hours, your career or business gets a positive boost. It is a matter of cycles. The moon will be in Aquarius, your tenth house, that section of your horoscope relating to promotion, success in business, and career. A flirtation gets going!

Saturday, May 4 (Moon in Aquarius)   This could be a "wild" Saturday, and the key words are "could be." Maintain your emotional equilibrium and your sanity! Some people, especially members of the opposite sex, are "leading you on." Know when to say, "I will not go farther. Enough is enough!" Libra is involved.

Sunday, May 5 (Moon in Aquarius to Pisces 11:45 a.m.) Your spiritual values surface. Don't block the way. Play the waiting game. Time is on your side. Define terms, and outline boundaries. Avoid self-deception. See people as they are, not merely as you wish they could be. Pisces plays the top role.

Monday, May 6 (Moon in Pisces) On this Monday, you will be "up and at 'em!" A business meeting is called, and your attendance is required. Show you are in the game, not merely a space-sitter. The moon in Pisces represents your eleventh house—this, in turn, indicates that your wishes will be fulfilled.

Tuesday, May 7 (Moon in Pisces) Finish what you start. Ask for what you need, as well as what you might like. With the moon in your eleventh house, this could be the start of a "winning streak." Elements of timing and luck ride with you. Aries and Libra play quixotic roles.

Wednesday, May 8 (Moon in Pisces to Aries 12:21 a.m.) Lucky lottery: 1, 8, 16, 18, 25, 34. Strike while the iron is hot. Make a fresh start. Emphasize independence of thought and action. You might be advised to "slow down" by people you trust—they could be sincere and trustworthy, but also lacking pertinent information.

Thursday, May 9 (Moon in Aries) A secret meeting is taking place, perhaps even as you read these words! Someone who has it in for you is going to learn a bitter lesson. Defend your position. Be sure people know you are willing to fight if the cause is right. A Cancer is involved.

Friday, May 10 (Moon in Aries to Taurus 12:30 p.m.) On this Friday, what had been held back will be released. A secret meeting turns out favorably for you. A conference will be scheduled. You'll be invited to participate fully. Gemini and Sagittarius figure in this dramatic scenario, and have these initials in their names: C, L, U.

Saturday, May 11 (Moon in Taurus)   Your cycle is high. The moon in your sign equates to creative juices, initiative, originality, and sex appeal. Move ahead. Don't wait for others. Heed your instincts and your heart. The spotlight is on your personality, and the ability to gain the confidence of "important people."

Sunday, May 12 (Moon in Taurus to Gemini 11:02 p.m.)   Your numerical cycle is 5, which equates to Mercury and blends favorably with your natal Venus. The new moon in Taurus means imprint your personal style; do not follow others. You are going places, know it, and act as if aware of it. Virgo plays a role.

Monday, May 13 (Moon in Gemini)   Focus on favorable investments, and additional knowledge about the stock market. Your cycle continues high, so act boldly, take the initiative, and express original thinking. Highlight your personal magnetism, and an aura of sensuality and sex appeal. Music is involved.

Tuesday, May 14 (Moon in Gemini)   You will be provided with various propositions or opportunities. Be selective; choose the best. Insist on answers to questions, not evasions. A family member confides that deception was involved in a recent transaction. Do not point the accusing finger!

Wednesday, May 15 (Moon in Gemini to Cancer 7:32 a.m.)   Racing luck—all tracks: post position special—number 8 p.p. in the ninth race. Pick six: 2, 6, 4, 4, 3, 1. Watch for these letters or initials in the names of potential winning horses or jockeys: H, Q, Z. Hot daily doubles: 2 and 6, 4 and 4, 3 and 1. Favorites will be in the money. Capricorn jockeys win photo finishes.

Thursday, May 16 (Moon in Cancer)   A relative relieves you of a burden you should never have assumed in the first place. Look into the possibility of a journey that could take you to a foreign land. Finish what you start; open lines of communication. Aries will play a significant role.

Friday, May 17 (Moon in Cancer to Leo 1:50 p.m.)   Emphasize the original approach. Stick to your own style. Thank well-wishers, without being obsequious. Avoid heavy lifting, if possible. Leo and Aquarius play "sensational" roles and will prove to be valuable allies. Your lucky number is 1.

Saturday, May 18 (Moon in Leo)   Choose what is new, but remember that all that glitters is not gold. A different kind of love is on the horizon. Focus on direction, motivation, and numerous proposals that include business and marriage. A Cancer will be involved.

Sunday, May 19 (Moon in Leo to Virgo 6:00 p.m.)   An excellent day for relaxation, for being quiet within. Enjoy the comforts of home. Reestablish communication with a family member who means much to you. Some dark spots in your home life will receive the benefit of more understanding. A Sagittarian plays a role.

Monday, May 20 (Moon in Virgo)   This starts out as a "dreary Monday." In no time, however, you have things to do and people to meet. You might be saying, "If this is dreary, I'd hate to spend a similar Monday that is lively!" Leo, Scorpio, and another Taurus figure in this scenario.

Tuesday, May 21 (Moon in Virgo to Libra 8:17 p.m.)
Get ready for change, travel, and a variety of experiences and sensations. The Virgo moon means your creative juices stir—you find an outlet and exude sex appeal. Part of this scenario will include entertainment, children, and submission of a format to the powers that be.

Wednesday, May 22 (Moon in Libra)   Lucky lottery: 6, 7, 12, 13, 18, 22. Attention revolves around where you live and family relationships. To make the most of this day, be diplomatic and sensitive to sound. There are music and flowers, you will muse, "This is what I call enjoying life!"

Thursday, May 23 (Moon in Libra to Scorpio (9:37 p.m.)   On this Thursday, you might be doing a "balancing act." You'll ask yourself, "Should I give up this in order to gain that?" Maintain your emotional equilibrium. Avoid going to extremes. Pisces and Virgo are "destined" to play major roles in your life today.

Friday, May 24 (Moon in Scorpio)   A clash of ideas is featured. You'll be stimulated and encouraged by your skill in defending your position. Higher-ups say among themselves that you belong with them, promoted and provided with more financial security. Capricorn plays a top role.

Saturday, May 25 (Moon in Scorpio to Sagittarius 11:21 p.m.)   A relationship smolders, but can't quite catch fire. You are capable now of predicting the future and making it come true. What was missing will be located. Aries and Libra will play outstanding roles, and have these initials in their names: I and R. Your lucky number is 9.

Sunday, May 26 (Moon in Sagittarius) On this Sunday, you feel invigorated and optimistic. The full moon is in Sagittarius, your eighth house. This means enlightenment in areas previously shrouded in mystery. Make a fresh start. Let people know your ideas are original, dynamic, and creative.

Monday, May 27 (Moon in Sagittarius) Questions continue to loom large concerning public appearances, cooperative efforts, your partnership, and marital status. A Cancer extends an invitation to dinner—accept, and plan on bringing fine wine. Capricorn plays an outstanding role in becoming your valuable ally.

Tuesday, May 28 (Moon in Sagittarius to Capricorn 2:54 a.m.) Don't give in to those who say, "Tell us everything, and we will keep it secret." Remember that discretion is the better part of valor. Gemini and Sagittarius will play outstanding roles. Hold back. Don't give in to temptation.

Wednesday, May 29 (Moon in Capricorn) Lucky lottery: 1, 5, 8, 10, 29, 40. Open lines of communication—a Capricorn wants to tell you something of significance. Leo and another Taurus are also part of this exciting scenario. You will overcome obstacles concerning distance and language.

Thursday, May 30 (Moon in Capricorn to Aquarius 9:35 a.m.) Focus on travel, and giving special study to a "different language." A flirtation is becoming more expensive and embarrassing than you originally anticipated. Gemini, Virgo, and Sagittarius play leading roles, and could have these letters or initials in their names—E, N, W.

Friday, May 31 (Moon in Aquarius) You exude personal magnetism, and an aura of sensuality and sex appeal. What was supposed to be confidential will be revealed for all the world to see. Assume a leadership role. Help those who are helpless. Get your ideas on paper; write and read.

JUNE 2002

Saturday, June 1 (Moon in Aquarius to Pisces 7:36 p.m.) It's your kind of day, although at first it seems the opposite. Focus on details, inner strength, and a willingness to overcome the odds. In matters of speculation, stick with number 4. Basic issues need further consideration. You will be tested and challenged, but you will not be found wanting.

Sunday, June 2 (Moon in Pisces) Keep your plans flexible. Some people, including Gemini and Pisces, would like to see you fail. Disappoint them! Have alternatives at hand. Someone of the opposite sex is intrigued and is bold enough to say so. Read, write, and learn through the process of teaching others.

Monday, June 3 (Moon in Pisces) On this Monday, you will be murmuring, "Home sweet home!" Many things and persons you took for granted will hold new meaning for you. A discussion with your parents proves fruitful and knocks down barriers. Libra, Scorpio, and another Taurus edge their way into this scenario.

Tuesday, June 4 (Moon in Pisces to Aries 7:50 a.m.) Your opinion regarding a Pisces is subject to change. The moon is leaving Pisces, and what had clouded your relationship will no longer exist. Extend a hand of friendship—you won't be sorry. Virgo will also play a dramatic role.

Wednesday, June 5 (Moon in Aries) Focus on secret information, hospitals, and the theater. The numerical cycle is 8, which responds to Saturn. This day for you will feature promotion, production, and extra responsibility. Cancer and Capricorn play feature roles. Lucky lottery: 1, 5, 8, 9 10, 50.

Thursday, June 6 (Moon in Aries to Taurus 8:05 p.m.) On this Thursday, you anticipate the moods of those who oppose you. You will be ahead of the game. Family members support your cause, which elevates your morale. Leo, Scorpio, and another Taurus figure in this dynamic scenario. Have luck with number 9.

Friday, June 7 (Moon in Taurus)   Strive for truth. Discard preconceived notions. Your cycle is moving up, so circumstances will soon turn in your favor. Be creative and selective, and assert your views in an original, dynamic way. Some people ask, "Do you always know what will happen in advance?"

Saturday, June 8 (Moon in Taurus)   The moon is in your sign, and your numerical cycle is 2—you obtain bargains in connection with your home and family. An excellent dinner tonight could be prepared by someone born under Cancer. The focus is on your personality, personal magnetism, and aura of sensuality and sex appeal.

Sunday, June 9 (Moon in Taurus to Gemini 6:28 a.m.) A very special Sunday! Your cycle is high. Therefore, you win friends and gain approval of those you admire and respect. Don't attempt to please everyone all the time—that would be a sure way to madness. Gemini and Sagittarius will be part in this scenario in a positive way.

Monday, June 10 (Moon in Gemini)   On this Monday, you'll be concerned with buying and selling. Your sales ability will reach new heights. Leo, Scorpio, and another Taurus figure prominently. Many "familiar" things occur. You ask, "Could this be déjà vu?" People watch as you solve a mathematical problem.

Tuesday, June 11 (Moon in Gemini to Cancer 2:13 p.m.) A breakthrough is indicated. This means more money for you. People express confidence by adding to your funding. The pressure is on. Others rely on you. You are up to it. The numerical cycle is 5, which equates to Mercury. That planet blends with your Venus, and you get all the "good things" you have desired.

Wednesday, June 12 (Moon in Cancer) Racing luck—all tracks: post position special—number 2 p.p. in the fourth race. Pick six: 2, 4, 6, 2, 4, 4. Watch for these letters or initials in the names potential winning horses or jockeys: F, O, X. Hot daily doubles: 2 and 4, 3 and 6, 4 and 8. Taurus and Libra jockeys win photo finishes.

Thursday, June 13 (Moon in Cancer to Leo 7:38 p.m.) Confusion exists in connection with appointments, relatives, and social obligations. The remedy is to do one thing at a time, to enjoy what you do and do not try to please everyone. Gemini and Sagittarius play major roles, and have these letters in their names: C, L, U.

Friday, June 14 (Moon in Leo) There's good news financially, but not-so-good in connection with pressure, responsibility, and overtime. Capricorn and Cancer play important roles and are likely to have these letters or initials in their names: H, Q, Z. Accept a challenge!

Saturday, June 15 (Moon in Leo to Virgo 11:22 p.m.) On this Saturday, your interests are broadened. Look beyond the immediate. Be willing to take a chance on creativity and romance. Shake off the tendency to adhere to preconceived notions. Be open-minded to a different language and different cultures. Your lucky number is 9.

Sunday, June 16 (Moon in Virgo)   You will be re-assured that your love is not unrequited. The moon is in your fifth house, so you exude personal magnetism, and an aura of sensuality and sex appeal. On this Sunday night, rest easy in the knowledge that indeed you are loved.

Monday, June 17 (Moon in Virgo)   Questions relating to cooperative efforts, partnership, and marriage will loom large. Answer what you feel you are able to. Don't become a victim of frustration. With today's Virgo moon, you will be ready for change, travel, and variety.

Tuesday, June 18 (Moon in Virgo to Libra 2:10 a.m.)   Entertain children, and put on a "happy face." The more joy you give others today, the more joy you will feel within. Gemini and Sagittarius play meaningful roles and could have these letters or initials in their names: C, L, U. Have luck with number 3.

Wednesday, June 19 (Moon in Libra)   Lucky lottery: 4, 7, 11, 21, 35, 36. Attend to practical matters; face challenges and obstacles. You have everything you need in order to win—thus, make this a "winning day." Leo, Scorpio, and another Taurus play major roles, and have these letters in their names: D, M, V.

Thursday, June 20 (Moon in Libra to Scorpio 4:41 a.m.)   Racing luck—all tracks: post position special—number 3 p.p. in the second race. Pick six: 1, 3, 5, 2, 2, 4. Watch for these letters or initials in the names of potential winning horses or jockeys: E, N, W. Hot daily doubles: 1 and 3, 2 and 4, 3 and 5. Speed horses get out in front and will be in the money.

Friday, June 21 (Moon in Scorpio)   Attention revolves around your home, family, and insurance. What you did two months ago might be coming back to haunt you. Do not attempt to play "invisible man." You must face the music, then resolve to protect yourself in the future at close quarters. Libra figures in this scenario.

Saturday, June 22 (Moon in Scorpio to Sagittarius 7:41 a.m.)   You go through a period of introspection on this Saturday. The moon is in Scorpio, your seventh house, that section of your horoscope depicting a clash of ideas, partnership, and marriage. Pisces and Virgo play top roles, and some have these initials in their names: G, P, Y.

Sunday, June 23 (Moon in Sagittarius)   Meditation this Sunday will prove of great benefit. The numerical cycle is 8, which equates to Saturn and blends with Venus, your ruling planet. Cold water is splashed on some of your romantic illusions, but in the long run, this will prove healthy.

Monday, June 24 (Moon in Sagittarius to Capricorn 12:01 p.m.)   The full moon is in Sagittarius in your eighth house. This means your interests wander from the practical such as accounting procedures to the mantic arts and sciences that include astrology and numerology. Aries and Libra play top roles, and have these letters or initials in their names—I and R.

Tuesday, June 25 (Moon in Capricorn)   The subject of travel, foreign lands, philosophy, and theology will dominate today's scenario. Allow yourself to have a fresh point of view. Toss aside preconceived notions. Realize that indeed, many possibilities exist. Do not close the doors of opportunity. Leo plays a role.

Wednesday, June 26 (Moon in Capricorn to Aquarius 6:35 p.m.)   Your numerical cycle is 2, which equates to the moon—the moon and your Venus make quite a combination! Your personality will be pleasing; you can achieve almost anything via your powers of persuasion. Ask for what you need, as well as for luxuries.

Thursday, June 27 (Moon in Aquarius)   Today can be called your "lucky day." Your numerical cycle 3 equates to Jupiter, the planet of luck. With the combination of Jupiter and Venus, you accomplish things that ordinarily appear to be impossible. You will receive compliments on your "lovemaking"!

Friday, June 28 (Moon in Aquarius)   Business and career areas could dominate—people look upon you now with new respect. On this Friday push ahead with plans that could, if carried out successfully, make you rich and famous! Leo, Scorpio, and another Taurus figure prominently.

Saturday, June 29 (Moon in Aquarius to Pisces 4:02 a.m.)   Focus on a variety of sensations and experiences. Within 24 hours you will have things "your way." Don't force issues; be willing to wait and it is only a short wait. Get ready for surprise invitations to social affairs. You might be startled by the attention given to you by a glamorous individual.

Sunday, June 30 (Moon in Pisces)   On this last day of June, attention revolves around your family, your home, and your ability to win friends and influence people. When it comes to fund-raising, you will be unbeatable. Your popularity is on the rise, and those who counted you out will be "eating crow." Another Taurus is involved.

JULY 2002

Monday, July 1 (Moon in Pisces to Aries 3:48 p.m.)   An element of luck is present. The moon is in your eleventh house. Be near water, if possible. Gemini, Virgo, and Sagittarius play leading roles, and have these letters or initials in their names: E, N, W.

You'll be asked to analyze the value of a product—be objective; tell the truth as you see it.

Tuesday, July 2 (Moon in Aries)   Attention revolves around your family, tradition, insurance rates, and buying and selling property. You win, if diplomatic. Obviously, it will not pay to force issues. Libra, Scorpio, and another Taurus figure in today's exciting scenario—turn on the charm!

Wednesday, July 3 (Moon in Aries)   Lucky lottery: 3, 7, 9, 16, 18, 25. With the moon in Aries, your twelfth house is activated. What had been held back will be revealed—you will feel aggressive about it, at least for a short time. Later, humor hits home and everybody will be laughing.

Thursday, July 4 (Moon in Aries to Taurus 4:15 a.m.) What a holiday! Your cycle is moving up. You will say and do the "right thing." Some people will be envious, but you cannot please everyone. Trying to make everybody happy is a sure road to madness. Capricorn and Cancer play amazing roles. Your lucky number is 8.

Friday, July 5 (Moon in Taurus)   Reach beyond the immediate. Make personal appearances wearing shades of blue. Today, you will be lucky in money and love! You'll exude personal magnetism, and an aura of sensuality and sex appeal. Aries and Libra play fascinating roles, and have these letters in their names: I and R.

Saturday, July 6 (Moon in Taurus to Gemini 2:59 p.m.)   Take the initiative—imprint your style; do not follow others. The numerical cycle 1 equates to the sun, which blends with Venus, your ruling planet. You could be helplessly, madly in love. Don't fight the feeling! Leo stands out, playing a dramatic role.

Sunday, July 7 (Moon in Gemini) Questions loom large about cooperative efforts, service to the city, partnership, and marriage. Cancer and Capricorn play outstanding roles, and could have these initials in their names: B, K, T. A Cancer-born sibling makes a special request—fulfill it, if possible.

Monday, July 8 (Moon in Gemini to Cancer 10:34 p.m.) Forces tend to be scattered, so take aim at your objective. An aura of fun and frolic dominates—spread the message of "joy of learning." Gemini and Sagittarius figure in this exciting scenario. Keep resolutions about exercise, diet, and nutrition.

Tuesday, July 9 (Moon in Cancer) The moon leaves Gemini within 24 hours. The emphasis then will be on your third house, meaning there will be much activity in connection with relatives, short trips, and visits. Attend to routine matters. Be thorough in reading proofs. You may not like little things, but they are necessary.

Wednesday, July 10 (Moon in Cancer to Leo 3:06 a.m.) Racing luck—all tracks: post position special—number 3 p.p. in the second race. Pick six: 2, 3, 4, 8, 5, 7. Be alert for these letters or initials in the names of potential winning horses or jockeys: E, N, W. Hot daily doubles: 2 and 3, 1 and 1, 5 and 6. Speed horses get out in front and win.

Thursday, July 11 (Moon in Leo) You could change your residence or marital status today. Money comes your way. You might be asking, "Where is happiness?" Answer: It is coming if you so permit! An excellent day for beautifying your surroundings, remodeling, and making a neighborly gesture to someone who is temporarily confined to home.

Friday, July 12 (Moon in Leo)   Good for meditation; excellent for evaluating your property. Put a dash of color in designs. Wear shades of red. Make personal appearances. A mysterious Pisces comes into your life—be gracious, not obsequious. Check accounting procedures. Your computer could go "out of whack."

Saturday, July 13 (Moon in Leo to Virgo 5:39 a.m.)   This could be your power play day! You gain a foothold toward your main objective. An important person dispatches a message, and wants to see you. Do not go hat in hand—be confident, dynamic, and eager. Capricorn and Cancer figure in this scenario. Have luck with number 8.

Sunday, July 14 (Moon in Virgo)   Your spiritual experience dominates the moon in Virgo, your fifth house, means creative juices stir. You exude personal magnetism, and an aura of sensuality and sex appeal. Don't break too many hearts—at the very least, offer tea and sympathy.

Monday, July 15 (Moon in Virgo to Libra 7:38 a.m.) The current cycle denotes energy, drive, sensuality, creativity, and sex appeal. Leo and Aquarius play dramatic roles, and could have these letters or initials in their names: A, S, J. Make a fresh start in a new direction; exercise independence of thought and action.

Tuesday, July 16 (Moon in Libra)   What was supposedly a prank should be taken seriously. Focus on cooperative efforts, an offer of partnership, and marital status. Cancer and Capricorn figure in this scenario, and could have these letters or initials in their names: B, K, T. Be near water!

Wednesday, July 17 (Moon in Libra to Scorpio 10:12 a.m.)   Test, challenge, explore, and discover. Very good for advertising, publishing, and becoming aware of what people want to view and read. Gemini and Sagittarius figure in this scenario, and have these letters in their names: C, L, U. Lucky lottery: 3, 4, 12, 37, 50, 51.

Thursday, July 18 (Moon in Scorpio)   The Scorpio moon is in your seventh house. The spotlight is on partnership, public relations, legal affairs, your reputation, and marital status. Expect and be ready for a "clash of ideas." A Scorpio adversary will eventually become your ally. Know it and proceed accordingly.

Friday, July 19 (Moon in Scorpio to Sagittarius 2:01 p.m.)   On this Friday, get ready for change, travel, and a variety of sensations. Someone of the opposite sex confides, "You attract me very much, and I confess that at times I can hardly keep my hands off you!" Read, write, and learn by teaching. Virgo plays a top role.

Saturday, July 20 (Moon in Sagittarius)   Your general health report is good. A coworker who had been rambunctious decides to cooperate and offers an apology. Be gracious in accepting. Be sure that your actions do not betray a feeling of resentment. Libra is featured. Lucky lottery: 6, 12, 18, 32, 33, 48.

Sunday, July 21 (Moon in Sagittarius to Capricorn 7:27 p.m.)   This Sunday is very good for meditating, and for making decisions that involve travel overseas. People respect your opinions; many count on you to dispense wisdom. There is pressure, but you are up to it. Pisces and Virgo play unusual roles, and have these initials in their names: G, P, Y.

Monday, July 22 (Moon in Capricorn)   The emphasis is on your career, business, production, and promotion. A long-distance communication verifies your views—transform the abstract into a working model. You are going places, and today you know it for sure. Capricorn and Cancer play fascinating roles.

Tuesday, July 23 (Moon in Capricorn)   Finish what you start. Someone in authority offers praise and promises of promotion. On this kind of day, you can expect love and money. The ninth house influence means spiritual values surface, so welcome them! Aries and Libra play outstanding roles.

Wednesday, July 24 (Moon in Capricorn to Aquarius 2:39 a.m.)   The full moon in Aquarius equates to your career or the fulfillment of a major objective. You can combine romance with work. But be careful of "prying eyes"! Basically your position is strong, and you will have assurance that you soon will be getting more money. Have luck with number 1.

Thursday, July 25 (Moon in Aquarius)   You will be asked direct questions about your intentions involving partnership and marriage. The spotlight is on your home, family, insurance, and the ability to make a gesture of reconciliation. Remember that pride does go before a fall. A Cancer is involved.

Friday, July 26 (Moon in Aquarius to Pisces 12:04 p.m.)   Within 24 hours, your popularity will be on the rise. Prepare now for what you want, desire, and require. You are due to win friends and influence people, some of whom urge you to try for political office. Gemini and Sagittarius will play outstanding roles.

Saturday, July 27 (Moon in Pisces)   On this Saturday, the moon in Pisces will be in your eleventh house. You learn the difference between generosity and extravagance. Today, you are an excellent fund-raiser. You can expect to have luck in matters of speculation. Stick with number 4 for best results.

Sunday, July 28 (Moon in Pisces to Aries 11:38 p.m.) Expect a largess of love, money, and health. You deserve it, so act as if you're aware of it and carry yourself accordingly. In matters of speculation, stick with number 5. Gemini, Virgo, and Sagittarius play top roles, and have these letters or initials in their names: E, N, W.

Monday, July 29 (Moon in Aries)   Remember everything has a limit, so don't expect good luck, praise, and romance to last forever. A domestic adjustment is necessary; be willing to change the appearance of your home. Vow to make a partnership or marriage work. Libra, Aries, and another Taurus figure in this complex scenario.

Tuesday, July 30 (Moon in Aries)   On this Tuesday, with the moon in Aries, you learn secrets, and should visit someone temporarily confined to home or hospital. Remove fire hazards. Avoid arguing with an Aries, who could be high-principled but lacking in basic information. Pisces and Virgo are also in this picture.

Wednesday, July 31 (Moon in Aries to Taurus 12:15 p.m.)   On this last day of July, you finalize activities connected with production, promotion, and career. The moon remains in Aries this morning, so it will be very difficult to keep confidential information secret. Know it, and prepare an alternative. Have luck with number 8.

AUGUST 2002

Thursday, August 1 (Moon in Taurus)   On this first day of August, your cycle is high—you will be at the right place at a crucial moment almost effortlessly. Attention revolves around the protection of your family, insurance payments, and possible change of residence, marital status, or both.

Friday, August 2 (Moon in Taurus to Gemini 11:44 p.m.)   Your cycle continues high, so play the waiting game. The numerical cycle 7, which equals Neptune, blends with your Venus significator. Be skeptical about "sweet talk." See people, places, and relationships as they are, not merely as you wish they could be.

Saturday, August 3 (Moon in Gemini)   Financial pressure is relieved. You win a dispute over money. This could be your power play day—Saturn figures prominently, which means there is serious consideration about your bank account. You will be exuding personal magnetism and sex appeal. Have luck with number 8.

Sunday, August 4 (Moon in Gemini)   Your financial status continues to dominate. You will find you have more allies than you anticipated. Look beyond the immediate; predict the future and make it come true. Aries and Libra play significant roles, and have these letters in their names—I and R.

Monday, August 5 (Moon in Gemini to Cancer 8:00 a.m.)   Make a fresh start in a new direction. Let people know you intend to hold tight to your principles. Someone of the opposite sex will be bold enough to tell you, "I have always been attracted to you, and I can hardly keep my hands off you!" Leo is represented.

Tuesday, August 6 (Moon in Cancer)   Attention revolves around cooperative efforts and public relations. A short trip is necessary, if legal documents are to be recovered. Capricorn and Cancer figure prominently, and could have these letters or initials in their names—B, K, T.

Wednesday, August 7 (Moon in Cancer to Leo 12:25 p.m.) Racing luck—all tracks: post position special—number 3 p.p. in the third race. Pick six: 2, 5, 3, 7, 2, 1. Look for these letters or initials in the names of potential winning horses or jockeys: C, L, U. Hot daily doubles: 2 and 5, 1 and 3, 3 and 3. Sagittarian jockeys will have "racing luck."

Thursday, August 8 (Moon in Leo) The new moon in Leo, your fourth house, indicates a different kind of arrangement in connection with buying and selling property. Advertise and promote. Don't be bullied by those who claim to have authority but lack credentials. Scorpio is involved.

Friday, August 9 (Moon in Leo to Virgo 2:02 p.m.) The numerical cycle 5 adds up to Mercury, which means your mind is revved up and your ideas will pay dividends. Keep plans flexible. Be ready for change, travel, and a variety of experiences. Gemini, Virgo, and Sagittarius will play significant roles.

Saturday, August 10 (Moon in Virgo) The moon in Virgo, your fifth house, represents children, creativity, and the ability to win your way with the opposite sex. Attention will revolve around your home and family. There will be music in your life tonight. Dance to your own tune; maintain your personal rhythm. Have luck with number 6.

Sunday, August 11 (Moon in Virgo to Libra 2:37 p.m.) Your spiritual values surface. Young persons look to you as a role model. In matters of speculation, stick with number 7. See people, places, and relationships as they exist—avoid any tendency toward self-deception. Pisces will play a mysterious role.

Monday August 12 (Moon in Libra) Get things done. Catch up with past obligations. Capricorn and

Cancer will play important roles and could have these letters or initials in their names—H, Q, Z. A coworker could become your friend, and share collections and hobbies. Give a smile to get a smile.

Tuesday, August 13 (Moon in Libra to Scorpio 4:00 p.m.)   What you thought had run its course will again be alive and kicking. Take seriously an offer to travel, perhaps overseas. You no longer will be playing "second fiddle." Aries and Libra are in this scenario, and have these letters or initials in their names—I and R.

Wednesday, August 14 (Moon in Scorpio)   Lucky lottery: 1, 12, 13, 18, 19, 29. A new love will replace a recent "breakup." Imprint style, dance to your own tune, and be creatively selfish. Leo will play an outstanding role and could become your valuable ally. An Aquarian is also in the picture.

Thursday, August 15 (Moon in Scorpio to Sagittarius 7:25 p.m.)   You perceive what could be. Keep your dream. Don't confide in the "wrong people." Someone who took credit for your efforts will confess. This could be termed your "vindication day." Questions arise about cooperative efforts, partnership, and marital status.

Friday, August 16 (Moon in Sagittarius)   Display humor; laugh at your own foibles. Highlight versatility and diversity, and give full play to your intellectual curiosity. Much of what will happen is currently in the planning stage. Gemini and Sagittarius play unusual roles, and have these initials in their names: C, L, U.

Saturday, August 17 (Moon in Sagittarius)   Check accounting procedures. Have everything clear in your mind. A key computer might have gone haywire. Know it, and demand a review of your accounts. What had been a mystery will be cleared up—to your advantage. The question of faithfulness will loom large.

Sunday, August 18 (Moon in Sagittarius to Capricorn 1:15 a.m.) Within 24 hours, your creative skills will be most pronounced. If you can wait, you win. Otherwise, you lose momentum and the "game." Questions about the occult will be part of this scenario. Gemini, Virgo, and Sagittarius are in the picture.

Monday, August 19 (Moon in Capricorn) The moon in Capricorn represents your ninth house—and places emphasis on spiritual values, travel, and the ability to "predict the future." Don't confide, confess, or ask too many questions. You will be tested and challenged. You will come out on top in a "sensational way."

Tuesday, August 20 (Moon in Capricorn to Aquarius 9:16 a.m.) Meditate. The answers you seek are within. You will come up with a plan of action. Your life will be more meaningful. Pisces and Virgo play outstanding roles, and will have these letters or initials in their names: G, P, Y. Take care in traffic!

Wednesday, August 21 (Moon in Aquarius) The emphasis is on business, career, promotion, and production, having more responsibility and gaining financially. On a personal level, protect yourself in emotional clinches. Demand promises in writing. Someone in a position of authority communicates and requests, "I would like very much to have a talk with you!"

Thursday, August 22 (Moon in Aquarius to Pisces 7:10 p.m.) The full moon in Aquarius represents your tenth house, which means completion of a business transaction. All of this is unusual, and if you confide in too many people, you will get discouraged. An airplane flight may be necessary in order to obtain the legal green light.

Friday, August 23 (Moon in Pisces)   Racing luck—all tracks: post position special—number 7 p.p. in the third race. Pick six: 2, 4, 7, 5, 8, 1. Watch for these letters and initials in the names of potential winning horses or jockeys: A, S, J. Hot daily doubles: 2 and 4, 1 and 7, 3 and 8. Leo jockeys will win photo finishes.

Saturday, August 24 (Moon in Pisces)   Your sense of direction returns. You will make a major decision in connection with cooperative efforts, partnership, and marriage. Someone wants to deceive you—know it and protect yourself in emotional clinches. Lucky lottery: 3, 9, 12, 16, 18, 34.

Sunday, August 25 (Moon in Pisces to Aries 6:47 a.m.)   You will have reason to celebrate tonight— within 24 hours, a secret is revealed which will work in your favor. Visit a friend who is temporarily confined to home or hospital. Make arrangements to speak well of each other. A Sagittarian is involved.

Monday, August 26 (Moon in Aries)   The moon in Aries relates to your twelfth house—covers institutions, hospitals, theaters, and intimate secrets. Face the music, and you will be fortunate. If you attempt to cover up, you lose in the court of public opinion. Another Taurus is involved.

Tuesday, August 27 (Moon in Aries to Taurus 7:30 p.m.)   Welcome changes occur—you will know that cycle is moving up, and by facing facts and being discreet, you will be victorious. The "scare" is over—a health report is good, and from now on, you will pay attention to resolutions relating to exercise and nutrition.

Wednesday, August 28 (Moon in Taurus) Lucky lottery: 5, 6, 12, 18, 22, 28. Attention revolves around security, home, mortgage payments, and a pleasant financial surprise. Libra, Scorpio, and another Taurus figure in this scenario, and have these letters or initials in their names—F, O, X.

Thursday, August 29 (Moon in Taurus) Your cycle moves up; circumstances turn in your favor. Be selective; insist on quality. Accept the challenge of being at the right place at the right time. Focus on personal magnetism, sensuality, creativity, and sex appeal. Don't break too many hearts!

Friday, August 30 (Moon in Taurus to Gemini 7:44 a.m.) Strike while the iron is hot! The moon is leaving your sign, so ask for what you need, as well as for what you desire. Stress wisdom and maturity, and do not be a "selfish lover." A Cancer declares, "I want and need you!" Have luck with number 8.

Saturday, August 31 (Moon in Gemini) On this Saturday, your ability to perceive future trends and cycles will surface. Give time to the study of language and cultures of people in different lands. Your prestige is on the upswing—you are more important to more people than you might anticipate. Aries is represented.

SEPTEMBER 2002

Sunday, September 1 (Moon in Gemini to Cancer 5:13 p.m.) On this Sunday, an interest in theology will surface. Be quiet within. Find a place where you can meditate. You are a spiritual person, even if you don't "broadcast it." See people and places as they are, not merely as you wish they could be.

Monday, September 2 (Moon in Cancer) On this second day of the month, you have more responsibility and a chance for bigger financial rewards. A relationship is intense, and could get too hot not to cool down. Be practical enough to protect your interests, and to get credit for work done.

Tuesday, September 3 (Moon in Cancer to Leo 10:34 p.m.) A relative makes a gesture of reconciliation—accept it without fanfare. Diversify; make inquiries. If a proposition seems too good to be true, it probably is. Aries and Libra play meaningful roles, and could have these letters or initials in their names—I and R.

Wednesday, September 4 (Moon in Leo) Lucky lottery: 1, 4, 14, 28, 32, 50. Make a fresh start in a new direction. Imprint style; wear bright colors. Don't wait for others; do your own thing and stand by your talent and ideas. Leo and Aquarius figure in today's dramatic scenario, and have these letters in their names—A, S, J.

Thursday, September 5 (Moon in Leo) Face the music! If you continue to put off saying what you mean, you only make it tougher for yourself. The moon in Leo is in your fourth house—this means that previously unattractive areas will receive the benefit of greater light. Cancer plays a role.

Friday, September 6 (Moon in Leo to Virgo 12:14 a.m.) Focus on art, music, and literature—you become more aware of land value, real estate, and where you are going to live. Gemini and Sagittarius play memorable roles, and could have these letters or initials in their names—C, L, U. Have luck with number 3.

Saturday, September 7 (Moon in Virgo to Libra 11:56 p.m.) Your career gets a boost. Don't sell yourself

271

short. Be thorough, count your change, and refuse to be the "fall guy" for anyone. The new moon position highlights basic values. Your personal economy requires attention—food, rent, and other living costs.

Sunday, September 8 (Moon in Libra) You'll be active, even though it is Sunday! People who were "out of touch" suddenly call, visit, and seek your counsel. Make a conservative estimate of what you need and what you intend to do. Gemini, Virgo, and Sagittarius play top roles.

Monday, September 9 (Moon in Libra to Scorpio 9:48 p.m.) There's music in your life. Your voice is emphasized. Use a diplomatic approach to the solution of a problem. The spotlight is on your home, and the necessity for beautification and repairs. Someone of the opposite sex declares, "You sound wonderful—why can't you be this way every day?"

Tuesday, September 10 (Moon in Scorpio) Keep track of time. You will beat the odds, if you're aware of a deadline. Focus on your general health, employment, and sharing interests and hobbies with coworkers. The door is open for a new, meaningful relationship. Pisces and Virgo make you aware of their presence.

Wednesday, September 11 (Moon in Scorpio) The question of marriage or partnership will loom large. Don't neglect public relations; get your message across. If people understand who you are and what you intend to achieve, all will be well. In matters of speculation, stick with number 8. Good luck!

Thursday, September 12 (Moon in Scorpio to Sagittarius 1:44 a.m.) Look beyond the immediate. Perceive potential, but be careful about committing yourself to a legal arrangement. Flaws could be involved, so avoid self-deception. Open lines of communication. Someone in another land wants to contact you. An Aries figures prominently.

Friday, September 13 (Moon in Sagittarius) This is Friday the 13th, but no "bad luck" for you! Make a fresh start in a different direction. Imprint style; do not follow others. Make personal appearances; wear bright colors that include yellow and gold. An Aquarian will set the pace.

Saturday, September 14 (Moon in Sagittarius to Capricorn 6:47 a.m.) A family member suggests changes and seeks your opinion about travel. An excellent day for reading, writing, and teaching. Take note of your dreams. Properly interpreted, they could be guideposts to the future. Focus on direction, motivation, and dealing with a stubborn relative.

Sunday, September 15 (Moon in Capricorn) A burden is lifted. Your financial status is better than you originally anticipated. A lost article will be found. You will be capable of mapping your future. Appreciate what others might say, but do not necessarily believe them. Gemini and Sagittarius figure in this exciting, dramatic scenario.

Monday, September 16 (Moon in Capricorn to Aquarius 2:54 p.m.) The spotlight is on future prospects, language, and dealings with people who live in foreign lands. Leo, Scorpio, and another Taurus play "amazing" roles. You accomplish what others said would be impossible. In matters of speculation, stick with these numbers: 1, 4, 8, 12, 15, 22.

Tuesday, September 17 (Moon in Aquarius) The moon in Aquarius activates your tenth house—this equates to leadership and the ability to "sell your program." Stress originality, creativity, and sex appeal.

What was lost two or three weeks ago will be found. This is reason to celebrate!

Wednesday, September 18 (Moon in Aquarius) The written word is your ally. The Aquarian moon means you should present unorthodox views, while making it crystal clear you are capable of including practical ways. Libra, Scorpio, and another Taurus figure in this puzzling scenario. Have luck with number 6.

Thursday, September 19 (Moon in Aquarius to Pisces 1:17 a.m.) While explaining a message, don't give away secrets. Protect yourself in emotional clinches. An element of deception exists, but it could be self-deception. Follow through on your psychic impressions. If people are skeptical, so be it. Pisces and Virgo are in this picture.

Friday, September 20 (Moon in Pisces) The moon in your eleventh house (Pisces) coincides with your ability to obtain funding for a major project. You win friends and influence people—not everyone will be hypnotized, but important people will be on your side. A Cancer declares, "You've got it! I'm with you!"

Saturday, September 21 (Moon in Pisces to Aries 1:10 p.m.) Racing luck—all tracks: post position special—number 8 p.p. in the first race. Pick six: 8, 4, 3, 1, 6, 2. Look for these letters or initials in the names of potential winning horses or jockeys: I and R. Hot daily doubles: 8 and 4, 3 and 3, 6 and 2. Foreign horses and jockeys will be in the Winner's Circle.

Sunday, September 22 (Moon in Aries) Everything points to a pioneering spirit, originality, a new direction, and the possibility of a new, passionate love. Protect yourself at close quarters. Make sure you know where you are going and why you want to get to that point. Do not follow others!

Monday, September 23 (Moon in Aries)   On this Monday, confer with family members. Be aware of safety measures and insurance to cover mishaps. The spotlight is on cooperative efforts, public relations, and your marital status. A Cancer will play an outstanding role. Dinner tonight is delicious, but exercise restraint!

Tuesday, September 24 (Moon in Aries to Taurus 1:53 a.m.)   Within 24 hours, the moon will be in your sign. This equates to your "high cycle." Circumstances are moving in your favor, so emerge from your emotional shell. Social obligations surface. Be sure others understand you have not deliberately missed appointments.

Wednesday, September 25 (Moon in Taurus)   Lucky lottery: 4, 11, 18, 22, 25, 29. Your cycle is high, so your energy returns, along with your optimism. Be willing to tear down in order to rebuild. Proofreading is necessary: you could uncover a flagrant mistake. Leo, Scorpio, and another Taurus play "fantastic" roles.

Thursday, September 26 (Moon in Taurus to Gemini 2:25 p.m.)   The moon continues in your sign; you exude personal magnetism, optimism, and sex appeal. Some members of the opposite sex tell you that you are very attractive and they have difficulty keeping away from you! A Sagittarian plays an important role.

Friday, September 27 (Moon in Gemini)   Money is involved. Be sure you obtain a guarantee of payment. Your services are valuable—know it, and act as if aware of it. Home decorating and the purchase of objects to beautify your surroundings will be part of this scenario. Libra says, "Let's do it all at once!"

Saturday, September 28 (Moon in Gemini) Count your change! A tendency exists toward wishful thinking, which could cloud your judgment about finances. Define terms, outline boundaries, and listen attentively to a real estate proposition. Time is on your side. You need not rush into anything.

Sunday, September 29 (Moon in Gemini to Cancer 12:59 a.m.) Relatives abound. If anything is needed, just ask a relative. Pick and choose. Capricorn and Cancer figure in today's scenario, and could have these letters or initials in their names: H, Q, Z. Your spiritual adviser suggests that you come to see him.

Monday, September 30 (Moon in Cancer) Trips, ideas, and visits dominate. You will be "on the go." A burden you should not have carried in the first place could be removed—much to your relief and advantage. Travel plans can be solidified—Aries and Libra will be involved.

OCTOBER 2002

Tuesday, October 1 (Moon in Cancer to Leo 7:56 a.m.) On this first day of October, you will be glad to admit, "I'm happy the preponderance of storms is over with." The emphasis is on security, family, insurance, and knowing how best to prepare for the future. Highlight versatility and humor, and decide: "It could have been worse!"

Wednesday October 2 (Moon in Leo) The Leo moon demonstrates a need for additional security. Look beyond the immediate; prepare for a cycle that ends rather abruptly. A Taurus becomes your friend due to a "shared experience." Aries and Libra also figure in this scenario. Your lucky number is 9.

Thursday, October 3 (Moon in Leo to Virgo 10:50 a.m.) Imprint style; stress independence and originality. The completion of a project could be the cause for celebration. The Leo moon stresses innovativeness, creativity, challenge, and children. Leo and Aquarius will play memorable roles, and have these letters or initials in their names: A, S, J.

Friday, October 4 (Moon in Virgo) Test, challenge, and insist on guarantees. Cancer and Capricorn will play admirable roles. Focus on home, security, and the renewal of a construction survey. Use your power of persuasion—keep your guard up! A financial settlement will favor you.

Saturday, October 5 (Moon in Virgo to Libra 10:50 a.m.) You did not expect to celebrate, but good news is received concerning money, payments, and collections. Gemini and Sagittarius play memorable roles, and could have these letters or initials in their names: C, L, U. In matters of speculation, try these numbers: 3, 6, 9.

Sunday, October 6 (Moon in Libra) The new moon in Libra equates to your work program, maintaining emotional equilibrium. Scorpio and another Taurus figure prominently, and could have these letters or initials in their names: D, M, V. Questions arise about legal affairs or marital status.

Monday, October 7 (Moon in Libra to Scorpio 9:57 a.m.) Give logic equal time with a tendency to act on impulse. You are a romantic soul, but don't plunge into something "mysterious." Gemini, Virgo, and Sagittarius will figure prominently, have these letters or initials in their names—E, N, W.

Tuesday, October 8 (Moon in Scorpio) You are not free to act in a reckless way. There are legal implications concerning your partnership or marriage. You'll be surprising yourself, but don't hurt others. Libra, Scorpio, and another Taurus play fascinating roles.

Wednesday, October 9 (Moon in Scorpio to Sagittarius 10:21 a.m.)   See people, places, and relationships as they are, not merely as you wish they could be. With the moon in your seventh house, be very careful about signing legal documents. The spotlight is also on your marital status—take care! A Pisces figures prominently.

Thursday, October 10 (Moon in Sagittarius)   People request that you participate in legal maneuvers. Decline politely, saying, "I cannot be impartial, I have already made up my mind!" Hold back; don't waste "ammunition." You will be vindicated, especially if you practice restraint. Capricorn is involved.

Friday, October 11 (Moon in Sagittarius to Capricorn 1:45 p.m.)   People around you are subtle, temperamental, and do not show their true feelings. Know it, wait and see, and refuse to commit yourself to a specific course of action. Look beyond the immediate. Communicate with someone in a foreign land.

Saturday, October 12 (Moon in Capricorn)   The moon in Capricorn is favorably aspected to your Taurus sun—you could be on the verge of a "love affair." Remain steady; do not fall all over yourself. Leo and Aquarius will play stimulating roles. Lucky lottery: 12, 13, 18, 22, 29, 48.

Sunday, October 13 (Moon in Capricorn to Aquarius 8:51 p.m.)   On this Sunday, there will be a family reunion. A Cancer who had been cool toward you will suddenly change. You will find yourself in the arms of this person, who whispers, "I'm sorry for the way I acted before!" Enjoy a gourmet dinner!

Monday, October 14 (Moon in Aquarius)   Highlight versatility; adapt yourself to "changing conditions." It will be as if people are just discovering you—many bow and kiss your hand. Gemini and Sagittarius will play dramatic roles. Have luck with number 3.

Tuesday, October 15 (Moon in Aquarius)   You'll be intrigued with an Aquarius who takes you into confidence. Be discreet; don't tell all. Realize you are being shown great Aquarian secrets. Show gratitude without being obsequious. Scorpio and another Taurus are also in the picture.

Wednesday, October 16 (Moon in Aquarius to Pisces 8:51 p.m.)   Racing luck—all tracks: post position special—number 3 p.p. in the second race. Pick six: 1, 3, 4, 2, 2, 8. Be alert for these letters or initials in the names of potential winning horses or jockeys: E, N, W. Hot daily doubles: 1 and 3, 2 and 2, 6 and 4. Long shots win. Speed horses take lead and keep it. Virgo jockeys shine.

Thursday, October 17 (Moon in Pisces)   A family member who has been "in hiding" makes an appearance. Avoid pointing an accusatory finger. Be as understanding as possible. Attention revolves around your family, home, insurance, and protection against damages. Libra, Aries, and another Taurus figure in this scenario.

Friday, October 18 (Moon in Pisces to Aries 7:12 p.m.)   Many of your hopes and wishes come true in a sensational way. You say to yourself, "I wish I had complete control!" Pisces and Virgo play significant roles, and could have these letters or initials in their names—G, P, Y. Your lucky number is 7.

Saturday, October 19 (Moon in Aries)   On this Saturday, you could win money and love! Focus on production, the way you build things, and your presentation of a program to a superior. Capricorn and Cancer will play fascinating roles. In matters of speculation, stick with the power number, 8.

Sunday, October 20 (Moon in Aries)   The moon in Aries represents your twelfth house—your cycle is moving up. Toss aside preconceived notions, fears, and doubts. Give more time and study to the mantic arts and science, including astrology. Aries and Libra play dominant roles.

Monday, October 21 (Moon in Aries to Taurus 7:55 a.m.)   You will know what to do while others thrash about aimlessly. Focus on creativity, change, travel, variety, and romance. What was hidden will be revealed—to your advantage. Leo and Aquarius figure in this scenario.

Tuesday, October 22 (Moon in Taurus)   What you thought got away will make a dramatic return. The moon in your sign represents your high cycle—so take the initiative. Circumstances turn in your favor. Questions loom large concerning public appearances, legal efforts, and your marital status.

Wednesday, October 23 (Moon in Taurus to Gemini 8:16 p.m.)   Lucky lottery: 3, 7, 15, 17, 20, 22. Your popularity is on the rise. You will be at the right place at the right moment, almost effortlessly. Gemini becomes your ally, declaring, "I would follow you anywhere!" A Sagittarian also makes clear he or she is your friend.

Thursday, October 24 (Moon in Gemini)   You might feel you are losing something, but it is just that, a feeling. In actuality, you are in control of your destiny. People look to you for leadership. Almost before you know it, the "loss" will be replaced. Scorpio and another Taurus play top roles.

Friday, October 25 (Moon in Gemini) Get ready for an active weekend involving money, romance, and creative projects. If you write, expressing your feelings, you will find it profitable. It takes courage perhaps to "bare your soul." You are tough and sentimental; show us just how tough and sentimental via your writing.

Saturday, October 26 (Moon in Gemini to Cancer 7:09 a.m.) Racing luck—all tracks: post position special—number 2 p.p. in the fourth race. Pick six: 3, 4, 1, 2, 2, 6. Watch for these letters or initials in the names of potential winning horses or jockeys: F, O, X. Hot daily doubles: 3 and 4, 2 and 3, 4 and 8. Local jockeys win; favorites will be in and out of money.

Sunday, October 27—Daylight Saving Time Ends (Moon in Cancer) You might feel like you're walking on a cloud. Your sense of practicality is nil—you might be "seeing things." Pisces and Virgo play astounding roles, and could have these letters or initials in their names: G, P, Y. Tonight you'll be in a romantic mood, and will know your love is not unrequited.

Monday, October 28 (Moon in Cancer to Leo 2:18 p.m.) Everything might seem to be going backward for you today. Example: a relative you usually help is now "helping you." Capricorn and Cancer play meaningful roles, and could have these letters or initials in their names: H, Q, Z. Have luck with number 8.

Tuesday, October 29 (Moon in Leo) Following initial confusion, you will be back on track—emotionally and financially. One part of your life may be gone; you wave "goodbye" to it. However, the other part will be fulfilling. A new love is on the horizon. Aries and Libra play dramatic roles.

Wednesday, October 30 (Moon in Leo to Virgo 6:58 p.m.)   Get started on a project. Put forth your creative resources. Many are stunned by your initiative, originality, and energy. You'll be dealing with Aquarius and Leo. Do not follow others; be original, and display the courage of your convictions. Lucky lottery: 2, 9, 11, 12, 18, 32.

Thursday, October 31 (Moon in Virgo)   On this last day of October—Halloween—pay attention to the desires and health of an older family member. A digestive problem should not be ignored. Do your best. Take care of people. Don't try to please everyone because that would be a sure road to madness. A Cancer is involved.

NOVEMBER 2002

Friday, November 1 (Moon in Virgo to Libra 8:27 p.m.)   You get off to an amazing start—your fifth house is activated, and your numerical cycle is 9. This adds up to recognition, vigor, romance, creativity, and optimism. Aries and Libra play major roles in your life today, and could have these initials in their names—I and R.

Saturday, November 2 (Moon in Libra)   On this Saturday, you face the facts and learn that your position is stronger than you originally anticipated. You are due for a fresh start in a new direction—you look and feel better. Leo and Aquarius play leading roles. Have luck with number 1.

Sunday, November 3 (Moon in Libra to Scorpio 8:09 p.m.) That Libra moon works well on this Sunday. The meaning is that you accommodate people, especially relatives, without abandoning your principles. The Libra moon puts you in a mood to be cooperative. Capricorn and Cancer will play exciting roles.

Monday, November 4 (Moon in Scorpio) The new moon in Scorpio relates to your seventh house—in turn, that highlights legal affairs, publicity, and marriage. None of this is to be taken lightly, since Scorpio is involved. Humor is the best weapon and defense. Laugh at yourself, if necessary, but laugh!

Tuesday, November 5 (Moon in Scorpio to Sagittarius 8:01 p.m.) Those who claim you are "behind the times" will change their minds. Today you make creative changes, you read and write, and you learn by teaching or sharing knowledge. Check details and color coordination. Be willing to revise, review, and rewrite.

Wednesday, November 6 (Moon in Sagittarius) What you "forgot" yesterday, you will do today. The transitting moon in your eighth house makes you keenly aware of potential, of what the future could hold. An excellent day for beginning a thesis, or for communicating with a member of the opposite sex who attracts you and thinks of you in a favorable way.

Thursday, November 7 (Moon in Sagittarius to Capricorn 10 p.m.) Your interest in the occult surfaces—people ask questions, not in a condemnatory way, but because they want information about their own lives and loves. With the eighth house influence, you learn more about the financial status of someone close to you, including your partner or mate.

Friday, November 8 (Moon in Capricorn)   You
might be restless to move, travel, publish. This realiza-
tion hits home: that people are aware of you. You
don't want them to forget you, and this gives you a
mild panic attack. Pisces and Virgo figure in this scenario, and have these letters in their names: G, P, Y.

Saturday, November 9 (Moon in Capricorn)   This
is your "comeback day." You see things as they are,
including a relationship. If someone tells you a wonderful story, ask him or her to please put it in writing.
That wise producer Samuel Goldwyn once declared,
"A verbal contract is not worth the paper it is written on!"

*Sunday, November 10 (Moon in Capricorn to Aquar-
ius 3:27 a.m.)*   Spiritual values will be much in evidence, even if you don't talk about them. The numerical
cycle, plus moon position, indicates you are ready to
move on to dimensions of authority, responsibility,
and intensity, where love relationships are concerned.

Monday, November 11 (Moon in Aquarius)   Wear
bright colors; make personal appearances; let people
know you are no "stick-in-the-mud." This means you
are knowledgeable about the arts of astrology, number
divination, and palmistry. Make a fresh start; put forth
original concepts.

*Tuesday, November 12 (Moon in Aquarius to Pisces
12:41 p.m.)*   Within 24 hours, your life undergoes
a transformation. When the moon enters Pisces, that
will be your eleventh house—during that cycle, many
of your fondest hopes and wishes can become realities.
Cancer and Capricorn will play featured roles, and
have these letters in their names—B, K, T.

Wednesday, November 13 (Moon in Pisces)   This
is one Wednesday you won't soon forget! All indica-

tions point to joy, pleasure, and satisfaction. There's plenty of social activity, and your popularity is on the rise. Gemini and Sagittarius figure in today's scenario and are all for you. Lucky lottery: 3, 14, 18, 19, 22 30.

Thursday, November 14 (Moon in Pisces to Aries 12:37 a.m.) You come down to earth, landing gracefully. Details pile up; you handle them skillfully. Leo, Scorpio, and another Taurus figure in this scenario, and could have these letters or initials in their names—D, M, V. During this day, you earn new respect and regain self-confidence.

Friday, November 15 (Moon in Aries) Get ready for change, travel, variety, writing, reading, and teaching. People comment, "You are so alive and vital, it is a pleasure to be with you!" You learn a secret today. You gain "different" impressions of people and places. Virgo is involved.

Saturday, November 16 (Moon in Aries) During November as a whole, the emphasis will be on public relations, legal affairs, and your reputation and marriage. Today you do and say things you should have done some time ago. You will be concerned with the basics, including protection of your family. Your lucky number is 6.

Sunday, November 17 (Moon in Aries to Taurus 1:22 p.m.) On this Sunday, spiritual values surface. The moon is leaving Aries and moving into your sign, all to the good. Define terms. See people, places, and relationships in a realistic light. Pisces and Virgo persons play "clinching" roles.

Monday, November 18 (Moon in Taurus) On this Monday it is a power play day. This could be your day all the way. Your numerical cycle 8 equates to Saturn, and the moon is in Taurus. These and other factors indicate you will be at the right place at a crucial moment. A love relationship is complicated, but hot and heavy.

Tuesday, November 19 (Moon in Taurus)   Focus on your personality, initiative, and original thinking. Today you gain insight of world events and how you personally can do something about what is happening. You are an important person, and it is time you recognized that fact.

Wednesday, November 20 (Moon in Taurus to Gemini 1:23 a.m.)   The full moon, lunar eclipse is in Taurus. You will be in the news. People point to you with favorable and unfavorable comments. Feel good about it, just so long as they keep talking about you. Make a fresh start; stress independence, originality, and a pioneering spirit.

Thursday, November 21 (Moon in Gemini)   Focus on cooperative efforts, partnership, and your marital status. Cancer and Leo figure in today's scenario and it would be best to accept their goodwill. Rediscover your home, family, and spouse. You are where you belong, although many times you doubt it.

Friday, November 22 (Moon in Gemini to Cancer 11:46 a.m.)   Perceive today's picture and situation in their entirety. Leave the bits and pieces to others. On this Friday, opportunity exists for a wonderful social gathering. By taking charge, you elevate your prestige and you will feel good about it. A Sagittarian plays a major role.

Saturday, November 23 (Moon in Cancer)   There's much ado about relatives, visits, promises, and accusations. The focus is also on trips and ideas which require further development. Leo, Scorpio, and another

Taurus figure in today's exciting scenario, and have these letters or initials in their names—D, M, V.

Sunday, November 24 (Moon in Cancer to Leo 8:01 p.m.)   An exchange of ideas with a neighbor or relative proves stimulating. Have the facts at hand. You are better at debate than you might have imagined. Gemini, Virgo, and Sagittarius play memorable roles, and could have these initials in their names—E, N, W.

Monday, November 25 (Moon in Leo)   Today's scenario is "crowded" with children, family, and prospects for the future. Today you exude personal magnetism, and an aura of sensuality and sex appeal. Listen, Taurus: Don't break too many hearts! At the very least, offer tea and sympathy. Your lucky number is 6!

Tuesday, November 26 (Moon in Leo)   The Leo moon is in your fourth house—that section relates to home, family, and security. With Leo involved, "dress it up." Improve your surroundings by color coordination, beauty, and illustration, so that when one enters your home, it is almost as if by magic.

Wednesday, November 27 (Moon in Leo in Virgo 1:40 a.m.)   Confer with a Virgo. Accept constructive criticism, but refuse to bow down to a false accusation. A new, more constructive understanding between the two of you could result from this meeting or conference. Have luck with number 8.

Thursday, November 28 (Moon in Virgo)   On this Thanksgiving, you learn more about the history of the holiday. You also will be personally thankful for participating with people you respect and love. People with you have an understanding of world conditions and will ask you to speak. A Virgo lends encouragement.

Friday, November 29 (Moon in Virgo to Libra 4:53 a.m.)   You have a new view of yourself! Be confident, direct, and daring. Wear bright colors, make personal appearances, and if asked to speak, do so. Some people suggest you enter the political arena. Leo and Aquarius figure in this scenario. Your lucky number is 1.

Saturday, November 30 (Moon in Libra)   On this last day of November, with the moon in Libra, you receive compliments and are given credit for making the holiday meaningful. Accept graciously, without being obsequious. Cancer and Capricorn figure prominently. The subject of politics and marriage will dominate.

DECEMBER 2002

Sunday, December 1 (Moon in Libra to Scorpio 6:14 a.m.)   On this first day of the last month of the year, you become more conscious of the world around you. The Libra moon means you are aware of legal affairs, public relations, your reputation, and marital status. Leo and Aquarius play sensational roles in your life today.

Monday, December 2 (Moon in Scorpio)   Questions arise about direction, motivation, shelter, home, and family. If you're married, you rediscover your mate mentally, emotionally, and sexually. If you're single, that "restless state" won't last much longer! Cancer and Capricorn will play influential roles.

Tuesday, December 3 (Moon in Scorpio to Sagittarius 6:57 a.m.)   Today investigate and discover—give full play to your intellectual curiosity. Remember those recent resolutions about exercise, diet, and nutrition. You are going places, so be sure you'll be in good shape when you arrive! Gemini is in the picture.

Wednesday, December 4 (Moon in Sagittarius) The new moon and solar eclipse falls in your eighth house. Interest in the occult is emphasized. The numerical cycle 4 relates to the solving of a mathematical puzzles. People who previously were not interested will now be fawning all over you.

Thursday, December 5 (Moon in Sagittarius to Capricorn 8:38 a.m.) This is your day to "break for freedom." The eighth house emphasis continues; you will mystify many people, some of whom may accuse you of being in the playground of the occult. Gemini, Virgo, and Sagittarius play roles, and have these letters in their names—E, N, W.

Friday, December 6 (Moon in Capricorn) Music "finds its way" into your life today. A visitor from another country could have a concert. One way or another, music will play a role. A domestic adjustment is featured. Libra and another Taurus play key roles. Have luck with number 6.

Saturday, December 7 (Moon in Capricorn to Aquarius 12:54 p.m.) You have many memories, and you could be asking, "Is this déjà vu?" Many claim you are psychic, a mystic who won't admit it. It is best to be discreet. If you tell all, people lose interest and will walk away. Lucky lottery: 7, 12, 17, 18, 22, 25.

Sunday, December 8 (Moon in Aquarius) Spiritual values surface. Important people pay attention to you, and some will claim to have "discovered you." Be your usual unorthodox self—do things your way. Your cycle is high, so circumstances are turning in your favor. Capricorn is featured.

Monday, December 9 (Moon in Aquarius to Pisces 8:46 p.m.) Your wishes are fulfilled. Some people, for whatever reasons, want to start a controversy. Focus on travel, investigation, and decisions relating to people and nations. Aries and Libra play key roles, and could have these letters or initials in their names—I and R.

Tuesday, December 10 (Moon in Pisces)   On this Tuesday, you could be the "number one" person. Your numerical cycle is number one, which symbolizes originality, passion, and love. Imprint your own style. Don't follow others; let them follow you, if they so desire. Leo plays a dramatic role.

Wednesday, December 11 (Moon in Pisces)   Despite confusion, you find your way to your ultimate goal—home. The moon in Pisces represents your eleventh house. During this cycle, you win friends and influence people. You have luck in matters of speculation, especially by sticking with numbers 2 and 11.

Thursday, December 12 (Moon in Pisces to Aries 7:57 a.m.)   You'll have reason to celebrate. Your popularity rating is on the rise. In matters of speculation, stick with these numbers: 2, 3, 5. Get ready for change, travel, variety, and social responsibilities. Gemini and Sagittarius figure in this scenario.

Friday, December 13 (Moon in Aries)   It is Friday the 13th, but quite the reverse of the general opinion, you will be lucky. There will be minor obstacles. You'll overcome them. By proofreading, you prevent an embarrassing, costly error. Scorpio and another Taurus will play roles.

Saturday, December 14 (Moon in Aries to Taurus 8:42 p.m.)   On this Saturday, you will be told, "There is something vibrant about you, but I can't quite figure it out!" This person of the opposite sex, a Virgo, is drawn to you and makes no secret of it. A very good day for reading, writing, teaching, and taking notes concerning dreams.

Sunday, December 15 (Moon in Taurus)   Within 24 hours, the moon transits your sign—when this happens, your cycle moves up and you can count on being at the right place at a crucial moment. Attention on this Sunday revolves around your family, home, insurance, and security. Your marital status also figures prominently.

Monday, December 16 (Moon in Taurus to Gemini 8:41 a.m.)   During this Monday, it might appear that everything is in "slow motion." Gather your forces. Get a second wind. The moon in your sign indicates you are getting ready to go on the offensive. Pisces and Virgo play key roles, and have these letters in their names: G, P, Y.

Tuesday, December 17 (Moon in Gemini)   This is your power play day. The numerical cycle is 8, which equates to Saturn, which blends well with your Venus. The fact that the moon is in Gemini spells out for you the time to submit material to your superiors. Capricorn is in the picture.

Wednesday, December 18 (Moon in Gemini)   A cash deal goes through—you will be pleasantly surprised, because you'll have more money than you originally anticipated. You also locate a lost article. You could be humming, "Everything is going my way!" Lucky lottery: 2, 11, 12, 13, 14, 25.

Thursday, December 19 (Moon in Gemini to Cancer 6:29 p.m.)   The full moon in your money house once again points to a cycle of financial transactions which see you coming out as a winner. You'll be asked pointedly your intentions where marriage is concerned. Leo and Aquarius will play sensational roles.

Friday, December 20 (Moon in Cancer) Many things appear "familiar" to you. You will be asking yourself, "Is this déjà vu?" Whether it is or not, the cycle for you today points to home, family, and people you are familiar with and who want you to be happy and successful. A Cancer person is involved.

Saturday, December 21 (Moon in Cancer) The pressure is relieved. Humor saves the day. You get the okay to diversify, to be versatile, and to be selective. Gemini and Sagittarius play top roles, and will help you with a current dilemma involving language and distance. Have luck with number 3.

Sunday, December 22 (Moon in Cancer to Leo 1:47 a.m.) On this Sunday, you get foreknowledge about a problem that relates to children close to you. Your spiritual values surface, and you are in the mood to gamble. In matters of speculation, stick with number 4. Leo, Scorpio, and another Taurus figure in this dynamic scenario.

Monday, December 23 (Moon in Leo) With the moon in Leo, you brighten your home. You could receive a gift which provides an elegant atmosphere. Takes notes, and be analytical. Don't be satisfied merely to hear that something occurred. Find out why it happened. Gemini plays a quixotic role.

Tuesday, December 24 (Moon in Leo to Virgo 7:04 a.m.) On this Christmas Eve, you will give and receive gifts. But in the giving and receiving, there will also be a spirit of sincerity. Be with your family if possible. Show affection and appreciation. A major domestic adjustment is indicated, involving a possible change of residence or marital status.

Wednesday, December 25 (Moon in Virgo) On this Christmas Day, whether real or imagined, you feel the presence of a spiritual being. Go along with it, and act in a "spiritual way." A major gift received has to do with water. Pisces and Virgo play fascinating roles.

Thursday, December 26 (Moon in Virgo to Libra 10:52 a.m.)   On this day after Christmas, your creative juices stir. You feel elated, creative, dynamic, and "sexy." People close to you, including children, compliment you on being confident and optimistic. Capricorn and Cancer figure in this scenario.

Friday, December 27 (Moon in Libra)   On this Friday, you receive news about your general health—it is good! You complete a project. The green light will flash for you to continue, which could mean an overseas journey. Aries and Libra play significant roles, and have these letters in their names—I and R.

Saturday, December 28 (Moon in Libra to Scorpio 1:40 p.m.)   This is a day for a fresh start in a new direction! You'll have almost intimate dealings with a creative Leo who gives you a vote of confidence. Do not follow others; stress your originality and inventiveness. In matters of speculation, stick with number 1.

Sunday, December 29 (Moon in Scorpio)   A partnership proposal deserves serious consideration. The spotlight is on direction, motivation, and questions concerning your marital status. You'll be interviewed on world affairs. Do enough reading so that you do know what you're talking about!

Monday, December 30 (Moon in Scorpio to Sagittarius 4 p.m.)   Social activity is indicated, along with public appearances, legal affairs, and public relations. With the moon in Scorpio, your seventh house, you'll be pressed to the wall about certain questions and opinions. Your marital status figures prominently. A Sagittarian is involved.

Tuesday, December 31 (Moon in Sagittarius)   On this New Year's Eve, make resolutions that you know can be kept. You'll meet people who delve into the occult. You learn more about family and friends. Steer clear of those who drink too much. Someone close to you provides good money news.

HAPPY NEW YEAR!

ABOUT THE AUTHOR

Born on August 5, 1926, in Philadelphia, Sydney Omarr was the only person ever given full-time duty in the U.S. Army as an astrologer. He also is regarded as the most erudite astrologer of our time and the best known, through his syndicated column (300 newspapers) and his radio and television programs (he was Merv Griffin's "resident astrologer"). Omarr has been called the most "knowledgeable astrologer since Evangeline Adams." His forecasts of Nixon's downfall, the end of World War II in mid-August of 1945, the assassination of John F. Kennedy, Roosevelt's election to the fourth term and his death in office . . . these and many others are on the record and quoted enough to be considered "legendary."

ABOUT THIS SERIES

This is one of a series of twelve
Day-to-Day Astrological Guides
for the signs of 2002
by Sydney Omarr.